Beyond Measure
Neglected Elements of Accountability in Schools

Patricia E. Holland, Editor

Routledge
Taylor & Francis Group
LONDON AND NEW YORK

First published 2004 by Eye on Education

Published 2013 by Routledge
2 Park Square, Milton Park, Abingdon, Oxon OX14 4RN
711 Third Avenue, New York, NY, 10017, USA

Routledge is an imprint of the Taylor & Francis Group, an informa business

Copyright © 2004 Taylor & Francis

All rights reserved. No part of this book may be reprinted or reproduced or utilised in any form or by any electronic, mechanical, or other means, now known or hereafter invented, including photocopying and recording, or in any information storage or retrieval system, without permission in writing from the publishers.

Notices
No responsibility is assumed by the publisher for any injury and/or damage to persons or property as a matter of products liability, negligence or otherwise, or from any use of operation of any methods, products, instructions or ideas contained in the material herein.

Practitioners and researchers must always rely on their own experience and knowledge in evaluating and using any information, methods, compounds, or experiments described herein. In using such information or methods they should be mindful of their own safety and the safety of others, including parties for whom they have a professional responsibility.

Product or corporate names may be trademarks or registered trademarks, and are used only for identification and explanation without intent to infringe.

Library of Congress Cataloging-in-Publication Data
  Beyond measure: neglected elements of accountability in schools / Patricia E. Holland, editor.
    p. cm.
  ISBN 1-930556-80-2
  1. Educational accountability—United States. I. Holland, Patricia E., 1944-
  LB2806.22.B49 2004
  379.1'58—dc22

2004043214

ISBN 13: 978-1-930-55680-5 (pbk)

Production and editorial services provided by: UB Communications

Meet the Contributors

Paula W. Adams, Ed.D.

Paula Adams is an Assistant Professor in the Department of Language, Literacy and Special Populations at Sam Houston State University in Huntsville, Texas. She has over 20 years of experience in various teaching and administrative positions in public schools. Her research and writing interests focus on teachers' professional development and the preparation and development of special education professionals. Recent publications include articles in the *International Journal of Leadership in Education* and *Assessment for Effective Intervention*, the journal of the Council of Educational Diagnostic Services (CEDS).

Her Ed.D. was awarded by the University of Houston.

Kimberly C. Agnew, Ed.D.

Kimberly Agnew is the principal at Ryan Elementary School in the Houston Independent School District. She has extensive experience as a teacher and assistant principal working with students from low socioeconomic backgrounds in the school that was the context of her doctoral dissertation research and her chapter in this book. She has also worked as a facilitator for Consistency Management Cooperative Discipline.

Her Ed.D. was awarded by the University of Houston.

Lynn M. Bullard, Ed.D.

Lynn Bullard is a counselor in the Alief Independent School District in Houston, Texas. She has over twenty years of teaching and counseling experience in public schools. She has presented her research on school advisory programs at state and national conferences.

Her Ed.D. was awarded by the University of Houston.

Patricia Gaffney, Ed.D.

Trish Gaffney is Principal of Middle Level Learning Center in the Fort Worth Independent School District. Her research interests include school, family, and community partnerships. She has been a presenter at AERA annual meetings and the National Conference for Educators of Newcomer Students.

Her Ed.D. was awarded by the University of Houston.

Patricia Holland, Ph.D.

Pat Holland is Associate Professor of Educational Leadership and Cultural Studies at the University of Houston. Her research and publications are in the subjects of instructional supervision and teachers' professional development. Recent publications include articles in the *Journal of Curriculum and Supervision, International Journal of Leadership in Education,* and the *Journal of Technology in Education,* and a chapter in *Current Issues in School Leadership* (Erlbaum, 2004).

Her Ph.D. was awarded by the University of Pittsburgh.

Deborah Masterson, Ed.D.

Deborah Masterson is the Reading Intervention and Dyslexia Coordinator for a large suburban school district outside of Houston, Texas. She is also an adjunct professor at the University of Houston at Victoria and the University of St. Thomas in Houston. She teaches reading and special education courses.

Her Ed.D. was awarded by the University of Houston.

Laura Wagner Smith, Ed.D.

Laura Wagner Smith is an Educational Diagnostician in a North Texas suburban school district. She has worked as a special education educator, a principal, and an assistant principal in public and private schools.

Her Ed.D. was awarded by the University of Houston.

Contributors

Janis S. Terry, Ed.D.

Janis Terry is Director of the Learning Center at Kingwood College in Houston, TX. Her recent work and publications focus on constructivist education, and include "Fostering Trust within a Constructivist Classroom," *Evaluation Study: The University of Houston Charter School of Technology*, and an article in *Reading Matters*. She has also published articles in *Texas School Business, Texas Library Journal, The Clearing House,* and *Phi Delta Kappan*.

Her Ed.D. was awarded by the University of Houston.

Table of Contents

FOREWORD BY JUNE DONMOYER ix

PREFACE BY O. L. DAVIS, JR. xiii

Editor's Introduction 1
    Patricia E. Holland

1 Building Trust as We Build Knowledge 9
    Janis Terry

2 Designing Effective Advisory Programs 39
    Lynn Bullard

3 Building Teacher Leadership Capacity 71
    Laura Wagner Smith

4 Supporting Teachers' Professional
    Development 101
    Paula Adams

5 Linking School Reform to School Culture 133
    Kimberly Agnew

6 Eliminating the "Christmas Tree School" Effect . . 161
    Deborah Masterson

7 Engaging Families: A Study of Parent
    Mentoring 193
    Trish Gaffney

8 Understanding the Language of Values in
    Educational Accountability 225
    Patricia E. Holland

Foreword

June Donmoyer

January 8, 2004. It is the second anniversary of No Child Left Behind (NCLB), and as I prepare to write this foreword to *Beyond Measure: Neglected Elements of Accountability in Schools*, President Bush is celebrating the accomplishments of his "historic legislation." Earlier today, in fact, he visited a Knoxsville, Tennessee elementary school—one of the "success stories"— where he proclaimed that American schools are finally learning to meet the needs of *all* students now that accountability is directly tied to federal funding. The people I see in the crowd on the evening news cheer with pride, joy, support, and—I suspect—relief. Their school will be okay for another year. I click the remote and with a still-clear image of the citizens in that carefully staged scene in my mind, I wonder for a minute how in this foreword I can capture the relief I felt when I first read *Beyond Measure*. My relief and theirs come from such different places.

The President will spend the week stopping along the campaign trail to visit schools like the one in Knoxsville. His enthusiasm will be hard to ignore, and his statistics will be difficult to dismiss. It will be tough for those of us who work in schools to reconcile the obvious joy of successful communities with our own frustrations and concerns as we try to make sense of how our schools are changing as a result of our quest to attain more impressive test scores and passing rates on standardized measures that are, at best, incomplete indicators of what we know really matters.

Any of us who want to *do something* about the current situation, of course, will have a particularly difficult time. The spin machines of politicians are not above characterizing those who challenge NCLB as being *against accountability*. No thoughtful educator would endorse such an anti-accountability stance, of course. Indeed, Pat Holland, the editor of this book, makes clear that it is not a polemic against standardized tests. The book does, however, challenge readers to consider what education might be losing as a result of current legislation and the resulting obsession with improving students' performance on standardized tests. This obsession all too often requires that educators ignore other important social *and academic*—but difficult to measure—goals. It also encourages a quick-fix mentality and, at times, even outright cheating. Under these circumstances, teachers tend to be treated as factory workers, and students often become products fashioned on an assembly line.

In *Beyond Measure*, Holland and the other authors provide alternative images of what schools can and should be, as well as alternative ways to think about school success. The subtext here is not subtle: All of the authors, in one way or another, suggest that the standardized tools we use to assess students and schools cannot capture many of the things that really matter. The authors also model alternative approaches to the systematical study of the complexity of schools and school success. Holland suggests that some of these approaches could be used to study and assess things that matter but that cannot be fit into standardized research and evaluation designs.

Clearly, the publication of *Beyond Measure: Neglected Elements of Accountability in Schools* is well-timed. For me, personally, this book has arrived at an especially opportune moment in my life as a teacher. After teaching for 17 years, I had spent the past two years helping teachers and administrators in a diverse array of officially designated "low performing schools"—in Austin, Texas; Monument Valley, Utah; and San Diego, California—serve their students better. My assigned task was to teach instructional skills and techniques. To do this, however, I often also had to help teachers and principals rebuild their professional confidence and morale, which had suffered as a consequence of demoralizing, but undoubtedly well-intentioned, reform initiatives put in place by national, state, and/or district policy makers. It was somewhat alarming at times, in fact, to see the extent to which experienced, competent teachers and administrators had become immobilized by confusing, and frequently unreasonable, mandates.

This year I decided it was time for me to return once again to the front lines. I accepted a position as an English teacher at a "low-performing high school" where I had worked as a consultant the previous year. Now I am on the receiving end of the debilitating forces whose effects I had witnessed and tried to mitigate during the previous two years. While I have found being back in the classroom to be more rewarding and thrilling than I ever expected it to be, I have also had to struggle almost daily to balance policymakers' expectations with what I know my students need to be able to grow and learn.

Because of this struggle, I began looking for literature that would help me make sense of what is currently happening in schools. *Beyond Measure: Neglected Elements of Accountability in Schools* provides such insight. It offers helpful perspectives on the contemporary education reform movement and how it affects life in schools. Even more important, the book describes elements of schooling that are, indeed, "beyond measure."

January 13, 2004. As I complete this writing task, President Bush is in Mexico attending the Summit of the Americas. NCLB is not on the agenda, of course, yet I cannot help thinking about how the conference's main agenda item—immigration—is linked to education, particularly in states like my own that serve large immigrant populations. More than half of the students in my current school, for example, have cultural roots in Central and South America, and many hundreds of these adolescents do not speak English at home. Regardless of the logistic and moral dilemmas that circumstances like these pose, however, our school, like thousands across the country, is expected to turn these students into reasonable facsimiles of native English speakers in a few short years of schooling.

What is most disturbing about this cookie-cutter mentality is its failure to acknowledge, much less build on, what is unique and special about these students. Even their budding bilingualism is not valued by those who write state standards and develop the tests that measure whether standards have been attained. Likewise, the amazing cultural code-switching ability that many of my students possess is something that, once again, is "beyond measure," at least if our measuring instrument is a standardized test.

Now, as I get ready to hit "send" and e-mail *Beyond Measure*'s foreword to the publisher, I wonder if our President will realize the connections between his work today and his efforts to reshape United States schools. In case he does not, we can only hope that more books like this one will soon become part of the national debate on education, offering something more to consider—something better and wiser—to those of us who strive to meet the needs of *all* children as we work in schools every day.

Preface

O. L. Davis, Jr.

Measurement is not necessary in education. This statement is as true as it may be contested. Of course, measures can be valuable. In addition, political realities may require measurement of various matters, most surely of students' achievement. That mandate, however, differs markedly from the reasonable contributions that the logic of measurement seems to offer to educational practice and improvement.

Commonplace practice in education has all but elevated the belief in the necessity, not just the importance, of measures to the status of a fundamental principle. How this article of faith in measurement developed may be an intellectually interesting pursuit. Maybe, for example, the call to measurement can be traced to twentieth century educational reformers' acceptance into the managerial cult of efficiency with its signature insistence on measurement. On the other hand, maybe educational measurement is more indebted to the rise of the influence of psychology in education than it is to industrial management and efficiency.

Recently, such curiosity and understanding are of little, if any, consequence. In the politics of the present, legislative responses to educational needs have insisted that accountability be the handmaiden of reluctant and grudging increases in educational resources, primarily school funding. In most of these accountability requirements is embedded the creation of "one-best tests" and their use as the major, if not the only, criterion of educational success. These heavy-handed mandates illogically assert that the same student test score legitimately drives decisions about the adequacy of student achievement, teacher quality, administrative leadership, and school system failure or adequacy.

Under these contemporary conditions, searches for the origins of measures, however intriguing, appear to be utterly irrelevant. Educational measurement, with its rationale and technology, seems to have won the day, to be firmly established, and unlikely to be abandoned. On the other hand, accountability's operations and consequences, even its rationale, responsibly may be revisited and modified.

Several elements of rationale simply must be attended to early. One assumption is that measurement is equivalent to evaluation. Another is that single assessments are sufficient to make educational decisions. Others surely include recognition of the illogic that converts student's performance scores into judgments of teacher quality and school adequacy or success.

Measurement yields a score based on some appropriate scale. Evaluation, on the other hand, is a judgment or decision about worth or value. The two ideas profoundly differ. For example, parents and physicians routinely measure children's height in order to build a record of physical growth. They understand, almost intuitively, that other measures such as weight also are valuable. All such measures, however, *never* yield a proper decision about the goodness or merit of any particular height. In fact, that a particular child is shorter than most children of the same chronological age is meaningful only in *comparison* of that child's height with the *norm* of the height of many other children who are of similar age. Such a comparative statement is *not* evaluative. Although parents may want their child to be taller than he or she is, most of them understand that their child's *worth* or *value* is utterly irrelevant to height.

Single measures are appropriate to single and even to simple events or behaviors. Children's learning and teachers' teaching, however, are anything but single and simple. They are complex and admit many variables that are interwoven and difficult to separate meaningfully. Also, even single measures, like high-stakes accountability tests, yield scores from which only inferences honestly may be made about causes of these single scores. Arrogant interpretations of such scores easily may be asserted. One such meaning insists that an "achievement" score relates only to the substantive content that students encountered in the official curriculum. Another is that the score reveals not only the level of the student's learning, but also an estimate of the teacher's efficient instruction. What lamentable and absurdly confounded simplisms!

Particularly troublesome is the assumption of the direct, linear relationship of students' single scores on an achievement test to teacher quality. Indeed, this misguided belief is more than troubling; it is erroneous. Simply, students take the tests and their scores are directly related to the current state of their knowledge (including their prior knowledge), their intellectual talents, the extent and quality of their own engagement with content, and a number of personal variables (e.g., home circumstances, parents' levels of education and their aspirations for their children). A century of research findings reveals generally low and nonsignificant correlations of students' acquisition of knowledge with both teachers' knowledge and judged effectiveness. This evidence notwithstanding, most people (including most teachers) continue to believe that teaching *causes* student learning. Phrased differently, teachers are only successful if their students learn. However this fiction continues to possess currency, it fails on the criterion of logic. Teachers teach and students learn. These two enterprises differ profoundly. To be sure, teaching may *influence* students' learning, but teachers cannot learn for students. More importantly, both teaching and learning are results of related but not independent actions. Teachers *intend* (that is, they want students to learn), but they can never *control* or *cause* students' learning. Students are not passive, only vessels to be filled. They must intend to learn as a prerequisite to their learning. Furthermore, students' learning is contingent not only on their intentions to learn, but also on the extent and quality of their own engagement with relevant subject matter. Clearly, teachers' roles in students' engagements are important and, on occasion, vital in the interactions of teaching and students' endeavors to learn. As Harold Benjamin sagely remarked more than half a century ago, students are "under their own command."

The logic of teaching and learning is unambiguously simple; the belief that they are causally related is irreparably flawed and, consequently, mischievous. Students' scores on achievement tests cannot rationally be translated into measures of teacher or of school effectiveness. Insistence on such action must signal that the advocate does not live in the real world, but only in a world that never was nor will be.

Important educational decisions depend on adequate evidence. They always have. Moreover, most teachers always have understood that tests, ones constructed by themselves and others developed by testing professionals, are valuable. Teachers, as well, have recognized the added value of additional assessments. Tests constitute one kind of assessment, but an assessment need not be a measure.

The need, even the imperative, for educators to participate in the analyses of accountability's measures and the creation and advocacy of justifiable alternatives to the ideology of a single score sparked the development of *Beyond Measure: Neglected Elements of Accountability in Schools*. In this book, Professor Pat Holland and her associates provide both theoretical discussions and practical insights. They celebrate rather than decry the complexity of the educational condition. To all readers, but especially to teachers and educational leaders, they offer encouragement to think seriously about the adequacy of individual, even multiple, measures. In order to influence schooling's liberation from its captivity by the cult of measurement, they challenge educators to invent means, particularly complex efforts, to gain much appropriately rich evidence which is practically useful to the making of fruitful educational decisions.

> O. L. Davis, Jr.
> Catherine Mae Parker Professor
>   of Curriculum and Instruction
> The University of Texas at Austin

Editor's Introduction

Educators, policy makers, and the public have always been concerned about the quality of schools, both in their communities and across the United States. In recent years, however, the emphasis on accountability for the quality of schools has become increasingly narrow. We have reached a point where schools are being judged on a single measure of students' performance on particular standardized tests. The merits of such tests are not in question. They provide valuable information about student achievement across schools, information that has been particularly useful in raising the achievement levels of those students who are at risk of failure and of being forsaken by their schools.

This book is not a polemic against standardized tests. Rather it is, as its title suggests, an attempt to look beyond the kind of learning that can be readily tested and measured, an attempt to build a case for the importance of identifying and including in considerations of accountability other elements of schools which are "beyond measure." It is a call to attend to those often taken-for-granted elements that are inevitable in schools where students and educators are eager to learn and work, schools that parents and community members consider good schools.

Attending to what is "beyond measure" also means that the limits of conventional strategies of accountability are exceeded. Such strategies are based in quantification and measurement and are limited to what can be counted and measured. Conventional accountability measures cannot capture the more subtle and ephemeral elements of schooling that are the subjects of the chapters in this book. These elements sift through the current grid of testing and measurement like sand through a fence. We see evidence that they are there but cannot control them.

The elements of schooling examined in this book are examples not only of the kinds of things that are neglected by the quantitative measures of accountability currently being used but also of the finer gauge of inquiry provided by qualitative methods of research and analysis. These methods focus more narrowly on specific school and classroom settings and on how those settings are experienced by the people who inhabit them. Although the narrow focus of qualitative methods yields findings that are of limited use in large-scale assessment and policy making, such methods do produce information that can be very valuable at the school level. Furthermore, the rich descriptions of particular settings produced by the narrow focus of qualitative studies may prompt educators to become aware of and to better understand the often neglected elements of schooling in their own educational settings.

This book, then, is designed for educators who have at any time questioned the wisdom of limiting the criteria for assessing the success of their schools and, by extension, of their leadership, to students' scores on standardized tests. It is also intended to offer rich illustrations of some of the elements of schooling that are being neglected in current discussions of what makes a good school. Finally, it is intended to provide educators with qualitative strategies that they can use to study these elements in their own schools.

The chapters are organized to reflect a widening perspective that takes the reader from a focus on the classroom, to a focus on teachers' professional development, to a focus on the school as a whole, and finally to policy issues that operate beyond schools.

The first chapter focusing on the classroom is Janis Terry's exploration of trust as an important condition in a positive and supportive classroom learning environment. This study grew out of the author's work as a program evaluator in a charter school where a constructivist approach to education is used. During her work in the school, one classroom stood out because of the ways students interacted and communicated among themselves and with their teachers. Terry characterizes this classroom as a place infused by a sense of trust, and describes trust in terms of the elements and conditions that interact to create and sustain such an environment. Her study not only provides a compelling description of a trusting educational environment, but also helps educators to see that trust-building is itself a constructivist process that develops inductively over time, involves risk, blends autonomy and collaboration, and values both emotion and reason.

Lynn Bullard's chapter also focuses on the classroom. She describes the importance of the "care" that teachers show toward their students in successful advisory programs. Too often, she explains, teachers are inadequately prepared for their responsibilities in classroom advisory programs, in part because they do not understand the goals, and also because they do not engage students in activities that are appropriate for the goals. More importantly, however, advisory programs fail because teachers do not model relationship-building behaviors in their interactions with students. This study offers a look at how teachers' relationships with students need to be based in a concept of "care." Such a concept is shown to be consistent with the goals of advisory programs and with a need for classrooms in general to be places where teachers are directed toward the social, ethical, and aesthetic development of their students, as well as their intellectual achievement.

The chapter by Laura Wagner Smith shifts the focus somewhat from the classroom itself to teachers and their professional development needs. She describes in-depth case studies of two elementary school teachers, both of whom were highly regarded by their peers and administrators but did not think of themselves as leaders in their schools. According to the author, the goal for these case studies was to determine whether teachers can be encouraged to develop their leadership capacities by focusing their attention on what they are already doing, as well as on what they can potentially do as teacher leaders in their schools. Two particular strategies were adapted to help teachers focus on their leadership. The first of these strategies was a modified version of clinical supervision that explored the teacher's leadership behavior in various situations that ranged beyond classroom settings to include faculty team meetings, school committee meetings, and parent meetings as well. The second strategy, Interpersonal Recall Process (IRP), gave the teacher-participants an opportunity to consider their own participation in the clinical supervision process and to reflect on what influence that process may have had on their thinking of themselves as teacher leaders. This study offers a richly descriptive account of two teachers' understanding of their own leadership and of how that understanding developed over time. It also points to the value of a strategy such as clinical supervision to assist teachers and the administrators who would support them in developing their unique capacities for teacher leadership.

Another chapter focusing on teachers' professional development is Paula Adams' study of an evaluation process for experienced, high-performing teachers that was designed as an alternative to conventional, observation-based evaluations of teaching. The study explores the use of teacher-designed Professional Development Plans that targeted areas of growth or instructional improvement of interest to the teacher. Adams' study shows the strong value teachers placed on self-assessment, the opportunity to choose the focus of their own professional development, and assessment of that development over the course of an entire school year. Although teachers attributed professional growth and instructional improvement to the Professional Development Planning process in general, the author adds understanding of how the process supports such experiences and improvements by classifying them as activities of professional inquiry. Data from the study offer rich examples of these activities that include reflection, the use of instructional innovations, collaboration, and teacher research. Adams' study is a well-documented example of a teacher evaluation process that moves beyond uniform, simplistic, and repetitive observations of classroom teaching skills to one that empowers teachers to take the lead in directing their own development as professionals.

The next chapter widens the focus to consider the interrelationship between a school-wide reform effort and a school's culture. This case study by Kimberly Agnew examines an urban middle school's implementation of Consistency Management and Cooperative Discipline (CMCD) over a seven-year period. Using evidence drawn from interviews, observations, archival data from the school and the CMCD program, and her own participant-observer experience, Agnew shows how the CMCD model's "themes" of prevention, care, cooperation, organization, and community reflect values and beliefs that were once part of the school's culture but had been lost or buried over the years. The information presented in this study encourages educators to give careful consideration to the values and beliefs that are part of their school's culture when planning and implementing school reform.

Another chapter with a school-wide focus is Deborah Masterson's description of an elementary school's struggle to deal with the fragmentation of its instructional program that occurred when two dozen special programs operating in the school and pulled students from their regular classrooms to attend programs for which they qualified. At the point where she began her study, a committee of teachers had volunteered to address what they described as a "scheduling nightmare." The author describes the problems created by this scheduling nightmare at two levels. The first level is that of the school itself. It includes a review of the legal mandates that gave rise to the increasing numbers of special instructional programs as well as a description of the solutions developed by the committee's collaborative leadership of the faculty in a schedule planning process. The second level is more general. Here the author offers complexity theory as a framework for understanding the proliferation of special programs in schools across the country. The author then links the two levels, the specific and the general, in terms of three major problems that schools face: the intent versus the impact of legal mandates, the effects of leadership, and the impact of structure on process.

The next chapter by Trish Gaffney addresses a concern of educators that takes them beyond the boundaries of the school itself, i.e., parental involvement. Gaffney's study of twenty-six sites that attempted to implement Parent Share, a community-based program in which experienced parents mentor other parents, grew out of her interest as a school administrator in engaging and supporting students' parents. Examples from the various Parent Share sites provide fascinating descriptions of the ways that parent mentoring has been conceptualized and carried out across the Parent Share sites; the manner in which mentors are recruited, trained, and supported at different sites; how the sites identify parents to be mentored; and the ways in which sites have evaluated their parent mentoring programs.

Gaffney also offers useful information about how schools can work with community organizations to offer parent-mentoring programs. She encourages educators to break out of the isolation within which schools often operate and become full partners with community agencies in customizing mentoring programs for the parents they both serve. Gaffney's research on the various forms that parent mentoring can take suggests that such programs extend the reach of the school and can lead to deeper family engagement in support of student achievement.

The concluding chapter by Patricia Holland considers the discourse that has emerged to contain and describe current policies of school accountability. The chapter provides educators with an overview of perspectives from which current policies and practices of accountability are critiqued. These perspectives include a dominant instrumentalist one that the author contends addresses only the particulars of standards and the tests used to measure them. Other minority perspectives attempt to extend the discourse of accountability. They are curricular critiques that raise questions about the impact of standards and tests on curriculum, and social critiques that focus on the negative potential impact of current accountability practices on schools as communities and social organizations. By providing examples of these various perspectives, the chapter prepares educators to pose questions from within the instrumentalist discourse of accountability and to expose problems with standards themselves and with the measures of them that are being used. Examples of the curricular and social critiques prepare educators to stand outside of the discourse and challenge it for what is missing or ignored—for what is beyond measure.

All of the studies in this book are intended to provoke consideration of those elements of schooling that are "beyond measure" and to draw attention to ways of studying what counts as well as what can be measured.

Acknowledgments

Several acknowledgments are in order at this point. First, to the loved ones, colleagues, and students of the authors of the chapters in this book, we appreciate their understanding and patience as we balanced our writing commitments with the other responsibilities in our lives. Second, to the reviewers of early versions of chapters, their suggestions were most helpful and sharpened our thinking and our writing. Finally, to our editor, Bob Sickles, it was he who invited us to consider developing a book on the topic of what is beyond measure in schools that some of us discussed in a session at a University Council of Administration (UCEA) conference. The pages that follow are our response to that invitation.

Patricia E. Holland
January 2004

1

Building Trust as We Build Knowledge

Janis Terry

When we talk about trust, we have to show it in our actions.
(DANIEL HANSON)

Carl Rogers was one of many educational leaders who believed that the presence of trust within an educational setting allowed more learning to take place (Baloche, 46). One may ask, "How do we know trust exists within a classroom or school?" and "If we determine trust is lacking, how do we encourage its growth?" Within this chapter, these questions will be addressed.

A recent study of a constructivist elementary classroom has provided great insight into the process of recognizing the signs of trust and methods of building trust.[1] The study took place during a school year in a constructivist classroom in which I experienced an atmosphere containing what I came to label "trust."

---

[1] A general qualitative, ethnographic case study methodology was used to gather data in its natural context, drawing from the perspective of the participants involved.

The Classroom Setting

On my first visit to this classroom I was introduced to a room full of energy, emotion, and investigation. The class met on the second floor of a two-story classroom building on a university campus. The school year had just started, and 19 students and two teachers were adjusting to their unusual space where they were beginning to learn together.

As I looked around the room, the lead teacher explained that all work was being completed on the floor because the tables and chairs that would serve as desks had not arrived yet. The lack of desks did not seem to affect the attitude or productivity of the students; in fact, they seemed to enjoy having an excuse to stretch out on their stomachs to read a book or play a game.

When I returned a month later to observe the students at work and play, I found an altered workplace with numerous tables and chairs filling the once cavernous room. Even with the furniture in place, there still remained a large, carpeted space adjacent to a fireplace where the group continued to gather for some learning activities and for all group meetings. The students were still afforded, on occasion, an opportunity to literally stretch out—an appealing alternative for any 8-year-old.

There was always a lot of interaction within the classroom: among students and teachers, between individual students, or through one-on-one conversations between a teacher and student. The constant activity that took place here was in dramatic contrast to what I had always experienced in traditional classrooms as a student, a teacher, and a parent.

Instead of disrupting the learning process (an outcome I would have predicted), ongoing movement and interaction seemed to enhance the learning. Students were allowed to openly discuss with others what they were doing and learning as they worked through their lessons and projects.

Vygotsky would have applauded this classroom atmosphere, because he saw speech and dialogue as important elements in the learning process. He believed that collaborative discussions are an important method of learning. True dialogue, he suggested, promotes deep contact with ideas, stimulating the development of an active thinker. Vygotsky's theory about the relationship between thought and speech supports the belief that people learn from other people through dialogue. "The relationship of thought to word," he said, "is a process; thought is not expressed, but completed in word" (Pressley & McCormick, 1995, p. 227). According to Vygotsky, participation in group dialogue about important content should have profound long-term effects on cognitive development (ibid, p. 259).

Traditional vs. Constructivist Philosophy of Learning

A key factor in the classroom being observed was the constructivist approach to learning. Constructivism is a polar opposite of the traditional educational approach. Generally, within classrooms, the attitude is that knowledge is categorized and sequenced logically. The goal is for students to know more and more, absorbing a lot of information. Curriculum is organized around discrete subjects with information coming from textbooks and teachers' lectures. The goal of education in traditional terms is for those who have it (teachers) to pass their knowledge on to those who do not (students).

In contrast to the traditional method is the constructivist approach. The principles of constructivism are based on a philosophy of how people learn. The methods utilized are a direct reflection of the philosophy that knowledge is constructed through experiences within the social world which are based on historical reference (Brooks & Brooks, pp. 4–5). By encouraging questioning and a discovery approach, constructivist educators see themselves as facilitators of learning rather than teachers. Students are encouraged to develop theories and to explore their ideas, often in a group setting. Mistakes in judgment or errors in reasoning are expected to occur as part of the learning process. Answers are not judged "wrong," but instead are used as a stepping stone to get to better conclusions.

In constructivist terms knowledge comes into existence when someone examines data and assigns meaning to it, making sense of factual information. In a constructivist classroom not all students have the same assignment or read the same novel. Students work with various data to construct their understanding of events (Brooks & Brooks, 1993). The goal of a constructivist teacher is to have a student know how to do something sensible with information rather than simply repeating it on request. The philosophy and goals of the two teachers in the classroom under observation reflected this constructivist approach.

Foundations of Trust Set in Teachers' Philosophy

The tenets of constructivist education were deeply ingrained in the personal teaching philosophy of the lead teacher, Mrs. Allen. As a teacher with 30 years of experience, she had spent many years working with leaders in the field of constructivism and had even spent time under the leadership of noted constructivist authority, Rheta DeVries.

In her definition of constructivism, Mrs. Allen named autonomy as the most important ideal in this approach to learning. She described autonomy as being "the opposite of helpless," and then explained how she perceives the value of autonomy: "We need people who can take risks, who can participate, who can be confident, and who initiate and propel things that happen in our world." I interpreted her definition to mean that a person who has achieved autonomy is a person actively involved in the world and able and willing to take risks and initiate change because of clear personal vision, purpose, and direction in life.

As she saw it, her role in helping students to achieve autonomy was helping them to construct their own knowledge by being aware of what goes into their thinking. Being cognizant of her students' past experiences, significant life influences, and special interests helped her to guide them in their quest for knowledge and understanding. She saw her ultimate goal as moving the student to "being an independent person capable of being responsible for himself and others, participating in a community and society in a positive way with knowledge and conviction that he is going to reason through things and stand up for those convictions." Mrs. Allen saw herself as having the very important position of helping children to grow up to be the kind of responsible citizens needed to participate in and maintain a democracy.

How exactly did she see herself accomplishing this? Throughout the interviews, she made numerous references to student growth and development. She talked about paying attention to cognitive development, following their ability to think, and connecting their experiences to integrate their learning. Letting them explore their interests was an important element in learning activities. Whenever they could explore an area of interest in meeting cognitive goals, students were encouraged to do so.

Because constructivists believe the social context is directly connected to the way students learn, much effort is given to creating a sense of community within a constructivist classroom. Mrs. Allen's classroom was no exception. She emphasized the value of discussing each other's ideas, experiences, and cultural backgrounds in order to understand the ideals and convictions that had meaning for each person. She also believed that respect for each other's convictions was a necessary outcome of sharing this information with others.

The emphasis on learning within a social context led to social goals receiving the same emphasis as academic goals. Regarding their goal setting Mrs. Allen explained: "They have a friendship goal, and they have an academic goal. Once a week in the group time we talk about goals and the ideas associated with them. When they have goals, then that influences the decisions they make about themselves throughout the week—what choices that they're making. So, that's one way I help them shape the choices that they're making within the community."

With regard to the self-concept of students, Mrs. Allen mentioned that despite her emphasis on not labeling students, one student had "labeled himself" through previous experiences "as being a kind of 'bad boy.'" She worked with him during the school year to help him construct a new, more positive view of himself "as someone who's successful, capable, participatory, and excited about new things." She was accomplishing this goal by meeting with the parents to understand his interpersonal situation at home and to determine how the parents and teachers could cooperatively reinforce a new self-image. Mrs. Allen recognized, after consulting with his parents, that some of his anger came from feeling overpowered at home, and she began offering him opportunities to engage in activities in which his natural abilities and interests would be utilized. By encouraging his artistic talents and by allowing him to create constellations in cardboard punch-outs for a science project, she instigated activities that empowered him, changing his attitude about himself and the learning environment. She also gave him opportunities to have more personal interactions and group work within the classroom so that he would be working with others to develop stronger relationships and to feel a sense of community.

Mrs. Allen's methods of evaluating students followed the approach commonly associated with constructivism. When determining a child's progress, she explained that she looked for flexibility of thinking; understanding of concepts, patterns, and applications; growth in vocabulary; and improved social skills. Evaluation was a constant, on-going process that was often one-on-one and sometimes in group settings. She stressed the importance of continuous evaluation because "what they are able to do structures what comes next." Spelling was taught through use in writing activities rather than in scheduled spelling tests. In reading they focused on application, and in writing the emphasis was on effective communication. Editing the work was often done with partners and in groups, with improved personal editing skills as the ultimate goal.

Mrs. Allen's teaching partner, Mrs. Roberts, had a natural tendency toward practicing constructivism. In contrast to the lead teacher, however, she had no training in constructivist education. In her initial interview she talked freely about her lack of training and, at the same time, emphasized her natural inclination to employ constructivist principles in her interactions with students. The following remark illustrates her philosophy:

> It makes really good sense to derive knowledge from what you know, to gather information for where you want to go. And, thereby, there will be a wisdom in that learning that could be applicable to any situation in your life.

Responses she gave in her interview confirmed that her philosophy of teaching was in alignment with the constructivist philosophy. In talking about the characteristics she thinks are associated with teachers, she mentioned empathy and shared something that is clearly constructivist in nature:

> I think a good teacher, someone who will impact students, is one who allows them to think and gives them time to process rather than imprinting personal views or their values, as if they [the views] are the ultimate choices for the students.

In her conversation she talked about how she believes in children and learns a lot from them. Mrs. Roberts also talked about empowering children and encouraging them to express their feelings. She sees herself as a guide and coordinator of efforts in the classroom. Her goals for the students are autonomy, critical thinking, and self-evaluation. In discussing her role regarding assessment of the students, she showed strong constructivist tendencies when she said:

> Assessment should be done in terms of where the child is and where the child should be. But that assessment should be in a way that is positive; the words are very important. The words should be well suited to achieving our goals. And any time you have the individual, in this case the child, being sacrificed for what people perceive as goals in education, you lose the child; thereby, you lose the purpose of being.

By examining Mrs. Allen's and Mrs. Robert's philosophies of education and their implementation strategies, we get a good description of the constructivist concepts that inform their teaching.

Foundations of Trust in the Classroom

In a pragmatic sense, however, the meaning and truth of concepts are determined by their practical results. In this study of a constructivist classroom, it was necessary to look at the practical results of what the teachers said in terms of what was occurring in the classroom. In this study, I was looking at the culture within the classroom in terms of quality rather than quantity. I was not looking at how many times something happened or how one incident exponentially affected another; instead, I was looking at the characteristics and effects of the action and the consequential outcome of observed interactions.[2]

As data from the classroom observations accumulated, I began to see patterns emerge. Some actions were acts of courtesy; others were signs of acceptance; still others were attempts to be fair. Upon examining the types of behaviors that consistently occurred, I saw that the teachers and students were "asking, acknowledging, complimenting, allowing, providing, discussing, permitting, and showing interest," to name just some of the behaviors. The interactions of the teachers and students were reflecting a distinct and positive approach of relating to one another.

As these patterns developed, I was led to identify four distinct elements: *respect*, *caring*, *cooperation*, and *communication*. These elements had emerged in the classroom because of the types of actions, behaviors, and remarks occurring within this social setting.

The presence of respect, along with a caring attitude on the part of teachers and students, gave birth to a feeling of trust, the feeling that I came to realize was the unidentified feeling that I had initially sensed in the classroom. The phenomenon that existed within this classroom could be compared to a garden with flowers of care and blossoms of respect that were nourished through cooperation and effective communication. Specific examples of these elements at work provide a clearer understanding of how they contribute to the development of a trusting environment.

---

[2] Observations and interviews with both teachers and students were used to provide a complete, "thick" description of the classroom being observed. Classroom observations were videotaped and then later transcribed. Field notes recorded during formal and informal observations complemented the data collected through observations and interviews. A short survey completed by the students also provided quantitative data. This information served as a consistency check to confirm meanings derived form data gained from the qualitative observations and interviews. Multiple methods of data collection assist the researcher in providing an analysis that is both valid and reliable. All data collected helped to provide a detailed, in-depth description of the classroom dynamics.

Respect

The presence of respect became more clearly apparent as I began to focus on specific dialogue heard during observations in the classroom. The following is one example of a discussion about respect. On this occasion the group discussion was in its final stages. The group was attempting to determine the best activity for their "end-of-the-year" party. The two most popular choices were a "water play" day and bowling. Allison, one of the students, was very much against the water day, and there were strong reactions from some of the other students. The students were beginning to get restless, and a lot of talking among individuals was going on. The conversation went like this:

> MRS. ALLEN (SHOWING THE PEACE SIGN WITH HER HAND HELD HIGH): This has not worked very well for me today. Sam, you are still not cooperating. I'm seeing some people being very respectful of others in the group meetings; others are not.
>
> It's not very easy to find something that everyone wants to do. As a group, you have to be willing to compromise. If someone has a different opinion than others, do they have a right to that opinion?
>
> When we decide things as a group, it's hard to decide on something that everyone agrees with. We try to give you some choices in here. If someone has a different opinion, do they have a right to their opinion?
>
> Raise your hands if you believe they have a right to their opinion. Look around you. It looks like most people believe that. Hands down.
>
> How do we show people who have opinions different from ours—(PAUSE)—What do we do to show them we respect them? What has to happen to respect people of different opinions? How do we show that? Sam? How do we show people with different opinions that they're still okay? (SILENCE)
>
> These are decisions that you are going to have to make throughout your life about how you are going to treat other people. Allison, how would you have liked to have been treated just now.
>
> ALLISON: I would want them to respect me.
>
> MRS. ALLEN: How would they show you that?

JOSEPH: They would listen in class meeting.

ALLISON: Listen to me. And, not argue with me.

MRS. ALLEN: Of all that you have learned this year, that is the most important thing—that you respect each other, and your teachers, and your parents. Treat people the way you want to be treated. When you say something, think about what you are going to say. Allison's feelings were hurt because she doesn't think water play is for her. She has a right to that opinion and a right in this school to be respected for her opinion. I want you to think about that.

Respect was addressed in this situation, and responsiveness to the feelings of Allison was apparent, too. In addition to the teachers' reinforcement of respect, the students' actions and words also expressed a sense of respect for their classmates and teachers.

Throughout my time with this group of students and their teachers, I observed a variety of actions within the classroom and on the playground. Respectful behavior was practiced by both teachers and students. The teachers, in true constructivist form, had strong feelings about respect. Not only did they mention respect in their interviews as an important value they wished to emphasize in their class, but they also addressed respect in group meetings and encouraged students to understand the concept. They modeled respectful behavior on a daily basis. There was strong evidence of their respect for the students in many of their statements and actions.

In her interview Mrs. Allen talked about a student who had been shy and passive when school began. This girl had gradually become responsive and had grown to be an interactive member of the class. Mrs. Allen attributed these changes to the structure of the classroom where a lot of effort was put forth to make the students feel accepted. This effort involved creating an atmosphere in which risks are encouraged and mistakes are okay. She said, "It's okay to take risks. And I'm hoping that the behavior has come because she feels that kind of trust and has received that message through what goes on in the classroom."

Specific references to respect came in her responses to two questions: "How important is parental involvement?" and "How would you define constructivism?" In her discussion of parental involvement, Mrs. Allen first talked about how parents can respect their children by being directive without being authoritarian, by setting limits and having expectations, and by giving children choices but at the same time limiting those choices based on safety and reasonableness. She then went on to say:

> The idea of mutual respect is extremely important in my classroom. And I try very hard to respect the children and the parents. And what they do in this classroom is respect other peers, adults, and the materials that are here.

In her discussion of the meaning of constructivism, Mrs. Allen emphasized the importance of students becoming independent and capable of being responsible for themselves and others, learning to participate in the community in a positive way, and developing knowledge and the conviction to stand up for what they believe. In talking about having convictions, she added, "We not only have our own convictions, but we also need to respect those of others." Clearly, she has linked respect and commitment with the principles of constructivism.

Mrs. Roberts also emphasized respect in her interview. She equated the development of trust to the power to listen to and also to respect the children. She said, "I do not allow children to be unkind to each other. You do not have to be friends with them, but you have to respect them, and you have to honor the fact that they have a place in the classroom and have the rights of a person."

Student interviews conducted late in the research process after trust had emerged as an important concept further confirmed that honest concern and respect were a significant part of the classroom environment. When asked how they would define trust, most students gave examples of behavior that proved to them that someone is trustworthy. Joseph said that if someone talks to you a lot, in other words, is a good friend, and if he doesn't tell secrets, then he can be trusted. Also, if the person "listens to me," then he shows "respect for me," which tells him that person is trustworthy. Basically, if a person shows respect and does not lie (like in telling a secret), then he can be trusted. Respect and honesty were a big part of being trustworthy.

Sean liked being a part of the class particularly because they got to talk a lot and share ideas, and his classmates were good friends. He said, "I love to share my ideas. I think my classmates like my ideas because they listen." A significant part of Sean's satisfaction with this class seemed to be having his feelings respected and appreciated by his classmates. In defining trust, he said, "Tell somebody to do something, and they do it." He shared this example: "If I handed a person my favorite t-shirt and they took care of it and gave it back to me in the same shape or better, then I can trust them." He translated someone's keeping his word, as illustrated in respect for a borrowed item, as his way of confirming trustworthiness.

All the students interviewed said they felt they could trust classmates who kept secrets and who were kind to them, basically students who were honest, showed sincere respect, and were consistently considerate.

Respect among students and teachers was a direct reflection of the teachers' philosophy and the students' values as expressed in the class rules they developed. Not only was respect the topic of classroom discussions, but it was also apparent in the words and actions of teachers and students alike. The manner in which it was addressed—with honesty and acceptance—showed a commitment to the principle of respect and generated a personal responsiveness to students in sensitive situations.

Care

The elements of care and respect are similar because they can be called values and because they are associated with positive actions or ways of being. Tronto defines care, or caring, as "a species activity that includes everything that we do to maintain, continue, and repair our 'world' so that we can live in it as well as possible" (1994, p. 103). With that definition in mind, we can reflect on the section about respect, realizing that some of the situations might also reflect care, in addition to respect, and then move forward to consider other situations that fit Tronto's definition.

Mrs. Roberts dealt with children in a very forthright manner, yet her direct approach was executed in a very caring way. She often rubbed or patted the children on their backs and gave them praise and words of encouragement.

Mrs. Allen's approach with the children was equally as caring. The following excerpt from the observation transcripts illustrates her caring manner:

> The students are involved in silent reading time. Grace is sitting with another girl reading from the same book, and Mrs. Roberts moves Grace's reading partner and lets her keep the book. Grace is not happy with this change. She frowns and says to Mrs. Allen: "That's why we were reading partners because we wanted to read the same book."
>
> MRS. ALLEN: Let's go find another book.
>
> GRACE: But, that was the only scary book.
>
> Mrs. Allen and Grace go to the bookshelf together. Mrs. Allen picks up *Beware the Megrimum*.
>
> MRS. ALLEN: This is a scary story. Let's start it together.
>
> Grace examines it for a few seconds, frowns, and puts it back.
>
> MRS. ALLEN (WITH A QUESTIONING TONE IN HER VOICE): That doesn't have interest for you. Here's one—*The Buried Eye*.
>
> Grace picks up *The Legend of Sleepy Hollow*. She puts it down and seems to be resistant to take any other book. Mrs. Allen hands her the book *Verdi* and says, "I'll read with you." Grace takes the book, goes over to an empty space on the floor, and lies down on her stomach to read. Mrs. Allen gets down on the floor, right next to her, reading along with her, making eye contact, smiling, and listening to Grace's reading and comments.

This special effort on Mrs. Allen's part to stay with Grace to find a book she could enjoy and to remain there to read with her and help her get involved in the story was a very caring gesture. By helping her discover a new story to read, Mrs. Allen made a difficult transition less stressful and increased the chances that Grace would have a successful and meaningful reading session that day. This act of caring took extra time and effort, but the outcome was positive.

In her interview Grace explained that she liked her class, classmates, and teachers particularly because they could talk a lot and share ideas and help one another. She felt that the sharing "helps you learn." When asked about trust, she replied, "Well, I think I should trust someone if they're my friend, or they always keep promises (honest), and they really care about me." We discussed a moment I observed during a group meeting in which she began crying when someone in the class hurt her feelings. She talked about the fact that several of the girls in the class moved over next to her and consoled her while she cried. She explained that this incident was an example of how her classmates show that they care. They sat quietly by her side until she had regained her composure and was able to participate in the group once again.

The atmosphere of caring in any classroom is often a reflection of the teacher's attitude and actions. Both teachers in this constructivist classroom had strong feelings about caring *about* and *for* others, which came out not only in the classroom observations, but also in their interviews. Mrs. Allen stated that one of her goals for the year had been to pay attention to the students' interpersonal relationships and their social–moral development. Illustrating her desire for them to develop a caring attitude, she said, "I think particularly third graders should be moving toward the idea that 'I do things because it's a nice thing to do or the right thing to do.'" Her actions and the subjects of her class discussions (respect, thoughtfulness, fairness) reflected a strong awareness of the importance of caring and a strong commitment on her part to share this with the students.

Mrs. Roberts said a lot about her interest in caring when she answered the question, "What do you think are the most important characteristics of a teacher?" The most important characteristic was empathy, and the second was being fair. Her caring attitude was evident in some of the things she expressed in interviews. In talking about allowing children to grow at their own pace, she remarked, "I treat the children the way I want to be treated. I accept that we all don't learn at the same level." In the answer to another question, she said, "I want to be as open to them and [let them know they can] tell me what they need to tell me. And even though I may not have a solution for them, I want them to feel that I care and I'm concerned." A few minutes later she added, "You need to align yourself with the children's feelings, to be sensitized to what's going on, so that the children will come to you on their terms. They have to trust you."

Mrs. Roberts also shared some advice that she gives to parents that reflects a caring approach. She tells them, "If you raise your child with love, children will forgive your mistakes. If you do the best you can and let the child know you're really trying, most children remember the trying, not the outcome."

Discussions within the classroom reflected that the students understood the importance of care. The following excerpt from a classroom observation is a good illustration:

> Mrs. Allen has just read about leadership in the book she is reading to the class. She stops to ask the class what leadership is.
>
> JOSEPH: I know.
>
> MRS. ALLEN: You have answered a lot, Joseph. Adam? (SHE IS ENCOURAGING OTHERS TO PARTICIPATE.)
>
> ADAM: Leadership is being (PAUSE) the first . . . ahead of everyone.
>
> Joseph raises his hand, and Mrs. Allen calls on him by asking him what he thinks?
>
> JOSEPH: Well, there's another way. It's like being kind to people (PAUSE), taking care of people if they get hurt.
>
> MRS. ALLEN: Okay, so you have to be an example for others.
>
> JOSEPH: Yes.
>
> MRS. ALLEN: They follow you?
>
> JOSEPH: Yes.
>
> MRS. ALLEN (CONTINUES READING): The quality of leadership is something you don't gain overnight.

In his explanation of leadership Joseph described caring, being kind to other people, as a way to be a leader. This statement said to me that caring was an important part of the dynamics within this classroom, at least for him. He is one of the more outspoken students and assumes a leadership role in many situations, especially in the area of maintaining enforcement of the class rules. It was interesting to see that taking a caring approach was an integral part of his definition of being a leader and taking a responsible approach was an integral part of his definition of being a leader and a responsible person.

Another good example of respectful and caring behavior on the part of the students was the incident that occurred on a day when the students built kites. Kevin had worked in a group with two other boys. This group built a parachute rather than a kite. All of the group members were active participants and were equally enthralled with their creation. However, when Kevin's dad came to get him out of school early that day, Lindsey generously offered the parachute to Kevin to take home with him. This thoughtful gesture was a perfect example of the caring attitude present in the classroom.

Cooperation

As with the other elements of trust within this classroom, cooperation was evident from the outset. Students worked together in groups regularly, and they appeared to be very supportive of each other. When conflict did arise, a situation that is sometimes unavoidable, the students were usually adept at mediating each other's differences. Sometimes the teachers would be involved, but it appeared that many times the teacher would appoint a mediator and allow the students to solve the problem.

One of the most memorable examples of conflict being converted to cooperation occurred on a day when I observed Kevin and Sean engaged in an unfriendly discussion.

> MRS. ALLEN: Sean, bring your work here. We need to talk about your problem.
>
> SEAN (ADDRESSING KEVIN, THE PERSON HE HAS A PROBLEM WITH): Kevin, let me talk, please. I don't know if you did this or not. I've been hearing from three people that you have done this.
>
> Sean is holding a piece of paper that apparently was a math assignment given to them by the teacher. It has some marks on it.

Building Trust as We Build Knowledge

> Mrs. Allen: How do you know this? How did Kevin know this was your work? (to Kevin): Did you think it was Sean's paper?
>
> Sean: The reason I care is I worked hard trying to do it, and I don't like people destroying it so I have to do it again.

Kevin refuses to get involved in the discussion; he looks down at the desk. (Kevin is seated. Sean is standing in front of his desk as he addresses him. Mrs. Allen is standing to Sean's side.)

Mrs. Allen is called over by another student and leaves the boys to discuss their problem. Sean begins to address Kevin, and Kevin gets up and walks away to the back of the room.

> Sean (calling out to him as he leaves): Kevin, I wasn't finished!

Kevin goes into the principal's office, which leads to the restroom. (Sean looks over at me, smiles at me and points a finger, like "just a minute." He rolls his eyes and looks at me with a quizzical expression as if to say, "What do I do now?") Sean walks to the back of the room and follows Kevin into the principal's office. They both end up in her office where she begins helping them talk through their problem. Meanwhile, the third graders are at the front tables; both rows of students are working diligently. Mrs. Allen is working with the students.

Suddenly Mrs. Allen misses Kevin. "Where is Kevin? Why isn't Kevin here?" She goes to look for him. In the meantime, both boys are in the principal's office. Mrs. Allen goes and stands outside the office, realizing that the principal is working with the boys. Rather than interrupting them, she listens outside the door. The conversation in the office continues.

> Principal (to Kevin): So, do you need to talk about something?

Kevin refuses to talk. It is possible that he is worried that the principal is angry. (I learn later that this is not the first time Kevin has had problems getting along with others in the class.) She senses that he is worried and assures him that she is not angry, but that she would like to see them work it out. She tells them that it can be handled just between the two of them. Sean starts to interrupt, and the principal intervenes.

PRINCIPAL: Kevin, do you have anything to say? What do you think would be fair to do? What should you have to do?

Kevin stares at floor. Sean starts to give an answer.

PRINCIPAL: Kevin, I want your ideas. If someone wrote on your paper and you didn't want him to, what should you have to do? Is this fair?

Kevin is silent. Sean tries to answer for him.

PRINCIPAL: Kevin, is it uncomfortable for you to say you did it?

Kevin is silent. Sean tries to speak for him.

PRINCIPAL (INTERRUPTING SEAN): Want time to think about it? Want us to give you a minute?

Kevin continues to stare down at the floor.

PRINCIPAL: Kevin, look me in the eye.

Teachers often insist that students look into their eyes. It is a way to encourage honesty and acceptance.

PRINCIPAL: You can answer this question. (TO SEAN): Do you think Kevin can time himself? (TO BOTH BOYS): Kevin, do you want to time yourself? Or Sean?

Kevin indicates that he wants to time himself. She allows him to do this. Sean is a little unsure about this decision. Sean watches over Kevin's shoulder as he times himself. Mrs. Allen enters the room. When the minute is over, the principal breaks the silence.

PRINCIPAL: Kevin, do you want to end this now? What do you want to say?

KEVIN (VERY QUIETLY): I'm sorry.

PRINCIPAL: Sean, you were really patient, and Kevin, you were really brave. Do you see now that you are not going to get in trouble for telling the truth? Do you see how you can be friends and work things out?

The principal shakes both of their hands and thanks them.

In this interaction the principal skillfully assisted the boys by taking a confrontation that could have gotten unruly and helping them to learn how to negotiate their differences in a peaceful way. She was very responsive to the fact that Kevin was nervous about being "in trouble" again, and she carefully worded her questions and responses to give him a sense of comfort. She used the art of silence in allowing him to calm down and think about what he wanted to do and say. She gently refused to allow Sean to talk for Kevin or interject his opinion while she was allowing Kevin quiet time to think about the situation. She also used the technique of having Kevin look into her eyes. This is a technique that I witnessed both teachers using many times when talking to students. Their insistence that students look into their eyes was a method for getting honest and sincere responses and also a way to be sure the students were listening to them. The principal ended the session with a compliment for each boy, showing sincere respect and allowing both of them to leave the confrontation with a sense of dignity. This interaction resulted in a positive lesson in cooperation.

On a closing note, I asked one girl during her interview if she had a best friend, hoping to get her to talk about what friendship meant to her. I had imagined that she would say "yes" and name the girl with whom she spent the majority of her time. But, she surprised me and said, "No, I don't have a best friend. Everyone [in this class] is your friend." At least for her, it seems that the element of cooperation was having an impact.

Communication

Communication played a big part in this constructivist classroom. Certainly there was a lot of talking, but there were many less obvious ways (facial expressions, body language) that conveyed numerous messages. Also, listening was an important part of the learning process—both cognitively and socially.

A good example of how students were learning to communicate is a situation that Mrs. Allen discussed in one of her interviews. She gave this example when asked about some of her successes for the year. Her story involved a shy second-grader who Mrs. Allen described as "rather passive in her interactions." For the first five weeks of school, she had refused to participate verbally in any group circle or activity. According to

Mrs. Allen, she rarely made eye contact or showed a change in expression when called upon. After five weeks, the student experienced a transformation. Her new style included active participation and sharing of ideas. Mrs. Allen attributed the change to the structure of the classroom. Her vision of how she sees her class explains why such a change could take place. Mrs. Allen explained that within her classroom students know they can make mistakes without ridicule, offer ideas without being rejected, and take risks without being punished. Her closing remark was, "And I'm hoping that the behavior has come because she feels that kind of trust."

Mrs. Roberts, in a discussion of the importance of being fair, said, "It's important to find resolutions and compromises." Through observation I know that she practices this because she was often involved with students in a mediating role, either as the mediator or enlisting the help of a student to be a peer mediator. An observation of one such mediation gave me an insight into how effective and also how ineffective the mediation process can be.

> One day, Cameron and David get into a heated discussion about some stories each boy had written. As it turns out, both boys have fictional characters who are so similar that it is hard to distinguish one from the other. The biggest problem seems to be that they have identical titles for their adventures, "Poke Wars," and they both, coincidentally, are just like the Pokeman stories. David claims that he developed his "Poke Wars" even before the Pokeman series was created. When Mrs. Roberts realizes that their discussion is quickly becoming an argument that is going down a dead-end street, she suggests that they enlist the help of a mediator to see if they can resolve their disagreement in a peaceful manner.
>
> > MRS. ROBERTS: I think we need to get a mediator. Charles! (CHARLES COMES OVER.) David and Cameron have a real problem and need a mediator. Can you help them? (HE AGREES TO SERVE AS THE MEDIATOR.)
>
> The boys once again share the facts they had just shared in front of Mrs. Roberts. Then Cameron makes the following statement.

CAMERON: I came up with it, so I needed a title, and I was thinking about it in bed. And I came up with the title "Poke Wars."

DAVID: Let me talk, Charles.

CHARLES/MEDIATOR (TO CAMERON): I think he's worried about the title.

CAMERON (TO DAVID): I have written the same words as you.

DAVID: I'm not talking about the words. I just need to show him. (DAVID CALLS CAMERON OVER TO THE CUBBIES SO HE CAN SHOW HIM HIS DRAWINGS.) I made this up way before he did.

After many words back and forth between the two boys who are in conflict and after watching Charles, the mediator, listen awkwardly as the two boys argue, Mrs. Roberts gets back in the middle of the discussion. She has never gone too far away, even though Charles is supposedly in charge. Mrs. Roberts, probably unknowingly, shows sympathy to Cameron, for she becomes rather argumentative with David when neither side will give in. David continues to break in with his arguments. They finally agree that they will take different titles and continue to draw their characters and write their stories. Then the conversation continues.

MRS. ROBERTS: Mediator, do you feel everyone has gotten what they want?

CHARLES: Yes, I think Cameron got the title and David got what he wanted.

MRS. ROBERTS: David, Cameron, do you feel like it is okay?

CAMERON: It's solved. . . .

DAVID: No, Cameron, stop. I can't even think! I have proof.

David goes off to his cubby, and Mrs. Roberts follows him. They talk until David agrees to continue his stories with his title and that Cameron can take a new title.

The mediation process was not very effective, however, for several reasons. First of all, Mrs. Roberts did not let the boys choose a mediator; instead, she appointed one. Second, she did not really leave the boys alone to work it out. She stayed close by listening to every word and then jumped back into the discussion after a few minutes. Third, she continued to interrupt David and did not really allow the process to work. She seemed to be determined not to give in to David and his arguments. The whole process seemed very rushed, and it was not surprising that both boys came out feeling dissatisfied with the results. When handled properly, this process can be very effective. But in this situation, the results were less than favorable or fair. A communication technique such as mediation can work well when it is practiced according to its guidelines. In this case a completely effective mediation did not occur.

Mediation, however, can be effective. In this classroom I witnessed informal mediation efforts on the part of the students that worked. They didn't always go to the teachers to arrange a mediation; instead, they used their mediation skills as a natural part of resolving disputes. Discussing mediation in the interviews, both students and teachers indicated that mediation was a tool they used, and the attitudes expressed regarding this approach were positive.

In an interview, Mrs. Roberts said something significant regarding the connection between communication and trust. First, she said that she is careful when dealing with parents to try to ask questions that do not make judgments. And she stressed the importance of listening to them. Her conclusion was, "They will come around if they trust you, and they will ask you for help." During the altercation between Cameron and David, she had forgotten the importance of listening, and the results were adversely affected.

Mrs. Allen, in her interview, made several references to communication. To quickly summarize some singular comments, she mentioned that she stresses listening skills, uses language that is not confrontational, and tries to have parents come in to "just talk."

A reflection on the importance of listening came when Sean shared his view that a couple of classmates could not be trusted because they "didn't keep secrets." But, he added when questioned about his own trustworthiness, "All my classmates trust me. I don't blurt out things." Obviously, communication is not all about talking.

Children sometimes have great insights. When interviewed, Lisa commented, "Words do hurt. And you can never take back words." This is obviously one important lesson she has learned somewhere in life, but one lesson she said she learned that year in school is a positive statement for this classroom and the emphasis on effective communication and interactions. When asked, "What are the most important things you have learned this year?" she replied, "Well, I think I have learned how to deal with people."

Communication within this classroom was more lively than in many classes, especially classes in traditional schools. The students were allowed not only to talk a lot as they worked in groups and shared ideas in class discussions, but also to express feelings and use their words to encourage each other. Their daily class meetings provided a forum for sharing ideas, experiences, and emotions; and their use of mediation and open communication provided a means for resolving differences. An emphasis on listening added to the foundation of trust that was built with the contributing element of communication.

Conditions of Trust

The conditions of trust that I identified are *honesty, acceptance, commitment*, and *responsiveness*. When the elements of care, respect, communication, and cooperation are tempered by the conditions of honesty, acceptance, commitment, and responsiveness, a trusting environment is more likely to evolve. Within the classroom observed, the conditions of honesty (keeping your word, following the rules), acceptance (looking someone in the eye, appreciating others' differences), commitment (following through with promises, meeting responsibilities), and responsiveness (acting on requests, listening attentively to others in the group) were as apparent as the four elements. These conditions enhanced the quality of the trust.

They are "modifying" conditions, much like an adjective modifies a noun. They make the elements more complex, more effective, more meaningful. They were a part of the classroom environment in both an implicit and explicit way. These conditions were part of the teachers' values, as witnessed in their classroom comments and interview responses, and they were also ingrained in many of the children, as evidenced by their behavior in class and their remarks in private conversations.

Through communication of ideas and feelings, we can experience freedom in our actions, words, and choices and emotional freedom in our reactions. The essence of honesty can emerge in this instance. When care is shown through eye contact, a gentle touch, kind words, or encouragement, we might witness nonjudgmental attitudes and a relaxed demeanor. Within these encounters, acceptance can be realized. Acts of respect, such as defending one's rights, treating others with dignity, or allowing responsibility, can result in an atmosphere of autonomous independence and/or cooperative, collaborative interdependence, which can translate into feelings of self-confidence or belief in others. An enthusiasm for learning may be an additional result. The conditions of trust that can surface in these instances are commitment and responsiveness. When cooperation exists in group projects or class meetings, the result can be spontaneity. Also, when cooperation exists between two or three individuals, it is possible that they may experience acceptance when they find positive ways to manage crises or mistakes. In these cooperative situations, the emerging conditions of trust are acceptance and responsiveness.

The expectations of exploration and ongoing discovery within the constructivist classroom can occur only if the teachers allow students the freedom to participate in appropriate ways in classroom organization and management. The effective teacher utilizes suggestion and persuasion and encourages self-regulation or autonomy. She also insists on student participation in establishing class values and rules, as well as involvement in class meetings and expression of thoughts and feelings. Learning experiences involve varied approaches. Group projects and interactions exist alongside one-on-one teacher–student or student–student discovery and problem solving. Affective consciousness is of equal value to cognitive growth in a setting where well-adjusted, functional individuals are the desired outcome.

Commonalities in the Construction of Knowledge and of Trust

After observing the construction of knowledge within a constructivist classroom and witnessing the construction of trust within that same classroom, one discovers that the similarities between the two are apparent. The following chart (Table 1) outlines the connection between constructing knowledge and developing trust within the classroom and the elements and conditions of trust that both have in common.

As one can see from the chart, the construction of trust occurs in much the same way that knowledge itself is constructed. Both

Table 1. Commonalities in Constructing Knowledge and Trust within a Constructivist Classroom*

Constructivism (constructing knowledge)	Trust (developing trust)	Common Elements/ Conditions
1. Inductive process.	1. Inductive process.	Commitment Communication
2. Knowledge develops over time.	2. Trust develops over time.	Commitment Acceptance
3. Involves risk.	3. Involves risk.	Caring Respect Acceptance
4. Blend of autonomy and collaboration.	4. Blend of autonomy and collaboration.	Respect Cooperation
5. Cooperation and communication with conflict and academic controversy.	5. Cooperation and communication with conflict and misunderstandings.	Cooperation Communication Caring
6. Class rules based on mutual values.	6. Shared values inherent in trust.	Respect Honesty Responsiveness
7. Emotion and reason are part of constructing knowledge.	7. Emotion and reason enter into creation of trust.	Caring Responsiveness Acceptance

* Knowledge and trust develop in same way. Building trust is a constructivist process.

are built through an inductive process and develop over a period of time. When involved in an inductive process, participants must have a commitment to realizing the desired outcomes. At the same time, communication is a key factor in the development of knowledge or trust in an inductive manner. Only through talking about what one has read or observed and listening to others' opinions and feelings, does one gain understanding and realization of the goal.

Any process that requires change involves risk, and the construction of both knowledge and trust demands that risks be taken. In building knowledge, students must take risks and make mistakes. When a caring attitude is present, people feel safe to take risks. A caring and respectful atmosphere makes risk-taking less threatening and allows errors to become steps to gaining knowledge. When caring and respect are present in a relationship, a sense of acceptance makes risk-taking more likely to occur. Building trust within a relationship is possible when care and respect are conditions within the personal interaction.

One goal of constructivist educators is to encourage individual autonomy and, at the same time, to facilitate a cooperative/collaborative attitude among class members. The autonomous individual develops a sense of self-worth and personal integrity that can be interpreted as self-respect. Concurrently, the constructivist philosophy encourages a sense of cooperation that establishes an integrated community of learners. Although it is important that everyone achieve a sense of independence, a connection with others through collaboration breeds an interdependence that is also desired. This interdependence can be defined as mutual respect.

The development of trust follows a similar approach. An individual should have a sense of trust in self—an autonomous inner wisdom—yet, at the same time, trusting in others is a necessary part of life. The development of trust with others evolves through the interaction of the elements and conditions identified in this study. The blend, or collaboration, of these factors creates an environment of trust. Again, self-respect and mutual respect are factors that enter into this formula.

Addressing conflict through communication and cooperation brings about new knowledge and new levels of trust. In the constructivist classroom, conflicts can be a healthy part of growth. When critical pedagogy has a role in the classroom, academic controversy is a natural consequence. This type of controversy is a method for uncovering different ideas and new approaches to problem solving. Through effective communication and cooperation, knowledge is built. In the same way, trust can be built through cooperation and communication. When misunderstandings arise, careful listening and cooperative mediation can lead to increased levels of awareness and new plateaus of trust. An underlying caring attitude in these situations provides a setting for smoother resolution of differences.

Mutual values are an important basis of class rules established in constructivist classrooms. Discussions related to these values often lead to enhanced insights and understanding within a trusting relationship. When integrity and worth are defined by all parties in the same way, a solid foundation of trust can be built. In the achievement of these results, mutual respect must be exhibited, and honest sharing of values is essential. Likewise, responsiveness to others' values in a non-judgmental way sets the stage for mutual understanding.

Reason and emotion are also integral pieces of constructing knowledge. The mind, the instrument for reasoning, is generally given credit for assimilating knowledge, but emotions also play an important part in the process. Knowledge supplies the tools for survival in our world. However, survival occurs on many levels—physical, mental, emotional, spiritual—and the tools must be able to accommodate all needs. Thus, emotional awareness combines with reasoning powers to develop the knowledge we need to exist.

Trust, as well, is conditioned by reason and emotion. When we witness certain actions or behaviors of others, our minds tell us whether or not we can "trust" those people. If they break a promise or hurt us in some way, we determine that they are not trustworthy. At the same time, emotions affect the way we experience others, and positive affection—caring, responsiveness, acceptance—can set a tone for trust to develop. Both reason and emotion enter into the building of trust.

Implications for School Leaders

Margaret Wheatley in her book *Leadership and the New Science* (1999) discusses the importance of relationships. Her ideas give us food for thought:

> We need to become savvy about how to foster relationships, how to nurture growth and development. All of us need to become better at listening, conversing, respecting one another's uniqueness, because these are essential for strong relationships. The era of the rugged individual has been replaced by the era of the team player. But this is only the beginning.
>
> Even organizational power is purely relational. Power in organizations is the capacity generated by relationships. It is an energy that comes into existence through relationships.
>
> If power is the capacity generated by our relationships, then we need to be attending to the quality of those relationships. We would do well to ponder the realization that love is the most potent source of power (pp. 39–40).

Although Wheatley is addressing adult leaders and potential leaders, the children whom we encounter in the classroom today are our future leaders. If they can learn in their formative years to develop healthy relationships, they will be the leaders who can help to create a respectful working environment when they are in charge. If the children in the constructivist classroom are learning to develop trust for others within their community, then hopefully they will continue to model those behaviors in other settings. The knowledge that they can gain in such a classroom goes far beyond the cognitive gains reflected in test scores or grade reports. These students can develop life skills that should allow them to interact successfully with others and enjoy the benefits of healthy relationships.

Those of us who are current school leaders can benefit from Wheatley's words and the lessons learned within the classroom that were the subject of this study. We can find several theoretical connections that heighten educational leaders' effectiveness. The first regards trust. As discussed earlier, certain elements can encourage a trusting environment when combined with the right conditions. The observations and interviews in a constructivist classroom provided data that show trust to be a construct that can be consequently developed in a social setting.

The results of this study provide valuable information for school administrators who wish to infuse a level of trust within their educational environments. The ideals and principles of constructivism, when practiced consistently, provide a foundation for developing a deep sense of trust within a school community. When the elements of care, respect, communication, and cooperation are infused with honesty, acceptance, commitment, and responsiveness, they become more powerful and combine more effectively to create an environment of trust.

References

Baloche, Lynda A. (1998). *The Cooperative Classroom*. Englewood Cliffs, NJ: Prentice-Hall, Inc.

Brooks, Jacqueline Grennon, & Brooks, Martin G. (1993). *The Case for Constructivist Classrooms*. Alexandria, VA: Association for Supervision and Curriculum Development.

Hanson, D. (1997). *Cultivating Common Ground*. Boston: Butterworth-Heinemann.

Pressley, M., & McCormick, J. (1995). *Advanced Educational Psychology*. San Francisco: Jossey Bass.

Tronto, Joan C. (1994). *Moral Boundaries*. New York: Routledge.

Wheatley, Margaret J. (1999). *Leadership and the New Science*. San Francisco: Berrett Koehler Publishers.

2

Designing Effective Advisory Programs

Lynn M. Bullard

An effective guidance program furthers the work of every subject teacher. Achievement in each subject will be increased if the ambitions of children to succeed in their school work can be aroused, if their attitudes and manners are improved, if they are happier. The homeroom program, to the extent that it is successful, benefits the teacher as much as it benefits the pupil. The strain caused by the teaching load would be cut in half if each pupil were a happy, well-adjusted individual who wanted to learn the subject he was taking and who saw his teacher as a friend rather than a taskmaster. . . . Every teacher knows that something needs to be done. Where else, if not in homeroom? (V. Ross, 1954, p. vii)

Especially during these times of high-stakes testing when so much time in the school day is spent preparing students in academic areas, conscientious administrators must remain aware of the need to educate students in the affective as well as the cognitive realm. A time for an advisory period during the school day offers an effective way to support the affective development of students. Advisory programs have evolved from what Ross

(1954) envisioned as a homeroom to provide a guidance time for secondary school students. Affective needs were to be addressed. Unfortunately, most homerooms simply became a time for administrative details such as attendance and announcements. The evolution from the homeroom of yesterday to the advisory program of today has been a slow and difficult process.

Moss (1969) took another step in that process and discussed a program that is one step closer to the current advisory program used in schools. According to Moss, the guidance counselor was to serve as a trainer of teachers and coordinator of the program. Teachers were to be trained in conferencing techniques, keeping records, and recognizing signs of distress in students that may require additional attention from the counselor, administrators, or parents. As coordinator of the program, the counselor was to visit classrooms to help teach the lessons as part of a guidance unit. Teachers were to be provided with the lessons and encouraged to teach them without the assistance of the counselor.

There is still more, however, to the progression from the concept of the homeroom to the concept of an advisory program. Eventually, there is the expectation that academic teachers will become a significant part of an advisory program. The teachers will be responsible for implementing what is taught to them during staff development. Although there may be a support system for the teachers in the form of a counselor or an administrator, the task of developing an environment to promote a healthy adult–student relationship will be up to the teacher.

The advisory program serves several purposes. It promotes opportunities for social and emotional development. Advisory is a time to assist students with academic issues and to facilitate positive involvement between adults and students. The primary purpose, however, is to provide activities that support both students' social and academic success (MacIver & Epstein, 1991; Clark & Clark, 1994; Allen, Splittgerber, & Manning, 1993; Alexander, Williams, Compton, & Prescott, 1968). During a daily advisory period, students should enjoy positive adult and peer relationships and attain skills which help them cope with the increased number of personal, social, emotional, and academic challenges they will encounter in adolescence. There are more interactions between the advisor and the students during advisory than during the traditional homeroom period.

As extensions of homerooms, advisory programs provide specific opportunities for students to develop within the affective domain. Advisory programs assist students in learning how to settle interpersonal conflicts, develop study skills, and improve social skills. Opportunities and learning experiences encourage students to assess what they value and what is important to them. Students learn to consider values and dilemmas that are created by conflicting or inconsistent beliefs. Advisory programs help students to become aware of these aspects of the affective domain and encourage them to conduct a continuous examination of their values and beliefs in order to develop an increased understanding of themselves (Curtis & Bidwell, 1977; Dorman, Lipsitz, & Verner, 1985).

Bandura (1982) adds another dimension of the affective domain that is addressed in advisory, the concept of self-efficacy. Self-efficacy describes the students' ability to produce and control events in their lives. When students feel competent, they are capable of carrying through with a course of action and achieving desired outcomes. Bandura states that when students give up, it is often because of a negative environment that is unresponsive to their efforts. The students' accomplishments are not recognized or rewarded. When teachers address the affective domain, their responsiveness supports and encourages students' self-efficacy.

However, achieving self-efficacy may produce conflict within the individual. Students may be confused about the desire to be either a member or an individual in different situations. This conflict can be addressed in advisory. Through advisory, students can become a members of a community of learners. Within this community, they participate in collaborative activities that foster collegiality, mutual respect, responsibility, and participation (Digby, Totten, & Snider, 1995). Students can assess and modify their social skills in a non-threatening environment. With respect to students' individuality, advisory provides an opportunity for students to develop a relationship with one adult who knows them personally, who cares about their happiness, and who is willing to listen, help find solutions, and encourage their individual success (Muth & Alvermann, 1992; Bushnell & George, 1993). The goal is for this individualized attention to build students' self-efficacy by improving their attitudes toward school, increasing their self-esteem, heightening their levels of academic achievement, and decreasing management and behavior problems (Andrews & Stern, 1992).

The inclusion of the affective component in the education of adolescents is crucial to their development. Adolescence is a period of tremendous physical growth, intellectual changes, and emotional instability. Schools must recognize the need to assist students in several affective areas: (1) understanding themselves and others; (2) self-concept; (3) values; (4) decision making; and (5) developing interpersonal skills (Shockley, Schumacher, & Smith, 1984; Curtis & Bidwell, 1977). Advisory, as it is used in the public schools, can be defined as the place where all aspects of exploration in the affective domain can be brought into focus, and more attention can be given to affective learning (Curtis & Bidwell, 1977; Bushnell & George, 1993). Personalization of education requires that some time during the school day must be devoted to evaluating the needs and desires of each individual adolescent. These elements of the affective domain must be considered equally as important as the intellectual skills that are part of the cognitive domain.

Goals of Advisory Programs

The role of advisory programs in addressing the development of the affective domain has been summarized by Curtis and Bidwell (1977) in terms of four goals: (1) development of emotional health; (2) ethical and moral development; (3) aesthetic appreciation; and (4) socialization. An advisory program curriculum based upon these goals stresses freedom of choice, student responsibility, and student initiative. Information and skills learned in advisory can and should be related and integrated across disciplines (Curtis & Bidwell, 1977; Alexander, Williams, Compton, & Prescott, 1968). Including these concepts does not lead to a weakening of the academic curriculum; instead, these concepts can bring a change in the structure of the learning experience. This change may improve student attitudes toward school, increase self-esteem, increase levels of academic achievement, and decrease management problems (Andrews & Stern, 1992).

A brief review of each of the affective goals of advisory programs may be helpful for an administrator who is concerned about developing or maintaining a quality advisory program. The first affective goal for advisory is to develop the *emotional health* of the student. Training in emotional expression should create potentially well-balanced and emotionally healthy adults. To achieve this goal, the school must design a learning environment specifically intended to facilitate the development of the student's potential. The depth of a student's emotional balance can only be assessed after an emphasis has been placed on higher-level thought processes and emotional development (Curtis & Bidwell, 1977; White & Greenwood, 1991; Galassi, Gulledge, & Cox, 1997). For example, during an observation in a teacher's classroom, a boy threw his books onto the desk when he became angry. Most of the books slid off the desk onto the floor. The teacher did not become angry. She simply stated that she would talk to him in the back of the room. They spoke quietly for a few moments. The boy then went to his desk area, picked up his books, and calmly sat down. In this case, the student's outburst was quickly contained, and both the student and the teacher acknowledged and addressed the inappropriate behavior without further consequence.

The second affective goal for advisory is to address the *ethical and moral development* of the student. Ethical and moral development can best be developed in an environment where the teacher provides freedom to explore alternatives in behavior (Galassi, Gulledge, & Cox, 1997). Renewed attention to this dimension of affective education in an advisory setting allows students the opportunity to test personal values which conflict with the values of other individuals or groups (Curtis & Bidwell, 1977; Alexander, Williams, Compton, & Prescott, 1968). A skilled advisor is one who can and is willing to help a student with the struggles adolescents often face. Such an advisor encourages freedom of expression and consideration of the moral and ethical implications of possible choices students might make. However, the advisor must be careful not to become judgmental lest the student feel devalued. When relationships are established that give students the opportunity to explore their options, the students will feel respected and be willing to participate more freely in the discussions. In one classroom, the teacher encouraged the students to give book talks. Several students gave presentations from above-level books they were reading. One student was reading a children's insert from the newspaper. He said his mother always saves that part of the paper so that he has something he enjoys reading. He went on to describe how he always got into trouble because he never had anything to read during advisory. The class chuckled. Then he continued by describing the things he had learned from that section of the newspaper. He asked the teacher if he had said enough. She said that he had, smiled, and thanked him. He returned the smile and returned to his desk.

The third affective goal for advisory is to help the student develop *aesthetic awareness and appreciation*. Such awareness and appreciation should involve both intellectual understanding and emotional expression. This awareness can apply to art, music, politics, or logical development in academic areas such as mathematics. The assumption is that the more perceptive the student, the greater the appreciation for the subject (Curtis & Bidwell, 1977; Alexander, Williams, Compton, & Prescott, 1968). This goal can be can addressed in advisory classes through discussion of the expectations of audience behavior in assemblies. Advisory can also help students to learn what is expected when they apply for elected positions such as Student Council. Advisory time could be used to help students to learn about making campaign posters and giving speeches in front of an audience.

The fourth affective goal to be addressed is *socialization*. Socialization is the gradual process whereby attitudes and values of the society will encourage in the individual the greatest possible emotional health within the framework of that society. Socialization is an important function of the school. Students must be taught how to cope with the problems and the changes they will experience not only in school but throughout their lives (Curtis

& Bidwell, 1977; White & Greenwood, 1991). Advisory should provide experiences that facilitate the development of socialization skills which students can use in their relationships with peers and others in the school, in the family, and in the community. For example, advisory time can be used to explore opportunities to participate in clubs and other activities. Such time should be made available as part of this goal to help students enhance their socialization skills (Alexander, Williams, Compton, & Prescott, 1968; Galassi, Gulledge, & Cox, 1997).

There are also specific programs available to schools that address socialization skills. One example of such a program that teaches socialization skills is Boys Town Social Skills. This program is designed to teach skills such as "How to handle criticism," "How to accept 'No' as an answer," and "How to disagree." Advisory offers a time in the school day for faculty to focus on helping students to learn and understand the importance of these skills. A competent advisory teacher will establish an environment in which guidelines for behavior are important teaching tools to help students toward desirable behavior. Teachers will discuss concerns with students who disregard the guidelines, and intervention becomes a teaching strategy, not a punitive stance, when the focus is on students learning appropriate socialization skills.

The importance of including the four goals of advisory in a school's curriculum becomes obvious when the developmental changes adolescents experience are considered. Adolescents often behave inconsistently, experience real and imagined fears, and display a myriad of emotions. It is these needs, feelings, and problems of adolescence that are addressed in the four goals of an advisory program. To ignore these needs, feelings, and problems of the students is tacitly to say that schools are not responsible for those parts of their development.

Obstacles to Implementation

Even with widespread acceptance of the importance of advisory programs, such programs often do not function as intended, thus limiting their effectiveness in meeting adolescent needs. Although there are cases in which advisory programs show positive results (MacIver, 1990), advisory remains one of the most difficult concepts to implement (Fenwick, 1992; Lounsbury & Clark, 1990). There are several obstacles to the implementation of advisory (Clark & Clark, 1994). All of these obstacles involve teachers whose commitment and competence are essential to the success of an advisory program.

The first obstacle is that teachers feel they do not have adequate knowledge or skills to serve as advisors (Clark & Clark, 1994; Ross, 1954). Some teachers feel that their role as an advisor is really a counselor's role that they are not willing to assume. Particularly those teachers who have been trained to teach on the secondary level consider themselves content specialists and not responsible for addressing the nonacademic problems, interests, or concerns of their students (White & Greenwood, 1991; MacIver & Epstein, 1991).

The second obstacle is the teacher's belief that the additional role of advisor detracts from his or her role as subject-matter expert (Clark & Clark, 1994). A corollary of this belief is the assumption that advisor and teacher are separate roles, and that teachers will experience great difficulty if they have to change from role to role. What teachers fail to recognize is that, consciously or unconsciously, classroom teachers advise students throughout the day.

A third obstacle that teachers face in implementing advisory is insufficient time to plan (Clark & Clark, 1994; Ross, 1954), and that what to plan is often out of their realm of expertise (George & Bushnell, 1993). There are many activities that schools can incorporate into the advisory time. School-wide themes such as recycling, study skills, and building and maintaining friendships can involve many people and therefore not become the responsibility of one person (Clark & Clark, 1994). Intramural and service projects can also be part of the advisory program. Activities may be organized depending on the needs of the school, of the faculty, and of the students (Clark & Clark, 1994).

A fourth obstacle is the lack of resources to plan advisory programs (Clark & Clark, 1994; Van Hoose, 1991; Ross, 1954). Teachers are often not aware of the availability of resources and feel all activities must be teacher-planned. Advisory programs differ widely in their approaches, but the focus should be on the intellectual, social, and emotional needs of the adolescent.

The day-to-day workings of a successful advisory depend on teachers who are comfortable with their roles as advisors and are committed to the philosophy behind advisory programs. However, fear, inexperience, lack of skills, and ignorance of philosophy are obstacles to successful advisory programs. These obstacles must be examined, understood, and remedied through staff development (Ayres, 1994; James, 1986; Ross, 1954). Staff development must help teachers to understand the relationship between affective and cognitive learning. Without this understanding, teachers often view advisory as a waste of time that could better be used for academics. Many teachers fail to see the value of a warm and caring classroom environment in which the teacher serves as a student's sounding board. Through staff development teachers will learn that it is not necessary nor expected that they be guidance counselors. However, they will learn to detect potential problems, handle immediate concerns (a crying student), and work with the counselor to prevent or solve problems. Staff development can convince teachers that advisory will actually lighten the teaching load (Ross, 1954).

Administrative Support

Staff development is not enough, however, to prepare advisory teachers to adequately address the needs of the students and teachers. School administrators must also take an active role. An administrator must support teachers and counselors as well as voice public support for the importance of advisory in the community. Sufficient time for planning and implementation must also be provided. The goals and functions must be clearly stated. Advisory programs must differ clearly from academic classes. An established length and time of day for advisory must be included in the daily schedule, and a budget for materials must be available. In addition, as discussed above, appropriate staff development must be provided for advisory teachers. Finally, administrators must assume responsibility for continuously evaluating the advisory program. Administrators who attends to these aspects of their role in an advisory program exhibit commitment to the program and, by doing so, can generate a total school philosophy of support for advisory (Allen, Splittgerber, & Manning, 1993; James, 1986; McEwin, 1981; Ross, 1954; Clark & Clark, 1994; Cole, 1994).

Studying an Advisory Program

Even when administrators and teachers accept the importance of advisory programs for students' affective development, designing and evaluating such programs remains a challenge to both administrators and teachers. Although there are "canned" programs that schools can use and the broad principles that advisory programs should address are generally recognized, there is little guidance in the literature about how to determine whether the four goals of advisory programs are successfully addressed. In order to provide administrators and teachers with information they can use to develop and evaluate advisory programs, I conducted a case study to gain a better understanding of how a middle school's administrators and teachers understand and implement the four goals of advisory programs.

Interviews of twelve volunteer faculty advisors, an assistant principal, and the principal were conducted. Teachers were asked to describe the purpose and goals of advisory programs and to describe how the advisory program in the school compared with what they consider the ideal for such a program. The teachers and administrators were also asked what factors contributed to the effectiveness or ineffectiveness of the program.

Each of the teachers was also observed two or three times during his or her advisory period. Each observation lasted between twenty and thirty minutes. Detailed field notes were taken during each observation. These field notes focused on the topic of the lesson; the format (whether it is discussion, lecture, role play); the number of students who participated; the frequency of student participation; and the nature of the interactions between teacher and students. Field notes included a description of the setting of the room, the movement of the advisor within the classroom, and how often and where the advisor moved to interact with a student. The number of interactions the advisor had with students was also tallied, and it was noted whether interactions were advisor initiated or student initiated. In addition, the principal was observed as she presented staff development training about the advisory program.

The field notes taken during classroom observations also included qualitative information about the teachers' interactions with students in advisory. For example, were students encouraged to initiate interactions with teachers? One teacher, for instance, seemed to have established a pattern in which the first few minutes of advisory were informal and students were encouraged to discuss their concerns freely with the teacher. Were these interactions spontaneous, or were the students required to raise a hand and gain recognition before speaking? Were comments from the students received by the teachers without criticism or judgment? Were students encouraged to interact with one another regarding topics about which they have differing opinions? Observations of another advisor revealed that a structured advisory class did not provide the freedom to speak, and students were not spoken to respectfully or encouraged to speak to one another with respect. Perhaps the most important information gained from the classroom observations is that experience does not appear to be a factor relevant to the effectiveness of a teacher as an advisor.

Three Questions

Three questions were developed from an analysis of all the data that were collected about the middle school's advisory program. It is important to emphasize that these questions were not imposed on the data before analysis; rather, each of the three characteristics that the questions address emerged out of the data. These questions offer administrators an important tool for selecting and assessing advisory teachers. They can be used not only to identify teachers, based on their answers to the three questions, who might be suited to be advisors, but also to provide direction for planning staff development to prepare teachers to be better advisors.

The first question is whether teachers can describe the *purpose* of the advisory program. Advisory programs often are designed to increase students' feelings that adults care for them and to create a sense of community among students. Additionally, programs may attempt to meet the students' needs in the areas of developing study, decision-making, goal-setting, and time management skills (Galassi, Gulledge, and Cox, May 1977). During interviews, teachers were asked to describe what they understood to be the purpose and goals of an advisory program. Some teachers were able to state the intended purpose of advisory easily. One teacher responded, "The purpose is to assist the kids, to get to know them, to teach kids that things can be discussed with a teacher and that kids can even disagree with a teacher." Another teacher stated, "Advisory should be an environment that the kids feel comfortable in, that they feel safe in. It needs to be safe for them to say, 'I have a problem. Could you or somebody help me?'" A third teacher replied, "The purpose of advisory is to build camaraderie with the kids." Another response when asked the purpose of advisory was, "It is a time to really get to know these children and develop a close relationship with them. . . . They need to feel the warm and loving atmosphere that is safe . . ." Six of the twelve people interviewed said in some way that the purpose is to provide time during the day to build a relationship with the students. They stated that the purpose and goals were discussed during staff development sessions about the advisory program. However, six teachers stated they had no idea what the purpose and goals are. Five teachers said that advisory is for checking attendance and completing paperwork while the students study or visit. Four teachers simply stated that advisory is a waste of time.

It is important to know whether teachers understand the purpose of advisory. Such information not only offers clues about teachers' perceptions of advisory, but also provides direction for staff development to prepare teachers to be more effective advisors. For example, the information gathered in the school that was the site of the study should bring an awareness to the administration that the message about the purpose of advisory is not being delivered as clearly as the administrator believes. The perception by some teachers that advisory is not their responsibility or that it is a waste of time may very well indicate that teachers do not have a good understanding of advisory programs. It appears that just delivering the information during a segment of a staff-development day has not been sufficient. The teachers may benefit from a more in-depth explanation and perhaps from opportunities to discuss and study the advisory program and its benefits to students' learning and development.

The second question is whether teachers complete the advisory *activities*. Teachers may be reluctant to complete activities if they feel they lack the skills necessary to direct the students through the advisory activity (Galassi, Gulledge, & Cox, May 1977; Ayres, 1994; Cole, 1994). Teachers who are uncomfortable may disguise it as a feeling of frustration about not using all of the school day for instructional/academic activities. Some of these advisors may only complete advisory activities that appear to be academic in nature, such as silent reading or study skills. However, when such activities are completed in the absence of the full scope of advisory activities, they are apt to contribute little to the students' learning or development. One teacher did not complete the advisory activities. She expressed frustration that students would not read or participate in discussions. She did not take the initiative to read to the students. The teacher stated that she did not have time to help the students look for books and that it was not her job to entertain them during advisory.

There was also a range in the degree of compliance—whether or not a teacher actually did the advisory activities. One teacher stated that she does the advisory activity every week and that both she and the students look forward to the activities. Another teacher said she sincerely tries to do all the activities. Sometimes, however, she modifies the activity to fit her students' needs and interests. She stated that because many of her students either have difficulty or dislike writing, she prefers to discuss situations during advisory. She felt the students still gain from the discussions. Five teachers stated that they seldom completed the activities despite the expectation from the principal that all activities be completed. "Sometimes, the lesson just cannot be done at that time," stated one teacher. "Advisory is too structured. I want to do what I need to do during that time," said another teacher. A third teacher reported, "Sometimes I try to do the activities, but some are just so dry."

This second question, whether or not advisors completed specified activities, raises the issue of whether completing the activities is enough to determine the success of an advisory program. Assuming this to be the case, then a highly prescriptive advisory curriculum should be all that is needed to guarantee that the four goals of advisory are achieved. However appealing such a conclusion might be, it is not one that is borne out by this study or by others. It would appear that more crucial to achieving the goals of advisory is an answer of "yes" to the third question about advisory teachers.

The third question is whether teachers model *relationship*-building behavior. Galassi, Gulledge, and Cox (1997) report that these behaviors might consist of availability, enthusiasm, a caring attitude, and an ability to relate to students in an informal manner as opposed to the formal manner often used in the classroom setting. Teachers must also be active listeners and facilitators of discussions. In effective advisory programs, teachers frequently demonstrate these behaviors. The conclusion of Galassi et al. that teachers who are not inclined to develop close personal relationships with students will not be as effective or successful in an advisory program is strongly supported by the data from the study considered in this chapter. In fact, the single most important characteristic of successful advisory teachers in this study is that they develop a relationship with their students.

Observations of teachers during their advisory period provided an opportunity to witness the presence or absence of relationship-building behaviors. Some teachers demonstrated relationship-building behavior by greeting the students as they entered the classroom. One teacher greeted each student by name and made a comment. One of her students was angry because his locker would not open. The teacher assured the student

Designing Effective Advisory Programs

that he could go to the office in a moment to remedy the problem. Another student entered and mumbled something to the teacher. She responded quietly, and the student went to his seat. The teachers took a moment to make personal comments to some of the students. There were also examples of teachers not working to build relationships. One teacher who did not work to build relationships simply attended to what she was doing at her desk and did not acknowledge the presence of the students. Another teacher did not say anything to students unless it was to redirect or question the students. "Today is silent reading day. Take out your book and read," ordered the teacher. The words and tone of voice were often sarcastic. A student was late to advisory. The teacher said to her, "You are late." There was no moment taken to conference with the student, no time provided for the student to explain.

Evidence of a relationship between the advisor and the student is the crucial element when considering whether a teacher gives more than lip-service to the goals of an advisory program. A teacher may be able to offer verbiage about the purpose of an advisory program and may complete specified advisory activities. However, if there is no relationship between the teacher and the student, neither the knowledge of purpose nor the completion of activities is meaningful, and the goals of advisory are not achieved. One teacher checked attendance and completed a lunch count with minimal conversation with the students. Then he began to speak by saying the advisory activity for the day was goal setting. He simply told the students to write a goal for themselves. There were no explanations, no discussion, no examples provided. The activity took about five minutes. Then he sat down and worked at his desk. There was no interaction between him and the students. When the bell rang indicating the end of advisory, he simply looked up and said, "See you later." In fact, the data from the advisors in this study indicate that even those teachers who could not articulately describe the purpose of advisory and did not complete prescribed activities could be successful advisors if they modeled a caring relationship to their students. One teacher frequently referred to the importance of having a classroom environment that "makes it easy and inviting for students to participate." However, she never did connect that importance to being the purpose of advisory. She did not complete the activities assigned. She talked to the students about Texas Assessment of Academic Skills (TAAS), but she did not do the study skills activity. She encouraged them to always do their best.

A careful look at whether teachers model and build relationships with their advisory students leads to several issues for administrators and teachers to consider. What are specific things that teachers who build relationships with their students do? Is there a way for teachers to learn and develop these specific relationship-building strategies? Is every teacher capable of building relationships with students? Should teachers who do not exhibit relationship-building behaviors or do not want to be advisors be assigned to other duties? If the success of advisory hinges on the ability of a teacher to develop a relationship so that a student can have a caring adult in whom to confide, perhaps only those teachers who either innately possess qualities that enable such relationships or teachers who are willing to improve on those skills through further training should be advisors.

A Matrix for Evaluating Advisory Programs

The results of the study of a middle school advisory program indicate that while the importance of teachers to the success of an advisory program cannot be overemphasized, it is possible to describe the characteristics of effective advisory teachers. Furthermore, these characteristics can be linked to the four goals of advisory programs to form a matrix (Table 1) that provides an overview of the kinds of things that successful advisory teachers do to achieve each of the goals as they fulfill the purpose of advisory, complete advisory activities, and develop relationships with their advisory students. This matrix not only offers an overall descriptive account of advisory, but also may function as a tool that administrators and teachers can use to develop and evaluate the advisory program in their school. The matrix is a chart comprised of cells that link the characteristics of advisory teachers with the four goals of advisory programs.

Table 1. The Evaluation Matrix: The Completed Instrument

Goals	Purpose	Activities	Relationship
Development of emotional health	♦ Safe environment ♦ Advocacy ♦ Support/ encouragement ♦ Responsibility	♦ Discussions ♦ Role playing ♦ Reading ♦ Projects	♦ Modeling ♦ Encouraging ♦ Support ♦ Availability
Ethical/moral development	♦ Safe environment ♦ Freedom of choice ♦ Rewards ♦ Consequences ♦ Understanding others	♦ Discussions ♦ Role playing ♦ Reading	♦ Modeling ♦ Encouraging ♦ Support
Aesthetic awareness	♦ Safe environment ♦ Awareness ♦ Appreciation ♦ Global view	♦ Discussions ♦ Assemblies ♦ Plays/ concerts ♦ Speakers	♦ Modeling ♦ Encouraging ♦ Support ♦ Availability
Development of socialization skills	♦ Safe environment ♦ Relationships ♦ Attitudes/values ♦ Coping skills	♦ Discussions ♦ Role playing ♦ Clubs ♦ Activities	♦ Modeling ♦ Listening ♦ Encouraging ♦ Availability

Key elements for teachers to address in advisory classes are presented in each cell of the matrix. For instance, the teacher may not demonstrate an understanding of the goals of advisory or may need help in ways to build relationships with students. A principal can look for the presence or absence of these elements in an advisory classroom. The absence of the elements may provide direction for a principal when making decisions about staff development. If many advisors are not able to address one of the goals of advisory, the principal may want to look in greater depth at in-service sessions in that particular area. The absence of elements in a teacher's classroom may also provide a basis for individual feedback to an advisor who needs more direction or training. The presence of the elements may also provide the principal with teachers to use as examples or mentors for teachers struggling with the concept of advisory.

Teachers can use the matrix as an instrument for self-assessment. Advisors can use the key elements in each cell to ascertain the presence or absence of their own knowledge, behavior, or activity in advisory period. For example, if a teacher does not exhibit the elements in the cell linking purpose and development of emotional health, the teacher may want to look for staff development opportunities to learn how to pay more attention to the classroom environment and to create an atmosphere of advocacy and support for students.

In the following sections, each goal within a column designating one of the three important characteristics of advisory teachers (abbreviated as purpose, activities, relationship) are discussed. Particular elements that contribute to the success of an advisory program are discussed within the respective cell that links the goals and teacher characteristics. Each section ends with a summary of the cells within that entire column.

Purpose and Advisory Goals

An advisor who has knowledge of the purpose of advisory is more readily able to address the first goal of the advisory program, which is the development of emotional health among students. The advisor knows that the purpose of advisory is to provide a safe environment for the student, to become an advocate for that student, and to be available for that student to discuss issues that are important to him or her. The advisor can encourage the student, provide support, and help the student to learn how to be responsible. The advisor needs to be conscious of whether she is doing these things in order to support the goal of emotional health in an advisory classroom. A teacher stated,

> One topic was "How to handle peer pressure." Some groups will discuss topics better than other groups. I usually see the same two or three students participating in discussions. My responsibility is to encourage the students to share freely. In this discussion about peer pressure, shoplifting became the issue. Students were talking about their experiences. They were not shy about it. But I had to try to steer them in the direction to see that shoplifting was wrong. I did appreciate that they felt comfortable enough to say things in front of me.

The second goal of an advisory program is moral and ethical development. In a safe environment, it is easier for a student to approach a teacher when troubled by a moral or ethical issue. Some adolescents struggle with issues of cheating, disobeying parents or teachers, or stealing. An advisor may become aware of a particular student's struggle with these or other issues and want to help students to be mindful about these issues. Students can feel free to discuss issues as they develop morally and ethically when they are in a safe environment. In such an environment students can demonstrate freedom of choice, operate within a system of rewards and consequences, and develop their understanding of others. One boy entered the room angrily and threw his books down. He had gotten into trouble in another classroom because he had been caught cheating. The student and the advisor spoke quietly. The advisor reported that the student was concerned about how he had disappointed the teacher and how angry his parents were on the phone when the teacher called them.

The purpose of an advisory program is also linked to the third goal of such programs, the development of aesthetic awareness. As an advocate of the student, the teacher demonstrates her awareness that one way for advisory to achieve this goal is by providing a safe environment in which the students can express and explore their aesthetic awareness. Willingness to take risks or explore new thoughts and behaviors may be easier if the student feels safe and sure that someone will listen. One group of students went to a nursing home. The teacher said that many of them were moved by the experience. The students talked about the fact that they had not been near older people. They did not know what they could possibly talk to older people about. One student exclaimed, "Hey, mine even dated behind her mother's back!"

The development of aesthetic awareness is often difficult for adolescents. Sometimes the students have not had opportunities to learn about the fine arts. They have not been to a museum or to the symphony, nor have they been encouraged to talk about their feelings. Although a principal can provide opportunities for the students to see plays, hear choir, band, or orchestra performances, or listen to speakers, it falls to the advisor to encourage students to express their reactions to these opportunities and to model for them such aesthetic awareness and appreciation. A student who is provided these experiences may be more likely to have a greater awareness of the fine arts. Interestingly, this awareness often transfers to the student's development in mathematics (Curtis & Bidwell, 1977).

The purpose of the advisory program to achieve the fourth goal, the development of socialization skills, also requires advisors to provide a safe environment and be an advocate for the students (Curtis & Bidwell, 1977). Students should be made aware that they are learning skills that will help them in their relationships with their peers and with adults in the school, in the family, and in their community. Opportunities to assess personal values and attitudes may be provided through activities completed during advisory. Coping skills may also be taught. And students may build confidence and develop skills that enable them to participate in clubs and activities that may have been previously unattainable by them. One advisor talked about opportunities for students to participate in the Shared Decision Making Committee. Each year, two students are elected, and she encouraged her students to become part of the process.

The thread that is woven throughout this column of the matrix that deals with the purpose of the advisory program is the idea of providing a safe environment for the student. Within the advisory setting, advisors must be able to understand the interaction between themselves and their students. The most important aspect of this interaction is that the student should be the focus of attention. Then the advisor may become an advocate for the student.

An administrator could use this column of the matrix to chart certain characteristics or specific behaviors in an advisory classroom. For example, a safe environment is one that allows a student to approach the teacher and question some aspect of school. There may be some classrooms in which it is obvious to an administrator that no student is ever allowed to question anything. The absence of this open and safe environment may become a building block for revisions in staff development, revisions in the selection of advisors, or discussion with an advisor during an evaluation of teaching.

Activities and Advisory Goals

The second column of the matrix concerns activities that may be used to help students achieve the goals of advisory. In addition to paying attention to the specific kinds of activities appropriate to the goals, administrators and teachers may find it important to consider how teachers complete particular activities or why teachers choose not to complete activities at all or just to complete some activities.

Many activities may be used to address the first goal of advisory, the development of emotional health. Discussions and projects, in fact, may address several goals of advisory. Discussions may provide thoughts for a student who is learning about freedom of choice, student responsibility, and student initiative. Discussions are usually easy to generate. Topics may be addressed through a variety of activities such as role play, reading, or projects. The students may role play some of the scenarios given as activities. Reading about people who have overcome obstacles may also be a way of generating discussion about what it is to be an emotionally healthy individual. Students may also make and display posters intended to promote a spirit of success. These are some of the activities that were observed during advisory periods.

Another goal of an advisory program is moral and ethical development. Students must learn what alternatives to behaviors are available to them. Some students do not know any other way to settle a disagreement but to fight. Others have difficulty expressing themselves verbally without yelling or cursing. The types of activities that seemed easy to implement at the middle school used for this study were discussions, role playing, and readings. One teacher reported that stereotypes often are associated with the racial issue. But she described how middle school students stereotype students who are overweight or who wear glasses. Discussions center on how the student who is overweight feels when someone calls him a name. She explained, "They are so nasty to each other.... They are quick to tell when someone has done something to them, and I try to get them to turn it around.... I want them to think."

To address the third goal, development of aesthetic awareness, advisors may allot time to discuss the importance of audience behavior in various situations. An administrator who is trying to evaluate the program may want to look at the activities being completed which address the goals of advisory. During an interview, the principal reported an incident that occurred at an assembly in the middle school.

> Some students booed at an assembly and exhibited some inappropriate laughter during a play. I asked advisors to address the issues during advisory. One teacher had no problem teaching her students the value of appropriate behavior through a discussion of what constitutes good audience behavior. The discussion expanded to detailing the opportunities available to students who may be interested in attending or performing in fine arts activities. On the other hand, some teachers grumbled about having to teach specific behaviors, believing the behaviors ought to be taught by the parents. I have to worry that this negative attitude may also be conveyed to the students.

Socialization as one function of the school (Curtis & Bidwell, 1977; White & Greenwood, 1991) is supported by development of socialization skills as the fourth goal of an advisory program. Many opportunities are provided by the schools for the students to acquire these skills. There are clubs, sports, and other activities available. The advisor may take time to discuss what is available to the students, what is necessary to get involved, and what behaviors are expected to continue being involved. A good advisory teacher will talk at length about becoming involved in school activities. Sometimes the students are unaware of what they may join or how to join. All they need is an advisor who makes the best use of advisory time and completes the activities. One teacher heard students complain about a school activity. She worked that complaint into a discussion of how schools make decisions and who is responsible for those decisions. After several minutes of interaction with the students, a couple of students said they had the solution to the problem. They were going to run for a Student Council position.

If an advisor completes the activities designated by an advisory curriculum, the student may learn some of the skills necessary to become emotionally healthy, to develop ethically and morally, to develop an aesthetic awareness, and to learn socialization skills. An administrator may want to use the matrix as a kind of checklist to plan activities in the advisory curriculum and to determine whether activities consistent with the goals of advisory are, in fact, being completed in classrooms.

Relationships and Advisory Goals

The third column of the matrix is concerned with how relationships between students and advisors promote the development of students with respect to the four goals of an advisory program. The information in this column may be used to help teachers evaluate themselves in terms of their relationship-building behaviors, as well as provide a tool for principals to use when evaluating the advisory program and the advisors.

The first cell addresses the question, how does a teacher use relationship-building behaviors to address the development of emotional health? The teacher may model behaviors that demonstrate emotional health. For example, one teacher observed an aggravated student enter the classroom. The teacher spoke calmly and modeled a positive, productive way to behave in a stressful situation. The teacher also demonstrated that talking about the situation can bring about resolution. In this example, by being available to the student, the teacher encouraged and supported that student in finding emotionally healthy ways to interact with others.

An advisor who is helping a student to achieve the second goal of advisory, to develop ethically and morally, must also be able to model his or her own ethical behavior in the relationship with students and be open about explaining the ethical and moral decisions behind certain actions. The teacher must be able to listen openly and attentively to students as they attempt to find their position on challenges they encounter on a daily basis. The teacher should be able to involve the student in questions about personal values and attitudes as they search for answers. One teacher was trying to have a discussion about a situation that might occur in a baby-sitting situation. The teacher expressed concern that she was not able to keep the discussion going as long as she wanted. However, she did state that several students participated in the discussion and that she hoped someone got something from it. Although such teacher behaviors may be teachable, it is impossible to teach the motivation of genuine concern about students that must underlie successful advisory relationships.

An advisor who is concerned about the students and wants to ensure personal development in their lives, takes steps to fulfill more than just the students' academic needs. The teacher also seeks to develop aesthetic awareness as a goal of an advisory program that broadens the scope of the academic to include the appreciation of the fine arts. Advisory relationships can support students' development of such aesthetic awareness. One teacher and her advisory group decided to do a service project for the school. They noticed trash by the fence and wanted to clean it on a regular basis. Then they wanted to plant flowers in the area. There was a lot of discussion because some students did not feel it was their responsibility to keep the yard clean. Others felt that it was similar to their home and they had a responsibility to keep it as nice as possible. The students were able to discuss their beliefs freely.

Teachers who have established a relationship with their students may be able to observe more quickly any changes in student behaviors that reflect the development of aesthetic awareness. Teachers may also model their own skills that illustrate their personal level of aesthetic awareness. Teachers can also help the students to focus on aspects of artistic and entertaining experiences that touch on issues or ideas that are important to particular students.

A teacher who models relationship-building behaviors also helps students to develop socialization skills by listening attentively to the student when personal interests are expressed. In one advisory group, a student wanted to explore the possibility of running for Student Council. The advisor listened and encouraged the student to pursue the position. During some discussions with the students in advisory, references were made

Designing Effective Advisory Programs 63

to demonstrate how student involvement may broaden the scope of that student's socialization skills. Having a relationship with the students also may support the students while they develop their own ability to learn and use socialization skills.

Modeling permeates the relationship-building behavior in this column of the matrix. It appears, however, that a teacher must establish the relationship with the student before the student will accept that teacher as a model. A personal relationship need not be time consuming. What is necessary is that the student be given undivided attention when there is a need. Teachers were observed exhibiting many acts that expressed attention to the student. Speaking quietly, patting a shoulder, and offering a smile are often sufficient expressions of the relationship between teacher and student. Such expressions may be brief and subtle, but they are examples of what an administrator might observe as evidence of relationship-building behaviors.

In addition, this column of the matrix on relationship building and the four goals of an advisory program is particularly valuable to the teacher. Using it, a teacher may self-assess whether or not certain relationship-building qualities are present in his every day interactions with the students in his advisory.

The question remains, however, about whether a teacher who does not exhibit relationship-building behaviors can be taught how to exhibit the behaviors or whether these behaviors are innate. Can the teacher who is woefully lacking these behaviors self-assess? Another question that can be raised about advisory relationships is what happens when the advisor does not get the response needed to continue. If the student does not respond to what the teacher models, the relationship is not going to flourish. Is the teacher then able or responsible to continue in an effort to get a favorable response from the student? Some teachers believe relationships need to be pursued. Such a teacher might well need to be supported in her efforts by administration and colleagues and helped to consciously consider whether specific behaviors identified in the matrix would help her build a relationship with a particular student.

An administrator who is trying to plan and evaluate an advisory program would want to look carefully at each cell of the matrix. Having the matrix as a guide may make planning and evaluating the advisory program easier. It certainly makes these processes more transparent both for administrators and teachers. The matrix equips administrators and teachers to recognize what it is that links the conceptual aspects of an advisory program (the goals) with the behaviors of the particular advisors in a school. In summary, the matrix may be used as an executive overview for planning advisory curriculum, for the professional development of advisors, and for advisory program evaluation.

The Ethic of Caring

According to Noddings, the primary aim of every school must be the maintenance and enhancement of caring (Noddings, 1984). All the stakeholders (parents, students, faculty, community members) must embrace this aim, but in the context of this discussion of advisory programs, the advisor's role in doing so is key. In an advisory classroom, a caring advisor establishes an environment in which the students feel at ease to talk to the teacher because they feel "cared for." A school that promotes such an environment is not abdicating its responsibility to train the intellect. Rather, the belief is that caring is the foundation necessary in order for teaching to begin (Noddings, 1984).

Noddings (1984) states that it is caring that supports the development of the relationship between the teacher and the student: "The one-caring desires the well-being of the cared-for and acts to promote that well-being" (p. 24). The advisory teacher in this case represents the one-caring. The student represents the cared-for. Noddings continues by stating that while an observer may not be able to accurately observe caring, the observer should be aware of an action bringing about a favorable outcome for the student, or seeming likely to do so, or of the teacher varying actions on behalf of the student. These things provide evidence that the caring relationship either has been or is being established.

The data collected for this study through interviews and observations, as well as the information in the literature, indicate that building a relationship is extremely important in determining the effectiveness of an advisory program. The relationship between the advisory teacher and the student develops into an affective response between the two people. Noddings (1984) calls this caring. It is the development of this affective response that links teachers' understanding of the purpose of advisory, their completion of advisory activities, and their relationships with their advisory students to the four affective goals of advisory programs.

Teachers exhibit the ethic of caring in their relationships with students in different ways. Some may greet the students warmly when they enter the room. The greeting may not be the standard "good morning." One teacher, for example, personalized her greeting of each student. For a student who had been ill, the teacher commented that she was glad the girl was back at school. This example also illustrates that evidence of a caring relationship can be something simple and not specific to the formal curriculum.

Although any principal wants advisors who care, there are limitations in caring even for the best advisors. It is impossible to care equally about all students, and conflict may occur when the student wants something the teacher does not think is best. Although a teacher may continue promoting appropriate activities and discussions during advisory with an overall positive attitude about her role as an advisor, it is easy, given the limitations on caring, to understand why the role of advisor is a difficult one.

Noddings (1984) also states what caring is not. A person cannot claim to care if the task is perfunctory or grudging. Five teachers in the study stated that advisory is a waste of time. These advisors also did not demonstrate relationship-building behaviors during the observations, nor did they describe examples of relationship-building behaviors during the interviews. They did not demonstrate care.

Noddings (1984) might appear to lend support to those teachers who expressed concern that advisory is a waste of time and that being an advisor is not what they were hired to do. The focus of attention for these teachers is inward. They care only about what they have to do to teach. One teacher, for example, expressed concerns that seemed to limit her ability to build a relationship with the students in her advisory. She described her concerns, saying:

> It is difficult for the kids to stay attentive all day with ninety minute classes. . . . We put so much emphasis on testing . . . I am not trained in counseling. . . . The things [problems] should be dealt with by the parents. I am not sure it is the school's responsibility to take on everything that the parent or society is supposed to provide and is not. And the classroom teacher is not necessarily the logical person to provide this help. . . . I can't do it.

The remarks from this teacher are indicative of one who does not care about the students' affective needs and who does not believe that building a relationship is important to her role as teacher or to the education and the development of the students.

It is interesting to note Noddings' presumption that what seems to be most valuable in the teaching–learning relationship cannot be specified without acquaintance and interaction (Noddings, 1984). Advisory, by its nature, seems to promote and support acquaintance and interaction. Only through acquaintance and interaction between the student and teacher can the characteristic of caring come through. The student must be able to freely associate with the teacher and must be able to initiate conversation. Only then can the student detect the attitude of caring, even in formal classroom situations such as lectures. Noddings suggests that teachers convey that the subject matter is both boring and exciting, useful and useless, creative and tedious, and that the regard between student and teacher will not diminish no matter how each views the subject. The bottom line is that the teacher must convey the message that the student is more important than the subject.

Caring involves stepping out of one's personal frame of reference and into the other's (Noddings, 1984). In this case, advisors' awareness of the issues affecting middle school students, particularly the students in their advisory, is reflected in how they address the goals of advisory. When a student entered one advisor's room late, that student was welcomed. The advisor noticed that the student seemed troubled and took a few extra moments to talk with her. When an advisor cares, there is this kind of specific evidence of regard for the student's point of view and needs. The advisor's behavior focuses on the student.

When an ethic of care is the basis for an advisory program, advisors are encouraged to maintain the spirit rather than the letter of the law. Noddings (1984) reminds us that caring may not follow strict procedures or rules. However, the caring advisors observed in this study managed to vary lessons to fit what was needed in the respective advisories without compromising the advisory program. One teacher, for instance, spent most of the advisory period on a study day discussing information about activities available to students. She provided information and also discussed how to make time during the day for some extra study time. She described the importance of becoming involved in school activities. Her efforts were rewarded by responses from some students who were interested. In this respect, she showed that she cared, and she was cognizant of the feelings and needs of the students. She also addressed the goals of development of emotional health and socialization skills.

Conclusion

School is a place where students learn from one another and from their teachers. The students learn how to respond with compassion and understanding to different people in different situations. To develop this learning, students must be provided the opportunity in a caring and supportive environment. The motivation in caring is directed toward the welfare and protection of the students. Teachers contribute to this learning by interacting with the students in several ways. They may tell stories, guide discussions, model kindness, and encourage open communication. There must be joint activity between the student and the teacher. All of these interactions constitute the development of a caring relationship between the teacher and the student.

Advisory is not a panacea for the development of students' affective domain. All problems will not be solved; not all activities will benefit every child at every meeting (Ross, 1954). However, for our educational system to continue to develop students who are well-rounded individuals and good citizens, educators must fill the void created by the current lack of attention to affective education. Educators must believe that the relationships created and the activities implemented in advisory programs are essential to both the affective and the cognitive development of the pre-adolescent (Alexander, Williams, Compton, & Prescott, 1968).

References

Alexander, W. M., Williams, E., Compton, M., & Prescott, D. (1968). *The Emergent Middle School*. New York: Holt, Rinehart, & Winston.

Allen, H. A., Splittgerber, F. L., & Manning, M. L. (1993). *Teaching and Learning in the Middle Level School*. New York: Macmillan.

Andrews, B., & Stern, J. (1992). An Advisory Program: A Little Can Mean a Lot! *Middle School Journal*, 24(1), 39–41.

Ayres, L. R. (1994). Middle School Advisory Programs: Findings from the Field. *Middle School Journal*, 25(3), 8–14.

Bandura, A. (1982). Self-Efficacy Mechanism in Human Agency. *American Psychologist*, 37(2), 122–147.

Bushnell, D., & George, P. S. (1993). Five Crucial Characteristics: Middle School Teachers as Effective Advisers. *Schools in the Middle*, Sept., 10–16.

Clark, S. N., & Clark, D. C. (1994). *Restructuring the Middle Level School: Implications for School Leaders*. Albany, NY: State University of New York.

Cole, C. G. (1994). Teachers' Attitudes Before Beginning a Teacher Advisory Program. *Middle School Journal*, 25(5), 3–7.

Curtis, T. E., & Bidwell, W. W. (1977). *Curriculum and Instruction for Emerging Adolescents*. Reading, MA: Addison-Wesley.

Digby, A., Totten, S., & Snider, D. (1995). Advisor-Advisee Programs: Uniquely Designed To Meet the Affective Needs of Young Adolescents. In Wavering, M. J. (Ed.). *Educating Young Adolescents: Life in the Middle* (pp. 277–306). New York: Garland Publishing.

Dorman, G., Lipsitz, J., & Verner, P. (1985). Improving Schools for Young Adolescents. *Educational Leadership*, 42(6), 44–49.

Fenwick, L. (1992). *Managing Middle Grade Reform: An "America 2000" Agenda*. San Diego, CA: Fenwick & Associates.

Galassi, J. P., Gulledge, S. A., & Cox, N. D. (1997). Planning and Maintaining Sound Advisory Programs. *Middle School Journal*, 28(5), 35–41.

George, P. S., & Bushnell, D. (1993). What Works and Why? *Schools in the Middle*, 3(1), 3–9.

James, M. (1986). *Advisor-Advisee Programs: What, Why, and How*. Columbus, OH: National Middle School Association.

Lounsbury, J. H., & Clark, D. C. (1990). *Inside Grade Eight: From Apathy to Excitement*. Reston, VA: National Association of Secondary School Principals.

MacIver, D. (1990). Meeting the Needs of Young Adolescents: Advisory Groups, Interdisciplinary Teaching Teams, and School Transition Programs. *Phi Delta Kappa*, 71(6), 458–464.

MacIver, D. J., & Epstein, J. L. (1991). Responsive Practices in the Middle Grades: Teacher Teams, Advisory Groups, Remedial Instruction, and School Transition Programs. *American Journal of Education*, 99(4), 587–622.

McEwin, C. K. (1981). Establishing Teacher-Advisory Programs in Middle Level Schools. *Journal of Early Adolescence*, 1(4), 337–348.

Moss, T. C. (1969). *Middle School*. New York: Houghton Mifflin.

Muth, K. D. & Alvermann, D. E. (1992). *Teaching and Learning in the Middle Grades*. Needham Heights, MA: Allyn and Bacon.

Noddings, N. (1984). *Caring: A Feminine Approach to Ethics and Moral Education*. Los Angeles: University of California Press.

Ross, V. (1954). *Handbook for Homeroom Guidance*. New York: Macmillan.

Shockley, R., Schumacher, R., & Smith, D. (1984). Teacher Advisory Programs: Strategies for Successful Implementation. *NASSP Bulletin*, 68(473), 69–74.

Van Hoose, J. (1991). The Ultimate Goal: AA Across the Day. *Midpoints*, 2(1), 1–7.

White, G. P., & Greenwood, S. C. (1991). Study Skills and the Middle Level Adviser/Advisee Program. *NASSP Bulletin*, 75(537), 88–95.

3

Building Teacher Leadership Capacity

Laura Wagner Smith

In the following chapter, I look at the importance of teacher leadership and the professional development of individual teachers in their school settings. In addition, I offer an alternative supervisory strategy for helping to develop teacher leadership capacity among faculty and for studying the more abstract concepts of teacher leadership. The strategy for teacher leadership development is based in the practice of clinical supervision, an approach that allows the supervisor more flexibility to engage the teacher in a personalized form of professional development. The chapter describes a study of efforts with two teacher participants to build their individual capacities as teacher leaders. In order to study the teachers' experiences of supervision and teacher leadership capacity building, I developed individualized plans of action with the teachers that allowed them to investigate their leadership interests and skills on a personal level, as well as at school administrative and organizational levels. The outcomes of this study suggest that an administrator's time spent helping teachers build their leadership capacity is time well spent.

Teacher Leadership and a Rationale for Its Study

The concept of teacher leadership is an emerging one in educational practice and research. Furthermore, it is not a concept that can, at this point in its development, be readily measured quantitatively, particularly for individual teachers. Prior to the 1980s, leadership theory in education concentrated on building and district administrators as the key forces of leadership and school improvement in the school community. During the 1980s, however, as the focus of school organizational behavior moved from autocratic and custodial models to more supportive and collegial models, the inclusion of teachers and other staff members in the decision-making and leadership process became more prevalent. With this shift, site-based decision making became a common form of governance within the school setting, and the teacher as leader was seen as an important contributor to the improvement of individual schools (Clark, 1998). Thus, the role of the teacher leader came to be seen as an important part of the school reform movement (Firestone, 1993).

Teacher leadership has continued to develop in various forms within school settings. Teachers have been given more opportunities to work alongside administrators as school leaders in more democratized settings that keep in mind the overall goal of school improvement. Whereas only a few select teachers initially benefited from being part of the site-based decision-making process, the infusion of shared power within learning organizations has opened the doors for teachers who traditionally were not given a voice or an opportunity to contribute their talents and assets. As a result, more teachers have opportunities to lead and to have direct influence on the overall business of schools.

But not all teachers are comfortable taking on leadership roles. Continued research done in the area of teacher leadership suggests that if the conditions that contribute to teacher leadership can be identified, teachers might more readily overcome obstacles and hesitancies to becoming teacher leaders (Katzenmeyer & Moller, 1996). This particular aspect of the research on teacher leadership was particularly interesting to me as a practicing supervisor. As I looked around my own school community, I saw excellent teachers with great potential in the area of leadership whose talents were not being recognized or utilized. The leadership role of the individual teacher on my campus seemed to be something that merited not only additional attention but also formal study. Such attention and study also appeared in line with existing research and practice in the area of teacher leadership capacity building. As this literature points out, many schools have teachers, as well as other talented professionals in the building, with a reservoir of untapped talent and only a limited venue, such as their classrooms, in which to utilize their talents. Administrators within these school systems may have excellent staff-development plans that address the needs of some of the more prominent teacher leaders such as team leaders but do nothing to help other faculty to develop their leadership abilities.

Part of the reason that teacher leadership development is not attended to may stem from the difficulty that administrators have determining exactly what they are expected to do to develop teacher leaders. There is a lack of consensus among various educational researchers who have elaborated on the concept of teacher leadership within the school setting. Definitions are wide and varied, depending on the researcher's viewpoint on the nature of teacher leadership. Some researchers define teacher leadership in terms of specific qualities that a teacher possesses that can be identified and described; other researchers concentrate on factors that may affect or influence these qualities (Suranna & Moss, 2001; Snell & Swanson, 2000; Katzenmeyer & Moller, 1996; Gullatt, 1995; Sergiovanni & Starratt, 1998; Bolman & Deal, 1994; Darling-Hammond, 1994; Whitaker, 1995.) Research in these areas has included both qualitative and quantitative perspectives, generating results and ideas that are linked to other research issues.

School accountability for improvement is one such issue to which research in teacher leadership has been linked. This area was particularly important to me as a supervisor in a school system that placed a great deal of energy and importance on high stakes testing and favorable outcomes for students. Linking the study of teacher leadership with school accountability also helped me to focus my interpretation of what constitutes teacher leadership and to build on existing research in the area of teacher leadership through my own work with the teacher participants in this study. Furthermore, as a scholar and a practitioner, it was important for me to have the credibility of research to back the study that I had asked two teacher participants to engage in with me.

For the approach that I would take to teacher leadership development, it was important for me to focus on teacher leadership qualities that were, at least to some extent, quantifiable by virtue of being observable and describable in empirical terms and that were also related to school improvement. What I needed was a conceptual framework for teacher leadership with categories that would help me better analyze and understand the individualized and qualitative supervisory work I was doing with the two teacher participants. It was in Linda Lambert's book *Building Leadership Capacity in Schools* (1998) that I found a conceptual framework that espoused my understanding of teacher leadership in regard to the school setting.

The framework describes distinct categories of teacher leadership within the school setting. According to Lambert, teacher leadership is broad-based, skillful participation in the work of leadership. It is inquiry-based use of information to inform shared decisions and practice. Teacher leaders assume roles and responsibilities that reflect broad involvement and collaboration. They engage in reflective practice and innovation, and they strive for and achieve high levels of student achievement. In her discussion of these categories, Lambert provides both quantitative and qualitative descriptors that were useful in shaping a vocabulary that I could use with my two participants to discuss teacher leadership and how it supports school improvement. These categories also provided me with an overall conceptual framework within which to locate my work with each teacher, a framework that could be used to study individual teacher leadership capacities.

In order to study teacher leadership development, I engaged in clinical supervisory experiences with two teachers in the school setting in which I worked. Each participant worked with me for the better part of a semester in a dedicated effort to examine her existing individual teacher leadership capacities. In addition, we were able to use the strategy of clinical supervision to address each teacher's professional development needs individually in the area of teacher leadership.

Each teacher was able to address certain aspects of her actual and desired teacher leadership. The results of my work with the two teacher participants suggested that the process of clinical supervision can be a helpful mechanism for school supervisors and teachers to explore professional growth in the area of teacher leadership. Discussion of these leadership issues with the teacher participants helped them to recognize and build their leadership abilities in relation to their teaching role within the school community and to see their leadership in the larger context of overall school improvement.

Within the course of the clinical supervision experience, I found four recurring elements related to teacher leadership that each teacher articulated in her individual way. The comments of the two teacher participants indicate that they came to take the presence of each of these elements somewhat for granted. However, their comments also suggest that these elements are necessary corollaries to their development as teacher leaders and that the presence of such elements has obvious benefits in terms of school improvement. The common elements are (1) mutual respect and trust between administrators and teachers; (2) the importance of collegiality between teachers and their peers; (3) teacher empowerment; and (4) the importance of fostering high student achievement. These elements are discussed in more detail following a description of the school that provided the context for the study of teacher leadership, as well as descriptions of the two teacher participants and the focus of their work in teacher leadership capacity building.

Setting the Stage: Two Teachers' Experiences

At the time of this study, I was employed as an educational diagnostician at the school site where I worked with each of the teacher participants. Not every school climate would have been conducive for the work that I was able to do with these two teachers. I had the good fortune to be employed in a school setting that fostered collaboration and collegial relationships, a school setting where each teacher is valued for what he or she adds to the overall school culture. The school is referred to as Willow Springs Elementary.

At Willow Springs, the pursuit and expectation of excellence has been a cornerstone in the philosophy of the school. With this drive for excellence, however, comes the price of even higher expectations for the individuals who work there. Turnover is not extremely high, but Willow Springs has experienced its share of teacher attrition, due in part to the high degree of involvement teachers are expected to have with peers, district supervisors, parents, and especially students. The two teacher participants I worked with as part of my study of teacher leadership were both active members of the Willow Springs school community and had been at the school for four and six years, respectively. I call them Betty and Stephanie.

My first participant was Betty, a talented and resourceful special programs teacher in the area of student social skills development. Betty might be described as one of those teachers who are noted for doing an exceptional job but who do not always receive recognition from their peers and supervisors for their work. Those who work closely with Betty, however, have been impressed by her excellent organization, knowledge base, classroom management skills, and high student achievement rate.

Betty might be described as the type of teacher that principals cannot easily replace and would hate to lose, but whose value may not be fully recognized until she resigns. Through my collegial relationship with Betty over the past four years, it was evident that she was a teacher whose full potential was not being focused on directly by her administrators.

Betty's impact at her current place of employment is quite evident, however, to those who work closely with her. For four out of her twelve years of teaching experience, she has worked closely with fellow teachers, parents, and other stakeholders at Willow Springs to foster a positive environment in which children's individual needs are met. Betty was a willing participant, who worked as a partner with me during the course of the clinical supervision process. Her particular interests in the area of teacher leadership capacities centered on her curriculum and programming efforts in the classroom and also on becoming recognized as a leader in her interactions with building and district-level personnel. She was particularly interested in her role as teacher in terms of leadership within the school system. Through my time spent with Betty, she came to a better understanding of how her specific actions and teaching practices facilitate leadership capacity both for herself and the Willow Springs school community.

My second participant, Stephanie, can be described quite simply as the quintessential master teacher. She has worked in elementary education for over fifteen years in both regular education and special education, with the last six years spent at Willow Springs as a special programs teacher in the area of math and reading improvement. Her knowledge of primary grade curriculum is one of her biggest strengths. She is the type of teacher that other teachers seek out to discuss strategies and interventions that target specific academic skills. In addition, Stephanie is always quick to share "success stories" concerning her students and delights in the their personal successes.

During our collaboration, Stephanie's leadership capacity building centered on her curriculum and programming efforts in the classroom, as well as her skills in articulating and reflecting upon these issues with peers and supervisors.

As described above, I used the ideas of Linda Lambert (1998) on specific teacher leadership capacities to guide discussions with each of the teachers about building her teacher leadership. Lambert's descriptors of teacher leadership provided us with a language to guide our discussions about which activities might constitute "teacher leadership" behaviors.

To begin the clinical supervision process with each teacher, she and I chose activities within the teacher's school day that we agreed were consistent with what Lambert describes as teacher leadership. Formal observations of each teacher engaging in these activities were then made with their consent. As the observer, I collected specific information about the teachers' performance of these activities and their interaction with others involved in the activities. I also made written comments during the observation process. In addition, each teacher was asked to provide artifacts within her teaching repertoire that supported her participation in teacher leadership activities. This information helped to support and document specific moments in a teacher's day that were aligned with the observable teacher leadership capacities suggested by Lambert (1998).

Within the scope of clinical supervision, the teacher participants and I were able to engage in an ongoing dialogue concerning the observation data and artifacts to help them better understand their leadership abilities and further their teacher leadership capacity. Interpersonal communication techniques were consciously used to allow the participants full opportunity to articulate their thoughts and beliefs about their professional development and the work that we did together, and to make our work as colleagues more democratic. As the process continued, it became clear to me that certain elements of teacher leadership capacity building were common for both teachers.

As stated earlier, these elements were mutual respect and trust between teachers and administrators, collegiality among peers, teacher empowerment, and the promotion of high student achievement. Such elements are important not only for teacher leadership capacity building, but also as aspects of a teacher's universe through which she is able to demonstrate knowledge and skill and over which she is able, at least in the school that was the site of my study, to exercise considerable control. I came to see a complex interaction among the four elements themselves, the ways that the teacher participants understood and expressed them, and the context in which they were enacted. All of these factors deserve consideration and further study as important influences on the development of teacher leadership.

Common Elements: Reconceptualizing Teacher Leadership Capacities

In the following descriptions of each of the elements that emerged from my study of teacher leadership, I have tried to convey the interplay of these four common elements with the teacher and the context of the particular school. The participants' own words convey this interplay and show how they were coming both to recognize and to build their own leadership capacity in their school community. Of course, the two teacher participants' experiences of their efforts were unique to them. However, the common elements that cut across their experiences offer food for thought about how administrators can shape schools and the relationships that occur within them in ways that recognize and encourage these elements and the development of teacher leaders.

Mutual Trust and Respect

The first common element I found was mutual trust and respect between teachers and administrators in the school setting. This element took into account the ways that both teachers were able to share their successful practices with administrators at Willow Springs in an atmosphere that was supportive and nurturing. Most interesting to me was how, once such mutual trust and respect were in place with me in the supervisory role, the teachers' engagement in the clinical supervision process provided a springboard for their reflection on their individual practices.

One of the comments made by Betty near the conclusion of the study revealed that such trust and respect is not automatic, even in a school such as Willow Springs. Betty shared some of her fears about participating in the study, fears that were later alleviated and even overcome through the process of clinical supervision:

> Well, at first, you know, when you picked me, I thought, well Mr. C. or someone asked you to be a mentor to me, and Stephanie said, "no," and I was a little hesitant at first, but you know, you kind of explained everything, and, you know, what started out to be hesitant, I've enjoyed very much.

Betty had come to realize that I had a true interest in working with her and supporting her in the area of teacher leadership. My supervisory role was more one of peer to peer, rather than evaluator and judgment-maker. Although she was more reluctant to verbalize her true hopes and dreams for her professional development in the initial stages of the clinical supervision process, this reluctance changed with time.

By the final stages of the of the study, Betty provided clear indicators to me that she saw clinical supervision as a safe venue to discuss specific teacher leadership capacities that she was working on. In addition, although still somewhat hesitant about claiming a leadership role, Betty seemed to enjoy the opportunity to discuss her professional development in a setting that supported individual growth, as evidenced by the following comment:

> I was very much, very proud of that and look forward to taking it to Jill and showing it to her, because, you know, it's kind of going beyond the call of duty; but it's also, I'm proud of the program, and I want to show it off, and if I can give ideas to other people, it might be useful and has to be, you know, to make it easier. You know, I think anyone would welcome that, and I would like to be responsible for helping someone make their day go easier. It's very, uh, hard enough to come into a classroom like this every day, so if you can make things be easier, I think that's good.

Critical to the process of a positive clinical supervision experience was this atmosphere of trust and mutual respect, in which the teacher participants and I experienced a collegial relationship that was nonevaluative in nature. By using a more democratic supervision process, I relied less on assuming power over the teacher participants and more on giving power to them. This type of leadership was already somewhat familiar to the teachers at Willow Springs. Stephanie, for example, talked of how the principal gives the teachers opportunities to make their own choices and decisions and makes it safe for them to take risks:

> This is a very calm school. It's . . . I have worked at other schools that were not as calm as this. At this particular school, our principal feels that we're professionals, and that we should know how to communicate the things that we need to do, and he, he kind of expects us to do what we, what we know best and what we know is right, and if we fail trying, well then at least we tried something.

The "calm" school setting in which it was possible to engage in progressive cycles of clinical supervision with each participant probably contributed to the success of the study by offering a supportive environment for the development of trust, respect, risk, and collaboration in the clinical supervision process. The high value that was placed on teachers' instructional development in this school carried over to our focus on teacher leadership capacity development. Each participant became free to express her individual leadership interests to me as the supervisor and was able to freely demonstrate and analyze her leadership behavior in order to gain a better understanding of what she was doing in her classroom setting and, more specifically, how what she was doing related to teacher leadership capacities and capacity building. Betty, for example, had this to say:

> I think that you made me more aware of it [leadership behavior] . . . and I think just from you, you know, making me reflect on what I've done, and the changes that I've made and things that I've improved on . . . it made me want to do that [leadership].

Collegiality

Mutual respect and trust were also parts of the second common element found in my study—one of collegiality between peers and other members of the school community. As Judith Warren Little has pointed out in her now famous study, collegiality is one of the hallmarks of good schools (Warren-Little, 1982). Collegiality definitely existed among the teachers and the other staff members in the Willow Springs school community. This judgment was supported by each teacher's description of instances of collaboration with other teachers, the importance of accountability, and the importance of others' perceptions about her as a "good teacher." Betty, for instance, said:

> I've always worked on portraying or trying to produce a more positive image of my classroom, and it's taken awhile, but in the four years that's what I've done. . . . They [other teachers] don't see it [special education] so negative. . . . It's a classroom, and it's just a more positive image. And I think that they're recognizing that, and saying that Betty has some things to offer.

Both teachers seemed to feel a strong sense of collegiality with their peers within their current job roles. Stephanie richly articulated how the school culture of Willow Springs contributed to her ability to participate in leadership processes. She talked about her feelings of collegiality at Willow Springs:

> It's not just my job, it's our job combined [staff members at Willow Springs]. It's a combined effort, to make these children gain as much knowledge as they can and to be all they can be, and I think that's very important.

Collegiality is also evident in the language that the two teachers used to talk about their work at Willow Springs. I noticed a sense of ownership in their comments, as they frequently referred to "we" and "us" in regard to the staff members of the school community. Rather than the traditional "us" versus "them" orientations of teachers with administrators, parents and even students, schools like Willow Springs seemed to possess more democratic orientations in which teachers see themselves as part of a team. Betty reflects this team mentality when she tells of drafting a specific plan for a student in need of specialized assistance. Her expectation of support from the other members of the school community makes apparent her positive sense of collegiality at the school.

> When [one of my students] was running away, I made up a course of action ... [so we would] not have this "if," "then" ... or "what do we do." I had a plan. We record what he is wearing every day, so we don't have to guess what he's wearing or look back. We will call the police, and this will be the procedure, and we will let the parent know. So we have these steps to follow, so we won't wish we could have done better.

Betty's description gives evidence of how she was able to do what she needed to do as a professional and of her assumption that her fellow teachers would positively receive the leadership role she took in this situation. She also implicitly conveys her expectation of support for her plan—and her student—by her colleagues. Betty saw this collaborative effort as an opportunity to let others know what she has to offer as a teacher leader, as well as a chance to build her leadership skills with others in a safe setting that nurtured her individual professional development.

Some of the most prevalent references to collegiality in the teacher participants' discussion of their leadership interests and experiences presented the teacher as a resource for her colleagues. This kind of collegiality was evident in remarks about being open to sharing ideas with others, such as Betty's description of "helping more or assisting more, facilitating more . . . and maybe being more of service [to other staff members], or providing some ideas or help to them."

Nurturing colleagues was another facet of collegiality for both participants. Sharing ideas about what she was doing in her classroom that could be easily adapted to other classrooms at Willow Springs was an instance described by Betty of this particular form of collegiality. Mentoring other teachers and para-educators in ways that were caring and supportive was another example. Stephanie, for instance, shared this comment about her participation in mentoring other staff members at her campus:

> I'm working with another teacher that is having a lot of problems with a special needs student. She's emotionally at the point where she is crying. I have been there before. And because I have been there, I have more empathy for this particular teacher, and I understand.

At another point in our work together Stephanie talked about her desire to help other teachers, especially teachers within her building who were in need of assistance: "I feel like I am able to help this particular teacher. . . . It's kind of crucial that I kind of help this teacher get through this. . . I don't mind helping if I can."

In yet another comment, Stephanie revealed her perception of the nature of her relationship with her peers:

> I feel like they [other teachers in the building] have gained a lot of trust in our department since I have started working . . . and I feel that, they, uh, look to me for answers . . . look to me to help the child, and I think they seem to be very grateful to that . . . they see that these children are learning.

These comments suggest that the teacher participants felt supported and empowered by their colleagues and comfortable taking leadership in their school setting.

Teacher Empowerment

Just as trust and respect between teachers and administrators relate to collegiality among teachers, so the third element of teacher empowerment relates to both of the first two elements. They all must coexist in a school setting if teachers are to be encouraged to develop their leadership capacity. Teacher empowerment was described by the teacher participants in terms of autonomy, open lines of communication, and the importance of being perceived positively by others.

Throughout the clinical supervision process the teacher participants revealed their perceptions about themselves as autonomous teachers who take available opportunities within the school setting to work with both colleagues and supervisors. In an example from Betty in which she outlines some of her personal goals, she indicates not only her sense of herself as an autonomous agent, but also her deep desire for the continuous professional growth that accompanies this sense of herself:

> I think I could be an asset and—not to pat myself on the back—but just to be an asset and to help other people. I really would like the idea of working, you know, and if I ever had my master's, teaching at a college level, to teach teachers to teach . . . I think that you want to go out and see what else is out there.

Similar evidence of autonomy and the empowering effect it has on Stephanie's drive to grow continually as a teacher is evident in this description of herself as a reflective practitioner:

> I'm pretty hard on myself. I'm my own worse critic . . . because I always try to go back and see what did I accomplish this week. So I try to do long-term goals so that I am focused; you know, what is the child going to benefit this week from the amount of learning that I'm trying to have take place. And I'm very goal oriented, and then I try to plan it out in my mind, and I try to execute those things. . . . Then I feel like there is something, that I've done something worthwhile with him, the child.

The example presented above shows Stephanie's ability to articulate for herself and, for me, her understanding of the importance of thinking honestly and systematically about her past, present, and future actions as a teacher. Her comments also show the value she places on self-improvement, as well as the importance of her continuous self-renewal as a teacher. Although she did not use the specific term *reflection*, Stephanie's remarks clearly describe a process of independent, professional decision making that characterizes what Schon (1983) has called "reflection on action."

Open communication was something else the teachers talked about in connection with teacher empowerment. Betty, for example, talked about the existing communication structure within Willow Springs:

> I want to mention again how much I feel comfortable having a team leader. I think that you go to the team leader and use her as sounding board, or even [to] other members of your team, colleagues, and use them as a sounding board . . . to practice your ideas or express your own thoughts or your own opinions, instead of going directly to the administrator. And I think that that's the purpose of a team leader, opportunities not to have to use administration so much.

Stephanie echoed this view with her comment, "We are a group that communicates well together and that understands one another."

A final aspect of teacher empowerment the teachers mentioned was the importance of being perceived positively by others. Within the clinical supervision experiences of both Betty and Stephanie, the importance of teacher empowerment was perhaps most obvious in the quiet pride both teachers took in being perceived as respected members of the school community. This pride is reflected in Betty's remark:

> I think every time you have something that can help you be prepared and have the answers, you're going to be more successful, or appear to be knowing what you're doing, And I think that that's it. I don't want anyone to doubt me. [I want to leave] no questions left unanswered.

Stephanie also paints a picture of the importance she gives to the way other members of the school community perceive her:

> Most of them [the teachers] say, "Oh, you know what to do, you know how to do, you know . . . curriculum, you know this, you know that, and you have a lot of good things that you're doing with your students. I can see their progress.

In a subsequent interview Stephanie leaves no doubt about the importance her colleagues' view of her role in the school: "I need a good name; I need to keep my good name."

Focus on Student Achievement

I almost hesitate to refer to the emphasis that the teacher participants place on high student achievement as a fourth element of teacher leadership capacity building because in the discussions I had with both teacher participants the success of their students always seemed inseparable from their teacher role. Although it is not surprising that teachers would be concerned about the success of their students, I chose to include the focus on student achievement as an element of teacher leadership because of the way these teachers view such success as a measure of their own effort and ability, and as something over which they have considerable control. Also, the fact that this emphasis on student achievement was present in every discussion with the teachers suggests that they consider their primary leadership role to be in their classrooms. I determined, therefore, that it is crucial to think about this element both in recognizing and in developing teacher leadership capacity.

Evidence of this element was found in frequent discussions of the teachers' decision making about classroom strategies that support student success and in the open lines of communication that the teachers created with parents, students, and district employees. Each teacher also mentioned the importance of her efforts to promote student choices, student empowerment, student accountability, and innovative programming to enhance student achievement. Throughout the clinical supervision process Betty's and Stephanie's personal leadership goals were largely about student achievement and about the kinds of adjustments they could make in their classrooms to enable students to be more successful. Furthermore, it appeared clear that each teacher perceived her students as unique individuals with unique strengths and weaknesses and that she saw herself as a powerful influence on her students' learning.

The focus of Betty's conversations during the first few cycles of clinical supervision always centered on her students. She painted an image of her students as good students who were working hard to achieve their individual goals. As Betty became more comfortable with me during the course of the clinical supervision process, I noted that she was more eager to discuss her own strengths and weaknesses as a teacher, particularly in terms of being better able to predict and influence student achievement. In one conversation she talked about her dissatisfaction with instructional materials that she had developed for herself and her team to use.

> Right now, this makes me think that there might be room for improvement. Right now, I did a pretty good job of submitting a program, or putting together a program in a handout, but now there are some flaws in it, but not exactly flaws but "what ifs" that could add more to it . . . [such as] being more specific in the wording of the program to where, when there is a situation, then there is an answer, instead of "I don't know; we've never had this happen."

As our conversations progressed throughout the course of clinical supervision, Betty also was able to talk at length about strategies and interventions she had devised to use with her students on a routine basis:

> I think because I am successful at it, and I'm not saying that it's easy, but I, I've made it easier for me; you know, the first year of teaching is, you know, a hellacious year, and you learn from it and how to always make it easier. . . . I've perfected it and try to always improve, and next year it will be something else that I will, you know, find to make better.

In her discussions about her efforts to increase student achievement, Betty provided an example of the teacher leadership qualities described by Lambert (1998). She took the initiative to work with colleagues to use information about their students to inform shared decisions and practices and to develop instructional materials based on information about these students. She assumed responsibilities beyond what was required of her, which made her teaching both reflective and innovative.

Although it was evident that student achievement was of the utmost importance to the teacher participants, their leadership in this area was also characterized by compassion and respect. Even when children and colleagues were not responding in the manner that each teacher felt they ought, the teachers were at once understanding and unwavering in their determination to persevere toward their goals of student achievement. Stephanie, for instance, described her efforts to be responsive to student needs:

> These children . . . my aide and I, we are both . . . seem to be adjusting better this week than last week. Last week we were adjusting as well, but I don't know if it's the planning. . . . Some of the children get tired of working . . . and I try real hard to listen to what they want. And that's been one of the challenges of working with . . . those large numbers.

Other significant comments regarding student achievement were comments that each teacher participant was willing to make about the mixed rewards and difficulties they encountered when they took on a leadership role. The following remark by Stephanie illustrates this point:

> I became a better person through this process because I learned a lot through it. Granted, I cried many times, and I also realize that it's not me; it's the other person that doesn't fully understand what we're doing, and how long and how far children can go.

While each teacher participant recognized the importance of her actions to influence what her students needed to be successful in the school setting, each teacher made very few comments about specific grades, testing information, or quantifiable record keeping that would quantify "student achievement." Both teachers clearly viewed student achievement as a process in which the teacher and students worked together in a progressive cycle of partnership, rather than as a single test or measure of accountability.

In summary, mutual trust and respect, collegiality, teacher empowerment, and a focus on student achievement appear to be four important elements in building teacher leadership capacity. These elements are interrelated with each other and depend on the overall context of a school. They are also interpreted according to the unique personalities and professional experiences of teachers, as well as according to the particular circumstances within which teachers work.

Building Teacher Leadership—One Teacher at a Time

Two primary concerns directed my study of teacher leadership: (1) the development of teacher leadership capacities and (2) the use of clinical supervision as a methodological strategy to facilitate individual leadership capacity building. The four elements that support the development of teacher leadership that were discussed above address the first concern. If these four elements are in place in a school that wishes to support the development of teacher leadership, what can then be done to focus attention on teacher leadership capacity building? This question led me to clinical supervision as a process that can be used to attend to building specific teacher leadership capacities.

Before arriving at clinical supervision as a good process for teacher leadership capacity building, I did a fair amount of investigation to determine what might work best for examining and building teacher leadership capacity. I began looking at how existing supervision techniques could be used within a school setting to investigate individual teacher leadership capacities in a manner that was natural to the school and to the teacher participants. What I was most interested in were techniques that were grounded in both theory and application.

I began by asking what type of supervisory strategy would best facilitate the teacher's becoming more aware of his or her teacher leadership potential? This is a question that does not appear to be addressed directly in existing research. Therefore, I looked to discussions of methods in the area of professional development for individual teacher capacity building in more general terms. What emerged as the best choice of tools in the instructional supervisory repertoire was what is commonly referred to as clinical supervision.

Clinical supervision offers a strategy that is meaningful to teachers in that it allows them to focus on those aspects of teacher leadership that are important to them in their own professional development. It is a powerful mechanism for building teacher leadership capacity in terms of the unique strengths and talents of each teacher. Furthermore, clinical supervision appeared to be well suited for examining and building teacher leadership capacity at Willow Springs because it reflected the kind of collegial supervisory relationship that was consistent with that school's culture for professional development.

Clinical supervision emerged in the 1960s in response to what supervisors working with preservice teachers perceived to be the ineffectiveness of the supervision intended to help these beginning teachers improve their teaching. The basic tenets of the method revolve around the establishment of a positive climate that fosters a healthy relationship between the supervisor and the teacher, the development of colleagueship between the supervisor and the teacher, observation of the teacher's classroom setting, and patterned analysis of observed data (Cogan, 1973; Sergiovanni & Starratt, 1998).

Clinical supervision has been described as a partnership in inquiry in which the supervisor acts more as a colleague to the teacher, allowing the development of a relationship that is based less on hierarchical authority and more on the supervisor as a resource (Sergiovanni & Starratt, 1998). In this sense, clinical supervision can also act as a component for individualized staff development, allowing teachers to lead their own inquiry concerning professional development.

Traditionally, the literature has described a number of phases of clinical supervision that the supervisor and the participant undergo in order for the participant to gain a better understanding of his or her teaching style. Although the number of phases differs according to different authors' views (Goldhammer, 1969;

Cogan, 1973; DuFour, 1991; Acheson & Gall, 1997; Sergiovanni & Starratt, 1998), the eight phases described by Cogan (1973) capture well the events of clinical supervision.

1. Establishment of the teacher-supervisor relationship.
2. Intensive planning of lessons and units with the teacher.
3. Planning of the classroom observation strategy by teacher and supervisor.
4. Observation of in-class instruction.
5. Careful analysis of the teaching-learning process.
6. Planning the conference strategy.
7. The supervisory conference.
8. Resumption of planning.

This cycle can be repeated several times throughout the course of a teaching year, helping to give teachers feedback concerning new instructional strategies in a collegial, democratic fashion. One of the benefits of clinical supervision is that it encourages teachers to develop their own ability to plan and analyze their own teaching and their students' learning. As teachers become more self-supervising, their need to rely on others, especially supervisors, to provide continuous feedback concerning professional growth diminishes. The reduced dependence on supervisors not only benefits the supervisors by protecting their time, but also helps to foster independence for teachers and more personal autonomy concerning their sense of efficacy.

The purpose of clinical supervision has been described as a process that enables teachers to change existing patterns of teaching in ways that seem meaningful to the individual teacher. The focus of clinical supervision is ultimately to support the professional development of teachers, one teacher at a time. The role of the supervisor in clinical supervision is to aid the teacher in highlighting areas of teaching that may be closely inspected and to help the teacher gain a better understanding of his or her teaching strategies. I came to assume that just as clinical supervision helped teachers to examine and develop their teaching practices, so it could be similarly used to explore aspects of their teacher leadership. It was this assumption that guided my use of clinical supervision with the two teacher participants.

Additional tools for communication can be used during the clinical supervision process. During the clinical supervision process with the teacher participants in this study, I chose to use interpersonal communication techniques derived from the counseling psychology model of Interpersonal Process Recall (IPR) to optimize the relationships built with each teacher. These techniques were added to clinical supervision based on the supposition that the process of clinical supervision inherently relies on strong interpersonal communication between the supervisor and the teacher. IPR communication strategies (Kagan, 1980), when used in a controlled setting, encourage an individual (in this case the classroom teacher) to "recall" specific moments of previous dialogue between the supervisor and the teacher that allow the teacher to elaborate on those moments in order that both parties might understand that previous dialogue much better.

The addition of interpersonal communication techniques provided both the teachers and me with a mechanism for reflecting on comments made during the clinical supervision process. Because many of the comments made during clinical supervision were prime for additional explanation or comments, it was helpful to give the teachers a chance to tell me "what they really meant" or to add comments that related to their developing understanding of teacher leadership skills. Being able to articulate their growing awareness of their own teacher leadership abilities and to consciously relate new terminology and practices to their own work within the school setting helped Betty and Stephanie incorporate some of their newfound understanding of teacher leadership into their sense of their roles as teachers. This process is illustrated in Betty's comment about her newfound awareness of her leadership potential. In response to a question during the final interview about which leadership quality she had become most aware of, Betty replied:

> Helping more or assisting more . . . facilitating more [in regard to other teachers within the school] . . . it never dawned on me that I could be of service to resource [teachers]. . . . I see some things that they [the students] could find helpful. And maybe being more of service, or providing some ideas or help to them [the teachers], it's made me kind of think that even

though I've proved a lot in my own program, there is still room to grow.

Clinical Supervision as a Mechanism for Teacher Leadership Capacity Building

Implications for the Clinical Supervision Process

Using clinical supervision as a vehicle for examining and developing teacher leadership has implications for the practice of clinical supervision in that it extends the range of possible uses for this supervisory model. It is, however, a logical extension. The characteristics that make clinical supervision appropriate for improving teaching skills also apply to its use for teacher leadership capacity building. Clinical supervision allowed each teacher participant to target particular aspects of teacher leadership based on her needs and interests in her particular teaching role. As teaching styles and philosophy differ from teacher to teacher, I also noted that their teaching leadership styles also vary, depending on the emphasis that the teacher places on various components of her job role. Clinical supervision allowed the teacher to highlight areas of teacher leadership that she believed merited closer inspection in order for her to gain a better understanding of her own teacher leadership behavior. For example, whereas Betty appeared to be comfortable talking about her teacher leadership practices both in the context of her classroom and beyond to building and district levels, Stephanie was much more comfortable talking about her teacher leadership only in regard to her students and her classroom practices.

Clinical supervision also allowed the teachers and me to study teacher leadership and its development in action as we examined observation data gathered from instances identified by the teachers that provided empirical evidence of their teacher leadership. The conference portion of clinical supervision provided an ideal forum for discussion of the observed data by allowing each teacher the chance to discuss her impressions of the data with me and to plan ways in which to extend and develop her leadership.

Finally, clinical supervision gave teachers a voice both in choosing areas of teacher leadership on which to focus and in interpreting data that documented their leadership behavior. It is this final aspect of clinical supervision by which teachers are empowered as decision makers about their own professional development—in this case, in the area of teacher leadership—that links clinical supervision to the four elements that help build teacher leadership capacity. Clinical supervision provided an ideal platform for an ongoing, open discussion of teacher leadership that promoted the professional growth of each teacher. Clinical supervision allowed each teacher to tailor her professional goals in the area of teacher leadership within her own comfort zone and skill level.

As a mechanism for teacher leadership capacity building, clinical supervision helped both Betty and Stephanie gain valuable insights into their own teacher leadership abilities. Clinical supervision made it possible for them to consider issues that neither traditional observation conducted for accountability purposes nor traditional in-service professional development training would have addressed. Clinical supervision, therefore, can be seen as a valuable tool for developing teacher leadership and for building leadership capacity in ways that are individualized for each teacher.

Implications for Individualized Professional Development

In my study of teacher leadership capacity building, clinical supervision allowed the teacher participants and me to explore individual areas of teacher leadership important to Betty's and Stephanie's professional development as teachers. During the clinical supervision experience, each teacher became more assertive and better able to articulate her individual wants and needs as a teacher leader. Such use of clinical supervision as a vehicle for teacher leadership capacity building not only extends conventional thinking about clinical supervision itself, but also extends the typical range of professional development that focuses only on aspects of classroom instruction. Identifying teacher leadership as an area for specific attention in teachers' professional development helps teachers recognize leadership opportunities and develop their abilities as leaders. The recognition that it is possible for teachers to assume leadership roles without leaving the classroom for an administrative position also makes it possible for teachers to grow in a career as a classroom teacher. As Betty put it, "I want to stay in the classroom, and this is the way for me to start up something new, something challenging, and just to branch out." Specifically, clinical supervision allows teachers to individualize their leadership capacity building, making it possible for them to choose the areas in which they will develop and exercise leadership. Clinical supervision also supports and sustains the kind of collaboration and trust that are important between teacher leaders and supervisors. Clinical supervision allows teachers and supervisors to move away from a relationship based on evaluation outcomes to one based on more reflective and individualized interactions.

The opportunity to discuss these issues of teacher leadership through the kind of reflective conversation about professional development that is a central feature of clinical supervision helped each teacher engage in what can be described as "framing action." Each teacher was able to "frame" or set off specific aspects or areas of teacher leadership and engage in individualized discussions to explore her interests and skills as well as the constraints to and possibilities for her exercising teacher leadership in those areas. Such framing made it easier for me in my role as supervisor not only to collect observation data about the teacher as an individual practitioner, but also to obtain teachers' input into data collection and data analysis.

I would argue that clinical supervision provides an invaluable tool in developing leadership capacity and in promoting professional development that is meaningful to each teacher participant. Powerful evidence of such meaningfulness can be seen in the fact that both Betty and Stephanie have engaged in ongoing discussion about their growth as leaders with either a supervisor or a peer since the cessation of data collection for the actual study. I suspect that these two teachers have continued to focus on their leadership capacity building because they see the benefits of a relationship of collegiality to their continued learning and professional development as teacher leaders. Perhaps the evidence that best summarizes how each participant was able to make clinical supervision meaningful to her professional development was epitomized in the comments made by Betty during the end of our time together:

> Well, the one thing that I mentioned to you before, kind of reflecting on what I've done . . . I think that you made me more aware . . . and I want to do more [in the classroom]. . . . I'm working on more . . . putting a book together for Pam. And I think just from you, you know, making me reflect on what I've done, and the changes that I've made and things that I've improved on, it made me want to do that.

I must add that both participants were ideal candidates to engage in the clinical supervision experience. They both had a vested interest in their own professional development and worked along with me to produce something positive and lasting from the experience. Above all, they were colleagues who were aware that I was undertaking this study as scholarly research. They were committed to supporting my research interests, and me, even if that meant taking time from their schedules. In many schools, teachers are not as willing to invest themselves either for their colleagues or for their own professional growth. In addition, Betty's and Stephanie's willingness to engage in a form of supervision that seemed novel to them demonstrated that a certain degree of trust existed between them and me as colleagues in that school.

Implications for Practicing Administrators and Supervisors

Just as clinical supervision has implications for the leadership capacity building of classroom teachers, so it has benefits for supervisors as well. The clinical supervision that I had the opportunity to practice for this study of teacher leadership has been invaluable to me now that I am a school principal. I have had the good fortune to experience supervision that balances the evaluative role of my job. Even though the observation-based evaluation form I am required to complete for each teacher homogenizes these teachers, clinical supervision allows me to work more collegially and democratically with them and gives them a stake in their ongoing professional development.

The experience I had with clinical supervision during this study strongly suggests the value of an administrator who observes, discusses, and builds teacher leadership capacities. Often, despite the best intentions of administrators, not enough attention is paid to the professional development of teachers in the school setting. The use of clinical supervision to develop teacher leadership capacity encourages and prepares teachers to assume leadership in their own professional development and that of their teacher colleagues. What better investment of an administrator's time than in a process that relieves some of the burden and time-pressures of his or her job by enabling teachers who have the greatest instructional skill and knowledge to become the leaders of professional development?

Developing such teacher leaders is also consistent with the No Child Left Behind Act of 2001 (United States Department of Education, 2002) that emphasizes the importance of school systems having "quality" teachers in order to satisfy increased accountability requirements. In an age when rising standards of accountability are placed on student achievement and on the ability of teachers to prepare students, school systems must look beyond quantitative and evaluative models of teacher assessment to determine what makes a "quality" teacher. Traditional one-size-fits-all evaluations fail not only to give a full description of a teacher's unique abilities or potential within the classroom, but also to address teacher leadership completely. Furthermore, the teacher has little input into the categories and outcomes on which evaluations are based. In the interests of time and efficiency, such uniform evaluation processes fail to recognize the way each teacher brings meaning to her teaching and how such meaning influences both student achievement and the teacher's own development as a professional. Because of these limitations, traditional forms of evaluative supervision do not encourage teachers either to conceive of themselves as professionals or to see themselves as developing during the course of their career the abilities to assume a leadership role within their profession.

Conclusion—Beyond Measure

The emphasis placed on school improvement and accountability by legislators and community stakeholders will continue to be important for school systems. Within the scope of school improvement, the teacher's influence on student achievement will receive increasing attention. If we continue to rely primarily on outcome measures of teacher quality in the form of student achievement, critical features of the instructional leadership provided by teachers and how that leadership contributes to overall school "success" or "improvement" may remain unnoticed. As practicing administrators, we must keep in mind that a thorough picture of any organization can be gathered only if we are mindful of all of the elements and individuals who make up that organization and if we work to ensure that their influence on the organization is optimized.

Studies such as the one described in this chapter help us as administrators to remember that a school is only as good as the sum of its parts. If parts of the school organization, such as the building of teacher leadership capacity, are not recognized or considered to be worth the investment of administrators' time, then the whole project of school improvement and accountability may be jeopardized. It is my hope that this discussion of teacher leadership capacity building will encourage school administrators and teachers alike to attend to the development of teacher leadership and to acknowledge its importance for the ongoing improvement of our schools.

References

Acheson, K., & Gall, M. (1997). *Techniques in the Clinical Supervision of Teachers: Preservice and Inservice Applications*, Fourth Edition. New York: Longman Press.

Bolman, L., & Deal, T. (1994). *Becoming a Teacher Leader: From Isolation to Collaboration*. Thousand Oaks, CA: Corwin Press.

Clark, D. (1998). Organizational Behavior. [On-line.] Available: http://www.nwlink.com/~donclark/

Cogan, M. (1973). *Clinical Supervision*. Boston: Houghton Mifflin.

Combs, A. (1999). On Becoming a School Leader: A Person-Centered Challenge. [On-line.] Available: _ HYPERLINK http://www.ascd.org/readingroom/books _http://www.ascd.org/readingroom/books_

Darling-Hammond, L. (1994). Will 21st Century Schools Really Be Different? *Education Digest*, 60(1), 4.

DuFour, R. (1991). *The Principal as Staff Developer*. Bloomington, IN: National Educational Service.

Firestone, W. (1993). Why "Professionalizing" Teaching Is Not Enough. *Educational Leadership*, March 1993.

Goldhammer, R. (1969). *Clinical Supervision*. New York: Holt, Rinehart and Winston.

Gullatt, D. (1995). *Effective Leadership in the Middle School Classroom*. Paper presented at the Annual Conference of the National Middle School Association, New Orleans, Louisiana.

Kagan, N. (1980). Influencing Human Interaction-Eighteen Years with IPR. In A. K. Hess (Ed.). *Psychotherapy Supervision: Theory, Research, and Practice* (pp. 261–283). New York: Wiley.

Katzenmeyer, M., & Moller, G. (1996). *Awakening the Sleeping Giant: Leadership Development for Teachers*. Thousand Oaks, CA: Corwin.

Lambert, L. (1998). *Building Leadership Capacity in Schools*. Alexandria, VA: Association for Supervision and Curriculum Development.

Schon, D. (1983). *The Reflective Practitioner: How Professionals Think and Act*. New York: Basic Books.

Sergiovanni, T., & Starratt, R. (1998). *Supervision: A Redefinition*, Sixth Edition. Boston: McGraw Hill.

Snell, J., & Swanson, J. (2000). *The Essential Knowledge and Skills of Teacher Leaders: A Search for a Conceptual Framework*. (Report No. SP 039409). U.S., Washington. (ERIC Reproduction Service No. ED 444958).

Suranna, K., & Moss, D. (2001). *Perceptions of Teacher Leadership: A Case Study of Inservice Elementary School Teachers*. (Report No. SP039203). U.S., Connecticut. (ERIC Reproduction Service No. ED 444096).

United States Department of Education (2002). No Child Left Behind web page. Available: http://www.nochildleftbehind.gov/next/overview/

Warren-Little, J. (1982). Norms of Collegiality and Experimentation: Workplace Conditions of School Success. *American Educational Research Journal*, 19:3, 325–340.

Whitaker, T. (1995). Informal Teacher Leadership—The Key to Successful Change in the Middle Level School. *NASSP Bulletin*, 79(567), 76–81.

4

Supporting Teachers' Professional Development

Paula Adams

Among the many competing demands confronting building administrators, it could be argued that none ranks higher than the role of "principal as instructional leader." It is in this role, after all, that principals actively support and facilitate effective teaching and the ongoing learning of students. Because they are instructional leaders, principals strive to recruit, develop, and retain the best teachers possible. While balancing the diverse administrative activities included in their busy job descriptions, effective building principals must also fulfill one of the most complex, although often undervalued, functions of educational leadership. They conduct classroom observations and evaluate teachers for appraisal purposes.

As leaders of instruction it is primarily building principals who supervise and evaluate classroom teachers. And so the question arises: If, in fact, the ultimate goals of teacher supervision and evaluation are to improve instruction and support ongoing professional development of teachers, how well do traditional evaluation practices meet these objectives? Some would argue that they do not. And many teachers and administrators might agree.

Often, the observation checklists of classroom behaviors used in typical teacher performance evaluation systems narrow the definition of "good teaching" to a predetermined set of tasks that occur in the space of an hour. In such systems, it is not unusual for the same instrument to be used as a basis for all summative evaluations with little or no differentiation between novice and veteran teachers. As a result, teachers who have been rated as high performing continue to be evaluated year after year on indicators they have already mastered. On the other hand, teachers most in need of improvement may not receive adequate supervisory support because of administrative time constraints that are exacerbated by such mandatory observation procedures. In either case, such systems deliver little benefit to teachers in terms of their overall professional growth or the improvement of their teaching.

There is little disagreement among school leaders that effective instruction delivered by highly skilled teachers is a primary means of achieving improved student learning. It seems ironic, therefore, that the critical elements of teacher supervision and evaluation that can best achieve those outcomes commonly receive little emphasis and often are completely absent. In order to have positive effects on classroom instruction and promote the professional development of teachers, supervisory practices, and performance evaluations in particular, must first recognize and honor the broad scope of skills and knowledge utilized by "good teachers," including those that may not be easily observed. Second, teachers should be encouraged and nurtured in their efforts to consciously study, develop, and expand their theories and understanding about teaching and learning in order to continuously improve their effectiveness as practitioners. After all, these are things "professionals" do. By some definitions, these are the very capacities (the ability to adhere to and contribute to technical and ethical standards within a field) that distinguish the professional.

Classroom teachers, through their daily interactions with students and by their selections of strategies and methods for delivery of content, are the greatest determinants of instructional outcomes. The practical and intuitive knowledge about effective instruction that highly effective teachers gain through their experiences and inquiry offers great potential for achieving goals of continuous improvement in students' learning and should be recognized as valuable to that effort. Unfortunately, traditional approaches to teacher supervision, professional development, and performance evaluation used by school principals seldom reflect this perspective and sometimes actually work against it.

For principals, who serve as instructional leaders and who are concerned with teacher professionalism as well as student achievement, the questions are these: How can schools provide supervision and evaluation experiences that promote growth and improvement for teachers? What can teachers and administrators do to continuously improve the quality of the classroom instruction and student learning that occurs in their schools? In considerations of these questions and the factors that contribute to quality schools and students' academic achievement, the impact of leadership that supports teacher inquiry and high standards of professionalism may, in fact, be beyond the measure of most school accountability systems. Nonetheless, there are compelling reasons why this element should not be ignored.

The study that this chapter examines was a nonconventional approach to teacher performance evaluation that greatly altered the teacher–supervisor interactions and professional development experiences of the participants. This alternative approach to teacher appraisal and evaluation shifted emphasis from a simple documentation of a prescribed set of observable teacher behaviors as evidence of "good instruction,"an "evaluation by inspection" approach, to one that encouraged professional inquiry activities of teachers and ultimately led to more innovative and learner-centered instructional practices. After a few years of experience with the process, principals and teachers so valued the benefits they perceived being derived from the system that when confronted with the possibility of a return to observation-based evaluations, they passionately exclaimed, "We can't go back!"

Teacher Evaluation Revisited

In order to fully appreciate the significance of the changes brought about by the new evaluation system, educators may find it helpful to consider the theories and purposes that underlie teacher supervision and evaluation practices. Presumably, evaluation is one goal of teacher supervision because evaluation of teachers supports and improves instruction by facilitating and positively influencing the professional growth and development of teachers. In practice, however, educators report that this potential is largely unrealized.

Research in the field of teacher supervision suggests many reasons for this failure. Common obstacles include (1) a lack of adequate resources, which results in insufficient time and training for supervisors to support the process; (2) supervisory approaches that are judgmental in evaluations of teaching practices; and (3) frequent misrepresentations of evaluation practices as "clinical supervision," which cause teachers to view the process as unpleasant (Holland, et al., 1992, p. 177). In many instances, teachers experience or perceive supervision as limited to or primarily involving those activities surrounding their performance evaluations. As means of addressing issues of accountability and meeting specific performance standards, teachers are often evaluated using high-stakes, observation-based measures that may be used to drive decisions about retention and compensation. Studies of systems that focus on demonstrating a prescribed set of observable teaching behaviors as a means of evaluating overall performance suggest that these measures predictably increase occurrences of the particular behaviors measured, but may actually decrease the occurrences of important nonobservable teaching behaviors (Darling-Hammond & Sclan, 1992). Research further indicates that teachers who know they will be evaluated on a given set of teaching behaviors can generally execute those behaviors on demand (Clift, 1989). However, it appears that evaluation systems that represent "good teaching" as a prescribed set of behaviors can result in decreases in important but less observable behaviors such as curriculum planning, diagnostic efforts on behalf of students having difficulty, or the coherent organization of units and lessons over time. For example, after describing the Florida Performance Measurement System (FPMS), a forerunner of various teacher evaluation plans later mandated by many states, Darling and Sclan (1992) point out its weaknesses:

> Teachers trained to teach to the FPMS indicators wouldn't learn to vary their behaviors according to the needs of students and the demands of the teaching situation ... The system consciously conveys to teachers that their use of pedagogically acceptable practices is not acceptable, and that they should ignore research which suggests that they should adjust their behaviors to different student responses or circumstances. (pp. 20–21).

Whether or not important teacher behaviors actually decrease with the use of such systems, it is clear that these types of instruments have serious limitations for defining and appraising the complex act of teaching. An instrument that focuses only on observable behaviors occurring during a given hour of instruction reflects a very limited and narrow definition of effective teaching.

Supervisory and evaluation practices that fail to support and nurture teachers in their efforts to grow professionally and to better understand and interpret classroom events overlook an essential resource for improving instruction. That resource is the rich knowledge gained by reflective practitioners who take ownership for the learning outcomes of their students. In order to grow as professionals, teachers need supervisory support that, first, encourages them to clarify and articulate their understanding and beliefs about instruction and, second, facilitates their growth and development as practitioners through ongoing inquiry and the reflective analysis of their classroom practices.

The Importance of Professional Inquiry

Some of the most valuable approaches to supporting teachers in their growth and development are those associated with the process of professional inquiry. Professional inquiry is the conscious development of teachers' own theories of practice. It is a process that provides continuing emphasis on the skills and experiences that help teachers grow in their understanding of teaching (Holland, et al., 1992). Activities such as reflective practice, peer coaching, collaboration, and action research are thought to be part of this process. Even though many good teachers instinctively do these things, such activities often go unnamed and, therefore, unrecognized by both teachers and their supervisors. They are certainly not behaviors awarded "credit" for evaluation purposes. However, many who conduct research and write about professional development have provided insights into these practices of professional inquiry and have created a language for talking about it.

Schon (1987), for instance, describes reflective practice as the process of interpreting and analyzing the "messy and indeterminate" nature of actual practice settings in order to develop context-specific solutions for the problems encountered in those settings. By engaging in reflective practice, teachers attempt to move outside the teaching act in order to examine it. They shed the "teacher as expert" role in the hope of discovering and building new constructs. Reflection is an essential tool and an important aid to teachers who seek to develop and implement effective classroom strategies.

Collaboration and peer coaching have also been shown to support and encourage teachers' efforts at reflection and instructional improvement. In writing about critical professional inquiry, Lester and Mayer (1987) summarize it this way:

> To be a professional is not to have all the answers. Rather, a professional is someone who can reflect on tentative solutions, collaborate with others on the possible avenues available, and risk making mistakes because mistakes are an inevitable part of building new roads. (p. 209)

In an article about the promotion of reflective practice through co-teaching, Celeste Brody (1994), an associate professor and co-ordinator of graduate programs at Lewis and Clark University reports the benefits:

> Reflective co-teaching encourages teachers to use collegial dialogue to clarify situations, recast them, rethink the assumptions on which the initial understandings of a problematic issue were based, and consider the range of possible responses they might use together. (p. 33)

The research and literature on collegial interactions such as peer coaching, co-teaching, and other forms of collaboration offer many examples of how these contexts for professional inquiry have supported instructional improvements and positive learning outcomes for students.

Classroom action research is another professional inquiry activity that has been shown to support teachers in their growth and development as effective practitioners. One study exploring the relationship between teacher-conducted research and professional growth observed that the teachers investigated research questions that were generated by their own classroom experiences, either as a response to specific incidents or issues, or as a way to validate experiential knowledge or beliefs (Brindly, 1991). Joanne Simmons (1985) examined the impact of assuming the role of action researcher as an example of inquiry-oriented professional staff development in a study of the experiences of K-12 teachers. She used a thorough review of the literature along with the interview and questionnaire responses of twenty participants in order to determine ways that teachers are influenced by reflectively analyzing their own practices in light of research regarding the teaching-learning process. Her conclusions point out numerous positive influences:

> These data indicate quite strongly that these participants believe that there have been positive increases in (1) their knowledge concerning effective teaching-learning; (2) their knowledge and skills concerning research; (3) their reflective thinking habits; (4) their attitudes toward the need for ongoing professional development for themselves as teachers; (5) their skills in identifying professional development goals for themselves; and (6) their overall effectiveness as educators. (p. 16)

All of these examples support the assertion that professional inquiry offers teachers and supervisors a way to think about teaching in terms of a continuum of skills and practices along which teachers develop during the course of their careers. An evaluation and supervision process should account for such development.

Improving Teachers and Teaching through Professional Inquiry

Most principals and teachers would readily agree that supervision should include the kinds of professional inquiry that have positive impact on teachers' growth and development. Yet, when teacher supervision is driven by and often limited to the activities surrounding observation-based evaluations, the process falls far short. As a result, a potent resource for effecting instructional improvements is neglected. In order to reap more fully the potential benefits, supervision should engage teachers in common practices that promote their development as skilled and reflective professionals. Supervisory interactions between teachers and principals should reflect these assumptions of professional inquiry: (1) learning or the development of one's teaching skills is an ongoing process; (2) teachers actively participate in determining the direction of their own professional growth; and (3) the focus of supervision is the effects and meanings of teachers' classroom practice (Holland, et al., 1992).

The experiences of teachers and principals involved in the study that is the basis for this chapter give credence to these assumptions in a dramatic way. Through a shift in the focus of supervision and evaluation practices, teachers reported significant increases in their own professional inquiry. As gratifying as the new evaluation process was for teachers, the more important implication is the fact that their perceptions of resulting instructional improvements concurred with those of their supervisors. School administrators who want to nurture the growth of teachers as professionals and who wish to boost the effectiveness of daily classroom instruction will find a preponderance of evidence here to indicate that these outcomes can be achieved through use of supervisory and evaluative practices that support professional inquiry.

Professional Inquiry in Action

The new evaluation system described below encouraged the professional inquiry activities of teachers by requiring that they reflect, self assess, and then design and implement plans for their own growth and development. This process, one that came to be known as professional development planning, drove the new evaluation system and had significant positive impact on teachers, supervisors, and classroom practices. It is safe to say that at the time the change was adopted, few of those involved in the decision would have predicted the specific advantages that would later come to be associated with it. Like so many innovations, this one arose out of a need. Principals and teachers generally agreed that the evaluation system they had been using was rote and time consuming. They did not believe the system had any enduring impact on instruction, and there was little they could find about the process that delivered any benefits to teachers in terms of their professional growth and development. In fact, particularly for veterans, the required observations had become little more than a "dog and pony show," a term that was not uncommon when teachers referred to the process. On the other hand, because of the time demand for implementation of the mandated observation schedule required for all teachers, principals found they had little time to devote to novices or to those who might be struggling. As a result, a district level committee of teachers and administrators was formed to closely examine the system in use and to explore possible alternatives.

Teachers and principals agreed that an ultimate goal of supervision and evaluation of teachers is the improvement of instruction and, consequently, student learning. They concluded that their current practices were not achieving those goals. At the time, the district was using a state-mandated teacher evaluation system that required at least one forty-five minute observation per year, per teacher, as the basis for an annual performance rating. Depending on years of experience in the district, prior performance ratings, and the discretion of the supervisor, teachers might receive two or more observations as part of the process. However, the same instrument was used for all teachers regardless of experience or prior ratings. Teachers were repeatedly evaluated according to 65 indicators of observable classroom behaviors that resulted in overall performance ratings of "Satisfactory," "Exceeding Expectations," or "Clearly Outstanding." The committee believed the system was contributing little to the professional growth and development of experienced and high-performing teachers who had already demonstrated consistent proficiency based on the instrument. Of even greater concern was the fact that the time required to observe all teachers actually impeded the delivery of supervisory attention to novice and less proficient teachers.

Acting on behalf of the school district and with full support of the superintendent and school board, the committee wrote an appeal to the state requesting a waiver from use of the mandated appraisal system. In the proposal the committee outlined an alternative system, expressing hope that it would be more effective in supporting improvements in teacher performance and student learning. As a result, the district received permission to evaluate some high-performing, experienced teachers using the proposed alternative method.

The alternative system essentially allowed teachers who had consistently performed as "Clearly Outstanding" on the observation-based measure to be evaluated based on the design and implementation of a Professional Development Plan (PDP). The PDP, which was reviewed and approved by the teacher supervisor, targeted an area of growth or improvement that was of interest to the teacher. Each PDP also included specifics about how the plan would be implemented and evaluated.

The use of PDPs for purposes of teacher evaluation and professional growth provided a sharp contrast to the state's observation-based system. A study was undertaken to determine how this alternative system influenced teachers' professional development activities, interactions with supervisor,s and instructional practices.

The study focused on teacher perceptions of PDPs and was designed to answer several questions. Given the opportunity to direct their own professional growth activities, teachers choose to do which things and why? Are they involved in the professional inquiry activities that have been described in the literature as effective vehicles for promoting growth and improvement? Do they experience professional growth through the use of the PDP? How does the PDP process impact their interactions with supervisors? How does the use of a PDP impact their instruction and the learning outcomes of their students? All of these questions were explored through the eyes of the veteran teachers who planned and designed, implemented, and evaluated PDPs.

Because the PDPs addressed targeted areas of interest or concern to teachers, it was important first to identify and describe not only the activities the teachers included in their plans, but also the underlying beliefs and understanding that led to their selections. Second, the supervisor's role with the use of PDPs shifted from one of inspector to one of collaborative consultant. It was important to determine the kinds of supervisory interactions teachers experienced throughout the process and their perceptions of the effectiveness of that supervisory support. Finally, because improved student learning was the ultimate concern and purpose for the alternative evaluation system, the study was designed to describe teachers' perceptions of how the PDP process influenced their instructional practices.

The study was conducted using a content analysis of 187 written PDPs, survey responses of those same teachers, and interview responses of 17 teachers selected as representatives of the larger group. Details of the methodology and data sources used in the study are provided in the endnote.

The Nature of Professional Development Plan Activities

For determination of which goals and activities had been selected by teachers and whether the PDPs appeared to involve teachers in professional inquiry, PDPs were examined for evidence of the professional inquiry practices of (1) reflection, (2) innovation, (3) collaboration, and (4) action research. These activities are all recognized in the literature on teacher development as practices that support professional growth.

Reflection

Study results showed that the PDP objectives selected by teachers involved efforts to analyze and interpret classroom events, teaching behaviors, and the resulting influences on learning outcomes. For instance, when teachers directly linked selected PDP objectives to specific needs or characteristics of students, that connection was considered evidence of reflection. An example of one PDP objective written by an elementary teacher follows:

> I would like to work with our special education team to modify and supplement the current fourth level language arts curriculum in order to better meet the needs of our resource and Chapter I students. I expect to enhance these students' learning by enabling them to work with instructional materials that more closely fit their learning styles.

The content analysis of the written PDPs showed that 70% of the plans included reflective statements or analyses. Likewise, in survey responses teachers indicated their PDPs prompted them to consider teaching methods related to students' needs. Teachers also spoke about these connections and their implications for instruction during interviews. Statements like the following make it clear that such reflections guided their decisions about PDP activities.

> It made me think, what is it that my students really need? What is the best way to meet that need? And then as I watched it develop, it made me consider: Is this working? Or do I need to make changes? How can I make this fit the students that I have? (Molly)

In addition, statements about the thought processes involved in the selection of PDP objectives and activities show that teachers valued reflectively thinking about instruction and identified it as an essential part of their growth experiences.

> The most beneficial aspect of the whole process for me was that it made me stop, think, and analyze what was going on in my classroom in order to find a way to make it [learning] more meaningful. (Lynn G)

Supporting Teachers' Professional Development

One teacher informant, who repeatedly referenced the reflective activities that characterized her PDP, summarized it this way:

> The most beneficial aspect of the process was partly the initial planning of it . . . thinking about it even before the implementing . . . thinking in my own mind what I could do with my particular group of students and my unique situation . . . what would be one thing that I could really work on and concentrate on this year that would impact them. And I think even if I'd only done a small segment of what I'd planned, I think it would have been worthwhile because it made me look at what the needs might be within my students that I could have a personal impact on within the school year. It made me take a look at myself and at my teaching and what I could work on. (Laura)

Through the process of designing and implementing their PDPs, teachers indicated that they were challenged to critically examine and rethink their existing instructional practices. Reflective self-analyses and self-assessments allowed them to redefine their theories of instruction and formulate new hypotheses. Traditional evaluation systems seldom place emphasis on this kind introspection. Considering how seldom typical performance ratings encourage or reward teachers for questioning their own classroom methods, one might argue that most appraisal processes actually inhibit reflective study of the craft of teaching. Yet, when asked about the role and value of reflection in the PDP process, teachers described it as very important. They recognized the fact that their reflections are essential for inspiring and ultimately evaluating their own professional growth. As they came to view instruction as a dynamic, problem-solving process, one that must evolve in response to learners, they were often ready to investigate and test new strategies and approaches to instruction. And so, reflections about their beliefs and observed classroom events led many teachers to innovative and creative endeavors.

Innovation

Many observation-based teacher evaluation systems credit demonstrations of predetermined instructional behaviors and, in effect, discourage innovation. By contrast, the teachers who implemented PDPs felt empowered to expand their classroom practices. The alternative system supported a degree of risk-taking because prior to implementation, teachers consulted with their supervisors regarding the PDP proposal and received approval of the plan. As a result, many expressed a renewed enthusiasm and optimism about meeting the instructional challenges they had identified. The alternative system supported teachers who were interested in trying fresh approaches and valued their efforts to continuously improve. For example, excerpts from the teachers' proposed PDPs illustrate such innovation:

> In cooperative groupings for science instruction, I will introduce a new lab role—the procedures manager.
>
> I hope to refine methods of presentation and have better, more modified lesson components so that all students will learn and feel successful. I will administer and refer to a learning styles inventory and use a variety of teaching methods to expedite learning for all types of learners.
>
> I will develop at least two alternative forms of assessment in my U.S. History class so that tests are not the only tool used to give major grades.

Innovation was determined to be present when the PDP activities involved a teacher's use or implementation of an instructional method, strategy, medium, or material which had not been used before or which would be used in a new or altered way. Whereas content analysis revealed evidence of innovation in 78% of the plans, when surveyed, 89% of the teachers stated that the PDP encouraged their use of new methods or materials. During interviews teachers were asked whether designing and implementing the PDP encouraged the use of instructional innovation and, if so, to describe examples. One teacher responded:

> Yes, because we tried many different things. We tried prepared innovations like portfolios and word banks, things that were out there that we had learned about in research and had been exposed to but really didn't get a chance to implement [prior to the PDP]. Plus, I found my own strategies. . . . I chose vocabulary development because I saw a need from test scores

and from the understanding and comprehension levels I observed in my students. I tried to use a lot of different techniques to develop vocabulary. . . . I sat and made a list of things that I felt the kids were weak in or things that I wanted to focus on for myself and for the kids, so we both would learn from it. From there, I just went through the list and chose strategies. I wanted to choose something new that I hadn't implemented before. I think it was a good problem-solving technique. I developed my own checklist for student assessments and realize now what I will do differently next year. A lot of the teachers I know worked on things that they felt they were weak on in the classroom . . . things that they thought would make them a better teacher. . . . So yes, I think you start developing your own tools for self-evaluation and for use with the kids. We can be innovative and creative and I think teacher generated things that we use ourselves are the best. (Kathy)

This teacher expressed an opinion shared by many of the teachers interviewed when asked about the influence of the PDP on instructional innovations. Teachers often reported that they had tried something new as part of their plans and that they had observed positive impact on student learning as a result. Innovative strategies spanned all areas of the curriculum and included varied materials, academic and behavioral strategies, modifications of instructional and assessment methods as well as the integration of technologies and individualized student supports.

Collaboration

Traditional evaluation methods apply ratings to teachers and sometimes rank their performance against that of their peers for considerations of salary, promotion, or merit pay increases. Such practices foster competition rather than collaboration and sometimes convey the message that only a limited number of the teachers evaluated can be truly "high performing." The focus of each teacher's PDP was to achieve a personal best. However, nothing about the PDP processes implied that "excellence" could be attained by only a few. On the contrary, the process of planning and implementing PDPs often involved teachers in collaborations with others as a means of successfully meeting the professional goals of all.

> I was in three other people's PDPs, and I don't really know how I got there. It's really not my field of expertise . . . but several of the teachers worked on computer PDPs and included me in their plans. Because I had taught myself, with the help of a friend, the Advanced Write program here at school, and I really used it and went in to the computer lab with my students every week, I sort of became known as the resident expert. So I didn't realize it, but three other people had put me in their PDPs as a resource. I did get to go in and help them with their lessons. I went with one teacher three different times to work with her class, and my students got to be tutors. So not only were the teachers interacting; the kids were interacting. Other interactions occurred when I discussed my PDP with teachers in other buildings. That gave me insights into other things that I wanted to do. So I think it's great for interactions between teachers. Now maybe everyone didn't have that experience, but I think the more we do it, the more we'll find our own teacher resources rather than going outside. We'll do it within. (Kathy)

Evidence of collaboration was identified when the PDP included consultations or collaborative exchanges between the teacher and other professionals, parents, students or community members as an action step for implementation. When examined during content analysis, collaboration appeared in only 25% of the written PDPs. However, 87% of the teachers surveyed stated that they had discussed their proposed strategies and PDP implementation with other professionals. Furthermore, interviews revealed a variety of collaborative activities surrounding PDP implementation that often had not been specified in the teachers' written plans.

> I talked to several people about ADHD . . . a pediatrician, a psychiatrist, and I searched out peer teachers, a couple in special education, because they tend to see more of a concentration of that in children than we do. A lot of times, just a peer teacher, possibly not even the same grade level, but someone you know who has worked with that [strategy] or has searched

out information, can serve as a resource. It [the PDP] causes you to really search for an answer rather than just depending on yourself. (Sunya)

I was so excited about it that I had to share it. We have a meeting with the three other middle school team leaders, so I had to share the PDP I had done because I was so pleased with what I was seeing with the children and the results. (Sharon)

The descriptions provided through the informant interviews gave testimony to the varied types of collaborative exchanges experienced by teachers during their PDP activities. Examples included informal sharing and discussions of PDP projects and results as well as more intentional and formal consultations that were conducted in order to facilitate implementation of their PDPs. These interactions often involved teachers in consultations with colleagues from grade levels or departments, campuses, and school districts other than their own. Teachers referred to consultations they sought with curriculum specialists both within and outside of their district as helpful resources utilized in the implementation of their PDPs.

Whatever the forms of collaboration reported, teachers uniformly described these encounters as beneficial to their PDP endeavors and conducive to their own professional growth. However, as noted earlier, it is interesting that such a small percentage of these collaborations were evident in the written professional development plans. It may be that prior evaluation experiences had done little to encourage or recognize the value of such collaborations and, therefore, teachers did not consciously plan for them or write them into PDP proposals. For many, it seems, the alternative evaluation experience prompted helpful professional collaborations and possibly increased appreciation for the importance of this particular form of professional inquiry.

Research

Many observation-based teacher evaluation systems utilize checklists of observable behaviors as a basis for performance ratings. Unfortunately, such systems can sometimes result in notions of "good teaching" that are limited to demonstrations of those very behaviors. When this happens, teachers learn to perform as instructional technicians of a sort. They learn to display on demand the behaviors that will be credited on the checklist and that yield high performance ratings. Less observable characteristics of good teaching, such as the ability to examine and test theories of instruction and apply new understanding, are often undervalued because observation-based systems fail to recognize and reward them. Applications of skills and insights developed through teacher research are certainly beyond the scope of most traditional appraisal methods. Yet, by contrast, this form of professional inquiry was an important element contributing to the growth and performance of teachers who were using PDPs.

Evidence of research, particularly action research, was noted when the professional development plan included a reference to any process of information gathering (surveys, grades, test scores, observations, etc.) which would result in documentation of new data for use in evaluation of instruction or for future planning and decision making by the teacher. Action research, by definition, deals with concrete problems in an environment where the researcher is a participant. The general focus of action research is to improve practice, improve understanding of the practice by its practitioners, and improve the situation in which the practice takes place (Brindley quoting Kemmis, 1982). As a professional inquiry activity, action research involves teachers in systematically investigating their own practices through cycles of planning, acting, observing, and reflecting. (Kemmis & McTaggart, 1988). Approximately 53% of the PDPs examined during content analysis show evidence of just such processes. In their survey responses, 88% of the teachers stated they had gathered information about instruction and student learning through the implementation of their professional development plans. In addition, 91% reported they had gained information that would assist them in future planning and decision making.

The descriptions garnered through interviews with key informants provided insights about the extent and nature of the research endeavors of teachers using professional development plans even when those activities were not formally recognized by the teachers as "research."

> It was informal, but I did write some things down. I kept some records after I'd give a test. I would write down the names of the kids who took the modified tests and their scores. At the end of the year, I looked through to see which kids passed more of the tests and which had failures. (Robin)

> If it [research] means coming up with a question, a problem, and collecting materials and the results of what you're doing and then coming to some conclusion, then yes. I've always been intrigued with it. I've always kind of wanted to become involved in it, but it's always been sort of a word.... [Until the PDP] I didn't feel adequate ... didn't really know what to do with it. But I think teachers are researchers. We're gathering data all the time. (Marilyn)

Often teachers stated that their PDP findings were difficult to quantify and, therefore, might not actually qualify as research. However, as they reflectively discussed the details of their particular inquiries, they began to acknowledge insights gained and implications for future instruction.

> I haven't done any statistical analysis, but then there is so much difference in my program and the program that was ... in my persona and the person that was; it's just incredible. There's such a difference that there's really no basis for comparison. So to compare would just be bogus data. But I know it made an impact on student learning because I've had feedback from teachers in classrooms. If I stay next year, this could be part of my doctoral work. I could compare the numbers we have this year to the numbers that we have next year and see if it [the program innovation] is indeed influencing kids' behavior. (Michelle)

During her interview, one teacher explained some recommendations she planned to make to the administrators in her high school regarding the make-up of classes for next year. The ideas for her proposals were a direct outgrowth of the insights about student groupings and interactions that she had gained through her PDP. Another informant said that while she had not actually conducted action research, her PDP had generated ideas for several possible avenues of research, as well as information about a topic she would like to present in a future professional journal article.

Like Michelle, quoted above, many of the teachers expected to use information gained through their PDP activities for future instructional decision making. The interviewed teachers often expressed this intent.

> Well, I think that the exercises and the things that I came up with are things that I will continue to do because they were successful . . . because they worked. So I think that I will definitely continue to use them. (Sammy)

> What I plan to do next year is to continue this with 5th grade only . . . to do one grade level instead of three. It was just kind of overwhelming, and I think that I would be more successful if I minimize it. I also think 5th graders are more capable of handling this than younger children . . . so I do plan to use it because I think it's worthwhile . . . but I wouldn't have known that if I hadn't jumped in with both feet. (Lynn S)

> Initially, I really assumed that if I gave them enough drill and practice, it would automatically come . . . and what I found out was that it did not. The next time I do this kind of activity, I'm going to include a structured 5 or 10 minutes of time for work on this. We're not only going to do choral response; we'll do more games . . . more active student involvement. I want it more structured. . . .The more experiences I can give them, the better off they're going to be. (Molly)

Research played a role in the PDP activities of teachers in more than one context. Whether or not they were actively engaged in action research, teachers who were interviewed each referenced some source of professional literature as part of their PDPs. In many instances, teachers' initial responses to the question about whether research activities were included in their plans were descriptions of the relevant professional writings they had reviewed. For many teachers in the study, the focus on a particular problem or issue of interest led to an investigation of the current research. When discussing their professional readings, these teachers revealed that they valued this pursuit as an important contributor to their professional growth and successful PDP implementation.

> I found a book from the Association for Curriculum and Development, and it was on how to help your child with ADD

or ADHD qualities. It was easy to read . . . much like a handbook. There were different chapters for different concerns. You'll not find one child that's the classic. I think there are all different ways in which children handle it emotionally and in different situations. I think understanding that fact in itself was probably most important to me. I bought the book, and I keep it right on my shelf. What normally works for those children who exhibit the ADHD qualities will more than likely work with other children . . . so why not use some of it with everybody? Some of the strategies needed to be extended a little bit more than what was suggested in the book. But overall, I used that source as my research base. The book gave quite a few statistics at the beginning . . . but not to the point of overuse. Because statistics do not mean anything to a child who is struggling in the classroom. So he may display those tendencies . . . the main focus is what are we going to do to help him and to help ourselves (laughter) survive the year! I think that's the most important part of the process . . . to realize that there's a problem and decide what we are going to do with it. I would say try innovations, and as far as research . . . you're going to have to do some. (Sunya)

The quote above is an example of the determination teachers displayed about becoming well informed about their PDP topics by enthusiastically reviewing professional literature and considering the implications of educational research for classroom practices.

The Administrator's Role in the Professional Development Plan Process

The alternative system clearly changed the roles of teachers in the evaluation process by involving them in reflective self-evaluations and other professional inquiry practices. It also changed the role of their administrative supervisors. Because the PDP process involved at least three exchanges with the teacher supervisor for planning, monitoring, and evaluating the plans, some teachers perceived their interactions with administrators as more collaborative. Teachers appreciated opportunities to discuss instructional issues with their principals rather than the typical administrative or disciplinary topics that are so often the focus of such interactions. The following comment captures the difference:

> I guess I interacted more. [I know it sounds kind of strange but] I interacted instructionally more with the assistant principal that's in charge of it [the PDP]. It seems that in my nine years of teaching, that I was always talking to administrators about challenging behavior problems or paperwork or parents or things that aren't. I mean it's all instructional, but aren't more academics instructional? I've had a lot more interaction with her talking about the content of reading/writing workshop, and especially with her being new and all, it has really helped me to know her a lot better. She's an incredible resource. I mean I'm always wanting to get to talk to her. . . . She's so busy . . . but that's caused me to talk to her a lot more about my PDP. (Jill)

The study revealed examples of how the PDP process, as compared with former observation-based supervision and evaluation methods, significantly changed the nature and quality of teacher and supervisor interactions. Through interview statements and survey responses, teachers consistently described the PDP process as teacher driven. It was critical that teachers feel free to honestly select those projects that they considered relevant and important to them. Although teachers perceived the process as beneficial to them because of this characteristic, they also acknowledged the facilitation and support of their administrators as a necessary ingredient for successfully planning and implementing PDPs. Responses such as the following clearly indicate that they welcomed this collaboration.

> Every teacher, every good teacher, knows what they need to do to grow. I've been teaching a long time, and I have been under many, many, many different types of evaluations. And the best I have ever been in is when you sit down with yourself and your principal or somebody who knows you best and who sees and observes you, and you say, "I think this is my strength and these are my weaknesses" and see if there's an agreement and then decide what you're going to do about it. Simple. (Jan)

Supporting Teachers' Professional Development

The written PDP format, coupled with a timeline for implementation that spanned an entire school year, served to strengthen a sense of commitment from both teachers and administrators. Teachers reported that the principal's participation, through the approval, monitoring, and evaluation of the plans, helped to reinforce and sustain their PDP efforts over time. The statements below are representative of the descriptions that many teachers provided when asked about their administrators' support throughout the process.

> I've been encouraged [by my supervisor]. When I did the first conference, I got a lot of support, a lot of encouragement, and a lot of freedom to design it in a way I felt I could best implement it. (Jill)

> By design, you get to interact with your teacher supervisor because the first one [conference] happens when you draw up the PDP and discuss what it is you're going to be working on. The second time that you do the mid-year [conference], you talk about what modifications you're going to make . . . what changes you felt like you have to make. . . . And the final one, of course, is where you meet with them to evaluate. So by design you meet at least three times, which is a pretty good set of interactions. (Molly)

Although PDPs are admittedly a teacher driven process, teachers repeatedly expressed an appreciation for input provided and the important roles of their administrators during the planning and evaluation of their PDPs.

> I think administrators need to know their teachers and make sure teachers are approaching this in an honest fashion—and that sounds like a negative statement against peers, but I don't mean it to be that way. This is the type of activity that can be taken lightly, so I think that for it to be meaningful, administrators really need to be in touch with their teachers, and if a teacher has not picked an appropriate area, then they need to be guided or encouraged to work on areas where they need work. (Lynn S)

> My administrator seemed pretty pleased with the plan that I had, although I will say that when I wasn't able to meet a

couple of the things that I had contracted for, I was a little hesitant on opening up and being honest about that. He was very encouraging and said, "Well, you know, that's part of the process, too. You don't always achieve necessarily everything." It helped me to feel more accepted that he realized that it wasn't a failure because I didn't achieve on every single level that I had anticipated. Perhaps I overshot with my goal a little bit. But I appreciated his understanding. It was great to see that he was more or less thinking practical[ly] and saw that human beings don't always do everything that they would like to be able to do. It'll make me feel freer next year to [set my] goal even higher if I choose. At first I felt . . . I have just got to do this . . . if I don't do this, then I have failed at this whole thing. But I realize now, while I didn't reach all I intended, I did come a long way. I'll feel more flexible in choosing a PDP for next year because I know that if I don't make it a 100% to my satisfaction, I will still have grown, and my teacher supervisor would still be accepting of what I am able to accomplish. (Laura)

The teachers quoted here express a value for collaborative supervisory interactions. They recognize such interactions as important for supporting their own self-assessments, goal setting, and other professional growth activities. The PDP process provided a framework and focus for the inquiry pursuits and supervisory interactions with school administrators that teachers considered conducive to their growth and improvement.

In many respects, the alternative system essentially reconfigured the roles that are typically associated with traditional performance evaluations. As professionals responsible for their own growth and improvement and capable of critical self-assessments, teachers were no longer passive recipients of performance ratings rendered by their administrators. Instead, they participated actively in their own evaluations and, in doing so, assumed additional responsibility for the process. Principals conducted evaluations in a more collegial manner. They assumed roles as facilitators of professional development by supporting the professional inquiry activities of teachers and collaboratively evaluating results. The PDP process provided a unique forum for teacher and principal interactions. In the alternative evaluation system, shifts in roles assumed by teachers and principals effectively expanded the degree of responsibility and accountability required of each.

Influences on Instruction

The ultimate goal of teacher evaluation is the improvement of instruction and student learning. In this study, teachers and principals referred to the evidence of the PDP's positive influence on instruction in terms of innovative practices that were used by teachers and the professional growth and development they experienced through the process. In survey and interview responses, teachers often compared the new evaluation system to the previous observation-based system and identified reasons for considering PDPs more conducive to effective instruction.

> When I consider what some of the teachers did, I just think that the opportunities for professional growth are really there. One group went to a three-week workshop where the works of minority writers were paired with traditional works taught within the high school English curriculum. Those teachers came back, and they made it part of their PDPs to include these Chicano writers and Black writers that weren't traditionally taught in the English curriculum. Things like that don't happen when all you're focusing on is one dynamite lesson for an observation. I think that this really does challenge us to improve as teachers as opposed to pulling out one little lesson. (Lynn G)

> You are forced to find something that you want to improve on and set goals for yourself, where[as] in the old system, you just had a 45-minute observation, and all you had to do was produce one lesson. A PDP is an ongoing thing over the entire year. You find something that you need to work with all year where you see that you're weak or the children are weak . . . and then do some research on how to improve it and read literature and see where you need to go. It's been a lot more work [than an observation] . . . but I think it's definitely been beneficial, and we've had great results this year with our [students'] writing. (Lynn S)

Teachers interpreted and described the instructional benefits of PDPs as specific and relevant to their particular plans and activities. The common element among all reports of instructional benefit, however, is the link teachers consistently made between their professional inquiry activities and subsequent instructional decisions. In describing their PDP results, teachers expressed their belief that in one manner or another, improved instruction was achieved as result of their increased skills, insights, and understanding about their own teaching. Furthermore, teachers in the study stressed a clear distinction between what they considered professional growth and any personal growth they may have derived from the PDP process. By their definition, professional growth was the achievement of improved instruction, whereas personal growth was self-improvement. This conclusion is illustrated by the following comments from the teachers:

> I think the students should always be the bottom line. I think through self-improvement, through whatever professional development we pursue, it should benefit the students.... Whatever knowledge we gain obviously needs to be put back into the classroom because there's really no other way to evaluate whether or not it's been successful except through evaluation with students... The student reaction to it or results from it [are] what's important. (Sammy)

> The focus should be student learning... what the impact is going to be on the students. The bottom line in any kind of professional development is what the students are going to get... at least that's the way I feel about it. (Molly)

> The focus needs to be something that can make a difference for your students... where you can see a visible difference... because you can grow within yourself, but if it doesn't make a difference in your teaching... It's wonderful for personal growth, but I don't think it really counts as professional growth. The bottom line is how can this help students learn better? (Laura)

In survey responses, teachers and principals overwhelmingly agreed that the PDPs resulted in improved instructional practices. Teachers offered many examples of innovations, developed and implemented through the PDP, that they felt had resulted in student learning and positive behaviors. These included various methods and strategies and altered uses of materials and technology, as well as efforts involving parents. To support their opinions regarding improvements in instruction and learning, teachers cited evidence. Some examples, such as student grades, test scores, daily class work, and homework, were easily measured and documented and provided data for evaluating the PDPs. Other evidence, such as increases in students' levels of class participation or changes in their behaviors and attitudes, were considered equally important but were recognized as more difficult to objectively assess.

> Kids were overwhelmingly positive in their journals in terms of what they liked about the classroom (Adventure in the Classroom innovation). I was really interested in trying to create a "we attitude" in the classroom instead of an "I attitude" among the students. I felt like it manifested itself in some neat ways . . . In terms of anything more specific, that's probably harder to assess because it's not something that can be easily quantified. (Lynn G)

Implications for Teachers

The supervision and evaluation process that is portrayed here appears to be one that supported the professional growth and development of teachers. For many of the participants in the study, the use of PDPs set in place conditions that supported professional inquiry. As teachers reflectively analyzed their instructional settings and practices, they identified problems and concerns, posed questions about instructional practice, and set professional goals. They worked collaboratively with others to plan and implement their PDPs, applied innovations, and evaluated outcomes. The teacher-driven quality of the process encouraged personal commitment and a sense of ownership of professional growth and instructional improvements.

The teachers in this study experienced growth and development through the use of the PDPs to the extent that they were engaged in the professional inquiry activities of reflective practice, applied innovations, collaborative interactions, and classroom research. The teachers themselves acknowledged these activities as important parts of their PDPs and attributed their own professional growth and improved instruction to these pursuits. Administrators were recognized as collaborators with teachers in planning and evaluating activities for achieving their instructional and professional goals.

Implications for Principals

This study of supervision and evaluation of teaching offers a message. In order to truly support the professional growth and development of teachers, evaluation systems must include elements that result in the kinds of inquiry experiences described by participants in this study. The PDP process engaged teachers as active, self-directed learners. It set the expectations for and, at the same time, placed trust in several critical assumptions. The first assumption was that, as professionals, teachers desire to learn and grow and genuinely want to improve their effectiveness. The second assumption was rooted in the belief that given the opportunity to reflect, focus, and plan, coupled with the supportive resources necessary for appropriate active response, teachers could devise effective instructional solutions. The final assumption was that as introspective, reflective practitioners, teachers can and do construct new meanings and understanding about learning that result in instructional improvements. The PDP process that was created on the basis of these assumptions occurred in a manner consistent with the concepts underlying more collegial approaches to supervision. It respectfully enabled teachers to function as masters of their own professional destinies and allowed administrators to adopt roles as supportive facilitators and collaborative evaluators. What principal wouldn't find these more desirable roles than that of traditional evaluation observer?

In daily practice, effective teachers make countless spontaneous decisions based on both theoretic knowledge and their instantaneous assessments of incoming information and evolving conditions. When doing so, they apply their technical skills in combination with intuitively devised strategies. It is this individualistic and creative aspect of the practice that is often referred to as the "art" of teaching. The use of PDPs or similar approaches to professional inquiry can give principals a way to acknowledge, discuss, critique, and support the development of that art.

Implications for Evaluation and Supervision

If the current educational discourse could be divided into two hemispheres, one would contain the beliefs that individuals extract transferable knowledge from their environments and experiences, that learning is primarily the result of such external influences, and that both knowledge and learning are discrete and measurable. The related terms and concepts that might reside here would include scientific method, quantitative research, generalizable results, outcomes-based curriculum, behavioral goals, objective measures, content-based instruction, accountability systems, and observation based teacher evaluation.

In the other hemisphere, one might expect to find terms and concepts like naturalistic studies, multiple and hermeneutic meanings, qualitative research, learners constructing knowledge, a process-based emphasis for instruction and assessment, and collaborative teacher evaluations based on reflections. The general beliefs supporting this second hemisphere of thought would be that individuals learn through their interactions with environments, that knowledge is constructed rather than acquired, that learning and growth are transformative in nature, and that they are fundamentally intrinsic processes which are not always possible to measure accurately. Although both perspectives on growth, learning, and ways of knowing are valid and valuable, practices representing the transformative tradition have too often been omitted from typical professional growth and development initiatives.

Traditional approaches to supervision, evaluation, and the promotion of teachers' professional development have spawned from the conception of knowledge as a reproducible commodity that is measurable and objective, and which can be possessed and transmitted from teacher to student or supervisor to teacher

(Jackson, 1986, p. 117). Using observational checklists and behavioral rating scales as the sole basis for the evaluation and support of teachers' performance and professional growth reduces the teaching act to a mere set of discrete skills. Such a practice devalues the judgments, ongoing assessments, instructional decisions and adaptations, and numerous other complex processes necessary for effective teaching. By attending only to the observable behaviors that represent what many practitioners regard as minimal competencies, such a practice ignores important evidence and the truths about growth and learning.

Methods of supervision and evaluation must begin to reflect a new tradition, one that supports teachers in their professional growth by embracing both the traditional and what can be described as the transformative theory of thought and practice. Accountability demands, as it should, that teachers excel in the basic skills required for adequate classroom performance. Traditional observations of their behaviors and conduct can provide useful information to this end. But if teachers are to work toward professionalism, if they are to practice in a mode which expects and nurtures continuous improvement, they must become skilled in monitoring their own effectiveness. Teachers and supervisors must do more than mimic the understanding of others. They must function as dedicated critics, become proficient in problem identification, work creatively and relentlessly to pursue solutions, and remain reflectively engaged in collaborative, ongoing self-evaluations. As education reforms provide increased emphasis on site-based management and allow more local decision making, educational leaders should aim for teacher evaluation systems and supervisory practices that reflect these transformative objectives and include the professional experiences and processes essential to growth.

Endnote

Three primary data sources were used in the study. A content analysis of the PDPs of all teachers who were eligible to participate in the alternative evaluation system was conducted to examine the actual elements included in the written plans (targeted objectives, activities, methods for evaluation, etc.). Through content analysis, initial evidence of the professional inquiry activities of teachers was identified.

An end-of-year survey was administered to the same 187 teachers whose PDPs had been used for content analysis. Survey items were designed to get information directly from the teachers about their perceptions and experiences of using the PDP. The objective portion of the survey allowed teachers to agree or disagree with descriptions of their own activities as well as those of their supervisors throughout the process. Open-ended questions at the end of the survey provided an opportunity for teachers to describe their experiences and opinions about the process more fully. These open-ended questions invited elaborations regarding examples and evidence of improved instruction and learning outcomes that teachers may have attributed to their PDP work. Teachers were also invited to describe their perceptions of their interactions with supervisors through the process and to offer suggestions for improving the alternative evaluation system.

Finally, interviews were conducted with individual teachers in order to gather descriptive details about the PDP process as the teachers perceived it. Seventeen volunteers, representing both elementary and secondary levels and various instructional areas, were interviewed in order to gather more in-depth insight about teachers' professional inquiry activities and their interactions with supervisors while working and evaluating PDPs. These teachers were selected to provide a group that mirrored and proportionately represented the demographics of the larger sample of teachers using PDPs. The interviews were conducted at the teachers' schools and were taped and later transcribed. Along with written statements included on the surveys, the interview data provided rich descriptions about the PDP process reported in the actual words of the teachers who experienced it.

References

Brindley, G. (1991). Becoming a Researcher: Teacher-Conducted Research and Professional Growth (Report No. Fl 022 039). In E.

Sadtono (Ed.). *Issues in Language Teacher Education*. Anthology Series 30. (ERIC Document Reproduction Service No. ED 370 362).

Brody, C. M. (1994). Using Co-Teaching to Promote Reflective Practice. *Journal of Staff Development*, 15(3), 32–36.

Clift, R., et al. (1989). Dogs, Ponies, and the Improvement of Teaching: English Teachers and Perceptions of the Texas Teacher Appraisal System. Paper presented at the Annual Meeting of the American Educational Research Association, San Francisco, CA. (ERIC Document Reproduction Service No. ED 312 221)

Darling-Hammond, L., & Sclan, E. (1992). Policy and Supervision. In C. D. Glickman (Ed.). *Supervision in Transition: 1992 Yearbook of the Association for Supervision and Curriculum Development* (pp. 7–26). Alexandria, VA: ASCD.

Evans, D. L. (1992). The "Instructional Leader" Must Go. (ERIC Document Reproduction Service No. ED 350 649)

Holland, P. E., Clift, R., Veal, M. L. (1992). Linking Preservice and Inservice Supervision Through Professional Inquiry. In C. D. Glickman (Ed.). *Supervision in Transition: 1992 Yearbook of the Association for Supervision and Curriculum Development* (pp. 169–181). Alexandria, VA: ASCD.

Jackson, P. W. (1986). *The Practice of Teaching*. New York: Teachers College Press.

Kemmis, S. (Ed.). (1982). *The Action Research Reader*. (Geelong, Australia: Deakin University Press).

Kemmis, S., & McTaggart, R. (Eds.). (1988).*The Action Research Planner*, 3rd ed. Geelong, Australia: Deakin University Press).

Lester, N. B., & Mayher, J. S. (1987). Critical Professional Inquiry. *English Education*, December, 198–209.

Schon, D. A. (1987). *Educating the Reflective Practitioner: Toward a New Design for Teaching and Learning in the Professions*. San Francisco: Jossey-Bass.

Simmons, J. M. (April 1985). Exploring the Relationship Between Research & Practice: The Impact of Assuming the Role of Action Researcher in One's Own Classroom. Paper presented at the Annual Meeting of the American Educational Research Association (ERIC Document Reproduction Service No. ED 266 110).

5

Linking School Reform to School Culture

Kimberly Agnew

One of the primary concerns of school administrators is the identification of school-wide programs that will result in the implementation of new structures and teaching strategies that will ultimately lead to improved student achievement. No longer can we think in isolated categories of staff development, schedules, budget, discipline plans, and parental involvement. That kind of "one-shot" approach does not address the larger context in which a school must operate to serve the needs and interests of its students, teachers, administrators, parents, and other community members. Today, as they pursue school reform through instructional programs and faculty and staff professional development, school leaders must examine and consider how all of the elements of their school interrelate to produce a positive school culture that supports members of a learning community. This view of school reform is exemplified in a case study conducted over a four-year period at an urban middle school,

Greenleaf Middle School.[1] The study examined how the interaction between a school's culture and a school reform model influenced, supported, and affected the implementation of the school reform program. I had the opportunity as researcher to serve as a participant observer at Greenleaf Middle School. Over a seven year time span, before and during the time of the study, I was a teacher, an in-house facilitator for the Consistency Management Cooperative Discipline program, which is a school reform model, and an administrator at Greenleaf. These positions allowed me to gain a rich understanding of the culture at the school and to develop a broad collection of the stories and rituals that had shaped that culture. I was also in a position to evaluate the school's repertoire of long-lived legends and more recent stories and to make informed assumptions about how they might account for the interaction between the school's culture and its school reform efforts. I was mindful, however, that in my role as a participant observer I was also a researcher. I was careful to triangulate material and recollections about the school's stories and rituals with the "harder" data collected from archival data about the school reform program and from the structured and semistructured interviews that were conducted for my study.

Greenleaf Middle School

Located on the north side of an urban city in the southwestern United States, Greenleaf Middle School was the first junior high school in the city. The Middle School Reform Movement of the late 70s and early 80s changed the school from a junior high (grades 7–9) to a middle school (grades 6–8). During its early days, the school was a vibrant learning community where high

---

[1]Greenleaf Middle School (a pseudonym) is an inner city school in a large city in the southwestern United States. The school population of over eleven hundred students is about 90% Hispanic and 10% African-American. Many of the students' families are recent immigrants, and most live in poverty. Approximately 97% of the students qualify for free and reduced lunch programs. The faculty is fairly evenly split between those with fewer than five years teaching experience and those with more than eleven years of experience.

levels of student achievement were taken for granted, and student discipline and appreciation for learning contributed to the school's success. Old school newspapers and yearbooks reflect a strong sense of school culture and pride that was supported by a community consisting of lower middle- and working-class Anglos and low-income African-American families.

During the mid-80s, the face of the community changed. Many of the neighborhood families that were economically able moved to the suburbs, and, in many cases, impoverished Hispanic families moving from Mexico replaced the once lower middle-class Anglo families. Many of the African-American families remained. This movement brought an influx of non-English-speaking family problems to the northside community, along with concomitant social ills associated with poverty: drugs, crime, and violence.

Consistency Management Cooperative Discipline Program

After years of struggling with low student achievement, negative public feedback, and poor student teacher relationships, the Greenleaf Middle School leadership team decided to pursue the Consistency Management Cooperative Discipline (CMCD) program. CMCD combines instructional effectiveness through consistency in teachers' classroom organization with student self-discipline that is developed cooperatively with teachers and fellow students in the classroom. The program's founder, H. Jerome Freiberg, and his staff of past and present teachers actively engaged Greenleaf teachers in learning experiences that were similar to the ones they would be expected to use with their students if they decided to implement CMCD. Eight years ago, 92% of the Greenleaf faculty voted to adopt the program in a secret ballot, a CMCD requirement. At that time, we as faculty had to find a way to change and make Greenleaf a more effective place for kids to learn. Mere survival had become the major issue at this school. Little did we know at the time we voted as faculty and staff to bring CMCD into our troubled school environment that hope and change were in our very near future. Nor were the faculty, staff, and administration, for that matter, very optimistic given their experience over the previous years as program after program plagued by weak staff development and implementation had resulted in little or no change for the school.

The CMCD program, on the other hand, offered a reform program that research had indicated was successful in changing teacher and student attitudes through staff development and coherent implementation in elementary, middle, and high schools in seven other states and other countries (Freiberg, Huang, & Stein, 1995; Opuni, 1996). Currently, the CMCD model is used by more than 70,000 students and teachers from inner city to rural schools (Freiberg, 1999a).

CMCD was first implemented in 1986 in five at-risk elementary schools. Student and teacher needs were addressed first within the context of the classroom and, second, within the context of the school. The program was designed to transfer research in classroom management, instructional and school effectiveness, school climate, and staff development into relevant classroom and school applications (Freiberg, Huang, & Stein, 1995). Classroom discipline and management were to be improved by giving students ownership and responsibility in the learning process.

Five themes are emphasized in the program: prevention, caring, cooperation, organization, and community. These themes, which provide a good understanding of the goals of the program, proved to be important for school reform at Greenleaf Middle School. *Prevention* includes teachers' having a vision and a plan for empowering students to become partners in the classroom and for informing students about important routines and procedures. In CMCD, 80% of classroom management is prevention. Teachers exhibit *caring* through simple tasks such as knowing students' names and unique qualities, surveying student needs, and recognizing each student's individuality. *Cooperation* occurs when students and teachers share classroom management responsibilities, when students work in cooperative groups, and when students support one another. *Organization* includes strategies that add structure to day-to-day classroom tasks and operations. *Community* allows teachers to reestablish relationships with parents, community partners, and businesses that build a sense of togetherness through school-wide campaigns and projects.

The program is built with the goal of changing school climate by building relationships between students, teachers, and the community through caring and cooperation. Teachers and students establish classroom rules and consequences at the beginning of each year by cooperatively developing classroom "constitutions" and "magna cartas." Classroom responsibilities such as taking attendance, collecting papers, distributing materials, and assisting substitute teachers are assumed by students who serve as CMCD "classroom managers." Students become managers by completing "job" applications that they submit to the teacher, who then interviews the job applicants. The classroom jobs are open to all students, and neither the students holding various jobs nor any other students are allowed to monitor or report classmates' negative behaviors. Instead, greater opportunities are provided for student self-discipline, leaving more time for teachers and students to engage in more complex instructional and learning activities. The teacher's role as "controller" is replaced by that of teacher as "facilitator." Students move from a role of being "tourists" to that of behaving as "citizens." Teachers and students also work together as a team to analyze and improve their learning environment (Freiberg, Huang, & Stein, 1995).

At the beginning of each school year, teachers socialize students toward values of cooperative learning, shared responsibility, and self-discipline. New students who enroll throughout the year are then socialized by both the students and the teachers. This process is one example of how teachers who participate in CMCD are challenged to rethink their views about learning and discipline. The CMCD program changes classrooms from teacher-centered to student-centered environments.

Unlike other discipline management programs, CMCD does not emphasize punishments; instead, it emphasizes cooperation and self-discipline (Freiberg, 1999a). Teachers are encouraged to weigh each misbehavior separately and not to designate certain fixed punishments for specific misbehaviors. Students receive different consequences depending on the circumstances of each misbehavior. CMCD combines instructional effectiveness through consistency in classroom organization by the teacher with student self-discipline, developing a cooperative environment in the classroom. The CMCD program provides a framework for teachers to improve instruction through cooperative discipline. Furthermore, the program's themes provide opportunities for schools to examine and reform their climate and culture.

School Climate

Earlier research about CMCD points to its impact on school climate. The research findings indicate that teachers and students in CMCD schools have more positive perceptions of school climate after CMCD implementation (Freiberg et al. 1989; Freiberg et al., 1990; Lorentz, 1998). Interview data collected over a two-year period of program implementation at five urban elementary schools reveal improvement in faculty morale and attitude at these schools (Freiberg et al., 1990). In one school studied by Freiberg, Huang, and Stein (1995), the findings indicate an improved learning environment, since the students perceived greater classroom order and had a clearer understanding of class rules than comparison school students. These students also exhibited a more positive perception of their learning environment than did students in 12 other non-intervention schools in the same school district. Teachers in the CMCD school appreciated the program because it offered them and their students clear indicators of success and provided them with specific strategies for emphasizing positive behavior. According to the teachers, CMCD offered an environment that they perceived as constantly encouraging (Freiberg et al., 1990).

Even more important research for Greenleaf Middle School was third-party analysis of school climate by Lorentz (1998) that spanned a four-year period at Greenleaf itself. This study was already part of the CMCD literature before my case study of the school began. Lorentz had surveyed Greenleaf teachers to determine their views about school climate in the period before and immediately after CMCD implementation. The results show a statistically significant, positive difference in teacher attitudes about school climate after implementation. The results come from a 90-item teacher survey administered during the pre-CMCD or baseline year, 1995 (n = 58), again in 1996 (n = 32) and in 1997 (n = 61), and finally post-CMCD in 1998 (n = 61). The survey measures school climate in three areas: teacher beliefs about the school, ways in which teachers spend time in class, and perceived discipline problems. Within these three areas are fifteen subscales.

Likert scale responses over the four administrations of the survey indicate positive changes in all three areas, although only nine of the fifteen subscales show statistically significant changes from the first to fourth administration of the survey, changes that may be attributed to something other than chance differences (Lorentz, 1998). The greatest positive change was in the area of perceived discipline problems ($F = 46.983, < .001$). In this area, subscale items addressing vandalism of school property, students cutting class, physical conflict among students, robbery or theft, and abuse of teachers by students show the greatest positive difference over time.

The findings about CMCD and the school climate provided important evidence, as I began to study the effects of school reform at Greenleaf Middle School, that dramatic changes had indeed taken place. I began to think that these changes went deeper, though, than the measurable aspects of school climate that Lorentz (1998) had been concerned with in his study. The consistently upward trend over time of teachers' positive opinions about Greenleaf in Lorenz's climate survey data suggested that the change had deeper roots in a less easily quantified concept, that of the school culture. I also considered whether there might be a synergistic interaction at work—that the changes in the school climate and culture were not only an outcome of the implementation of CMCD, but also of teachers' growing interest in and attention to that implementation. In other words, the positive changes subtly altered teachers' perceptions about the program and inspired them give greater attention to the implementation of CMCD.

School Culture

Before examining the interrelationship between CMCD and school culture at Greenleaf Middle School, one may find it helpful to consider how school culture is described in the research literature. In perhaps the best definition, Deal and Peterson (1998) define school culture as the "underground stream of norms, values, beliefs, traditions, and rituals that has built up over time as people work together, solve problems, and confront challenges," (p. 28). Another aspect of culture noted in the literature is its function as an integral part of school life that deeply influences the way that individuals in a school behave, think, feel, and interact with one another (Deal, 1993). School culture gives meaning to what the members of a school community say and do; how they think, feel, and act; and how they interpret daily actions (Deal, 1993; Deal & Peterson, 1999). Finally, school culture is an integral facet of school leadership (Hoy & Miskel, 1991; Stolp, 1994) and a determining factor in the outcome of school reform efforts (Stoll, 1992). In fact, the lack of supportive culture can cause reforms to fail, teacher motivation and morale to falter, and a faculty's level of commitment to decline (Deal & Peterson, 1999).

My reading about school culture resonated with my experience before, during, and after the implementation of CMCD at Greenleaf Middle School. I was led to the question that became the focus for my case study: How has the implementation of CMCD been influenced, supported, and affected by the interaction between the CMCD model and the school's culture? The importance of this question clearly extends beyond Greenleaf and the experience with CMCD at this school. It is a consideration that is important for any school reform effort, i.e., the way that the design and implementation of school reform take into account the culture of a particular school.

Case Study

A wealth of material was readily available for a case study of Greenleaf. Archival data from the school, program materials from CMCD, and climate survey and structured interview research data that were a part of the CMCD program evaluation gave a sense of the impact of CMCD on the culture at Greenleaf. Some results that warranted additional corroboration and elaboration led to open-ended interviews with four teachers who had been at Greenleaf since before CMCD began. These teachers were also selected based on their varying roles and levels of involvement in the school. One teacher had been at Greenleaf for twenty-one years, was a department chair and member of the Curriculum and Instruction Committee. Another was an eighteen-year veteran at Greenleaf who taught seventh- and eighth-grade Special Education Language Arts, was a cluster leader for Special Education, and had chaired the Climate Committee for four years. The third had taught Physical Education at Greenleaf for fifteen years and was a cluster leader. She also taught Special Education and English as Second Language. Finally, a teacher who taught only eighth grade Social Studies and had been at Greenleaf for five years was interviewed.

The data were analyzed to determine values that individual teachers held and school norms. Of interest, the evidence consistently reflects the very values that CMCD itself was designed to promote and uphold. Both the data gathered by CMCD researchers as part of the program evaluation of CMCD at Greenleaf and the interviews I conducted as part of my case study cluster quite naturally within four of the CMCD themes (prevention, cooperation, organization, and community). Although these themes were not directly articulated by the teachers, they easily describe what Greenleaf teachers perceived to be important or valuable. Furthermore, the data within each theme indicate that, for the most part, teachers shared a common understanding of these values and, therefore, of the CMCD themes. In addition, a new norm of collegiality appears with great prevalence, particularly in the interview data.

Prevention

The value indicators for the CMCD theme of prevention appear more frequently in the data than any other value indicator, and this theme is particularly evident in the comments made by teachers during interviews. Teachers who participated in the structured program evaluation interviews as well as the open-ended case study interviews spoke of boosting student esteem and morale and of improving student attitudes about school and learning as a result of CMCD. These teachers acknowledged the program's impact on their students. They indicate that the CMCD strategies of giving positive feedback to students and providing opportunities for students to feel empowered prevented discipline problems and negative feelings that students may have developed about school and learning. More than anything, the teachers referenced ways in which they used consistency management to encourage and motivate students, as well as to prevent negative behaviors. One teacher, for example, discusses methods of encouragement:

> We have a behavior manager who gives out awards for students who are doing well. . . . I have some notes that I have of my own that say that so-and-so student did well in general behavior; please give a hug.

Another teacher talks about a new emphasis on praise:

> Yes, I'm using Consistency Management. . . . I have classroom rules, rewards, and consequences, the Learner's Creed. . . . I was not rewarding students or praising them. I'm praising them more than I used to at the beginning of the school year.

Another teacher describes the spread of the prevention theme throughout the school when she says:

> We have students who excel, and we have students that you have to prod. We have students that you have to coax . . . seven or eight students in one class need encouragement, that "Come on, Jerome, you can do it" kind of thing. I see that more now than I did back then [before CMCD].

In yet another interview, a teacher recognizes that the school's prevention efforts are part of a larger project:

> I think that one of the big things is that Catamount Cash hasn't had the same force that it had during the first year. I don't know whether it is because we didn't have as nice of surprises in the raffles or never got the grasp of the raffle.

She is referring to a schoolwide incentive program for students that rewards them for appropriate behaviors such as arriving to class on time, bringing supplies to school, and participating in class. Catamount (the school's mascot) "cash" is usually issued during times when students are more likely to forget the "tools of learning." After several years of CMCD, this teacher recognizes that prevention includes encouraging positive behavior, not just eliminating negative behavior.

Additional support for the value that teachers attach to the prevention theme comes from Lorentz's survey of teacher climate at Greenleaf, which reveals that teachers' perceptions about discipline problems reflected the greatest change from 1995–1998. Lorentz reports that there was improvement in every area as determined by reductions in vandalism of school property, students cutting class, student tardiness, physical conflicts among students, robbery or theft, and physical abuse of teachers by students.

As a teacher at Greenleaf during the time CMCD was implemented, I remember that teachers were energized by the suggestions that CMCD offered for prevention. Given the chaos that existed prior to CMCD, teachers were willing to try anything that would work. It appears that the CMCD model helped teachers better enact their values. CMCD provided teachers with strategies that reflected the importance they attach to empowering, encouraging, and rewarding their students, values that had been lost in an atmosphere of disruption and mistrust. These values were recalled by CMCD strategies, and they interacted with the school's culture in such a way that teachers readily implemented innovations that reflect what they truly believe. CMCD brings teachers' values and beliefs closer to the school's norms of behavior and rituals by introducing new innovations that become a part of what is routinely accepted and practiced by Greenleaf teachers.

The prevention theme also permeates the other CMCD themes, supporting them and encouraging their growth and development. Prevention strategies not only solve problems, but also block obstacles before they infiltrate the relationships and supportive structures created through the other themes. At

Greenleaf, the CMCD prevention strategies were readily accepted because they were consistent with values about empowering and rewarding students that were historically held at Greenleaf. One example of how prevention reflects Greenleaf values is that students now receive "good citizenship" awards for reporting conflicts (such as gang conflicts) that students may be having or that seem likely to erupt. In the past such conflicts had caused severe discipline problems and disorder, with students and faculty alike feeling powerless to intervene. Conflicts are now likely to be reported and stopped before they even get started. Prevention as a strategy for reporting actual or potential conflicts is linked to the Greenleaf values of empowerment and reward. Thus, prevention and the values associated with it serve as a kind of shield for the other themes and values.

Cooperation

When CMCD was introduced at Greenleaf, the school was plagued by student fights that stemmed from gang rivalries and other in-school conflicts. Many teachers had borne the brunt of these conflicts by being hurt physically while trying to protect the safety of other students or themselves. Students did not seem to care about the welfare of their classmates, nor did they see themselves as members of a support system for one another. Yet, when I went to the school as a teacher two years before the CMCD reform effort began and the school was in the midst of this turmoil, teachers would openly discuss their desire for students to get along better. These discussions, which often could be heard at the lunch table and in the teachers' lounge, attested not only to the teachers' faith that students were capable of getting along, but also to the value that these Greenleaf teachers placed on the teamwork and the unity they envisioned for their students. CMCD brought these values together under the theme of cooperation and provided strategies for students and teachers to work in teams.

Comments made by teachers during interviews attest to the benefit they see in these CMCD strategies. One teacher, for instance, explains that the "students work in teams because we want them to be productive citizens; therefore, they need to learn how to work consistently as a team." The comments of a novice teacher also underscore the benefits of teamwork for students:

> I think that students working in teams with each other has been a wonderful idea, and it is a support system for each student. . . . Students are expected to be courteous to each other.

The value of teamwork also applies to teachers working together cooperatively. One veteran teacher talks about the team of five teachers that she works with to instruct and discipline the same 150 students (her "cluster"). She believes that her cluster's ability to exemplify strong teamwork values is reflected in their students:

> But my cluster is beautiful. . . . I think for the most part, they [students] see adults who are kind to one another, and they see adults who work well together for the most part. Perhaps the students see some of that model, and some teachers do take the time to reinforce that kind of behavior . . . so maybe that has helped the students. . . . Whatever we seem to do, some of them take it and say, "Well, this is important, so I'm gonna do this."

Teachers at Greenleaf implemented active cooperative groups for two reasons. CMCD staff development facilitators informed them of the positive academic benefits that cooperative learning could have for students. In addition, teachers cared about students and wanted them to experience more positive social relationships.

Cooperative learning is also a strategy valued by Greenleaf administrators. It was so important to the principal at Greenleaf that during the first year of CMCD, he removed all single desks from the classrooms and replaced them with either tables or connecting desks that could be used for cooperative learning. Teachers were warned that if they chose not to include cooperative learning in their instruction, it would be reflected in their state evaluations. The interview data from teachers indicate that they too appreciate and value the concept of having students practice cooperation.

Another way in which CMCD supports the value that Greenleaf teachers place on teamwork is through the Consistency Management discipline program that all of the teachers are expected to use as a part of CMCD. It can be argued that the teachers readily accepted this program because it was consistent with the teamwork they valued but had found difficult to implement. One teacher, for example, when asked to name elements of CMCD that are helpful, mentioned "working as a team." The term *team* occurred four times in her interview. In addition, she spoke of a "wholeness" or "joined togetherness" that now existed on the Greenleaf staff. She specifically described the value of teamwork in Consistency Management:

> With Consistency Management you have a faculty and staff as a whole ... it is an altogether jointed program. You are working as a team with Consistency Management, and with other programs you might only have certain areas of the building working on inservice, and it is not a team effort.

Lorenz's (1998) survey of the changes in school climate at Greenleaf before and after CMCD corroborates the teachers' interview comments about greater cooperation among students and teachers as a result of CMCD strategies. Prior to CMCD, Greenleaf had a reputation as a school that had very negative relations between students and teachers. After CMCD, Lorentz found statistically significant positive changes in teachers' opinions about teacher and student relations. In particular, more teachers felt that students get along well with teachers, and that teachers make students feel important. Conversely, fewer teachers felt that Greenleaf teachers had a negative attitude about students. Lorenz attributes changes in these areas to the CMCD theme of cooperation and to the strategies used to realize that theme.

Although it appears that all along teachers at Greenleaf had valued or wanted students to have positive relationships, they may not have known how to make them a reality. CMCD developed this value by providing strategies that teachers could use to teach students to work cooperatively. Again, the CMCD model reinforced beliefs and values that previously existed at

Greenleaf and provided opportunities for teachers to reflect these values through their practices. Students at Greenleaf are currently accustomed to working together in groups, and when new students enroll and do not know cooperative grouping "rules," they are frowned upon by their peers.

Organization

According to the literature on school culture, a school's values can be determined by its norms, by what seem to be acceptable modes of behaving and operating. Years before CMCD, the teachers at Greenleaf had developed clear norms and expectations about the level of efficiency or accuracy with which routine tasks such as making grade reports, checking materials in or out at the beginning and end of school, and finalizing class rosters should be completed. When I began teaching at Greenleaf, I noticed that for teachers who had been at the school for fifteen or more years these norms or expectations were noticeably different from those of the administration. The veteran teachers told tales of how the school was once highly organized and how this organization had enhanced student achievement. In fact, many of the "old timers" loved to sit at the lunch table and give personal accounts of days of yore when things at Greenleaf were structured and organized. School year openings and closings were smooth, and teachers and students benefited from working and learning in an organized, structured environment where they knew what to expect.

For the most part, the other novice teachers and I were like our veteran peers at Greenleaf in that we did not like surprises when it came to school operations and did not appreciate the Greenleaf administration's lack of organization prior to CMCD. We knew that the teachers had, in better times, been accustomed to receiving information and materials in an organized fashion, to having paperwork processed efficiently, and to having accurate student records (especially for special needs students). This was "the way that things had been done" at Greenleaf, and it persisted as an expectation. It was an expectation that arose from the value that teachers placed on consistency in the organization and management of the school and of their own classrooms.

However, at some point point in time, the administrators in the school (all of whom had been at the school for less than five years) had not fulfilled the faculty's expectations.

When CMCD was adopted in 1995, Greenleaf teachers, old and new, embraced the organization theme and quickly connected its emphasis on consistency with their own value of that quality. In interview comments teachers place an emphasis on consistency because it makes for more organization. Some teachers, for instance, talk about the benefits of consistency and organization for students:

> Anything you can do to set standards or have a schedule really helps students of this age . . . The big thing is that you have to be consistent and you need to be consistent across the board.

Another teacher also emphasizes the benefits for children:

> And so that is one thing I think has really helped over the whole school, consistency. They need, these kids especially, need structure because they have none. I mean, nobody tells them when to eat; they eat chips for dinner; their parents aren't home; they stay up all night.

Other teachers recognize that consistency in their own behavior received more attention as a result of CMCD. One teacher is particularly appreciative of the renewed emphasis on consistency at the end of the school year thanks to the CMCD theme of organization. His remarks also note that the decline in consistency and organization at Greenleaf prior to CMCD had spread from administration to the teachers themselves:

> By this time of the year, before we had CMCD there wasn't a place where you could write anything else in the bathrooms. . . . [Before] you would see more students out in the hall than you would see inside the classroom, because everybody was just tired and nobody wanted to deal with the kids. . . . And now we're looking forward to the end of school along with the kids. But, you know, we're looking forward to it because of the celebrations, because of the things coming up . . . Now [at the end of the year] I tell the kids how important it is that they continue to bring their "tools for learning" because we are still

working, grades are still counting. Where before I would allow the kids to get by—if they didn't want to keep writing with pen, they didn't have to . . . You know, we pretty much let it go. . . . The end of this school year [with CMCD] has been very smooth.

The value of consistency that was already in place at Greenleaf made CMCD a good fit with the culture of the school. Granted, at the time CMCD started at the school, faculty and administration were willing to try just about anything to address the conflict and chaos on the campus. It is important to remember, however, that CMCD was not the first attempt to improve the situation at Greenleaf. CMCD succeeded where other programs had failed. One plausible explanation is that the CMCD themes reflect the values at Greenleaf. With its theme of organization, the CMCD program reflects in its very name the value of consistency at Greenleaf.

Community

The fourth of the CMCD themes that shows itself as part of the culture at Greenleaf is that of community. Again, this theme was a value that had been honored in Greenleaf's better days but had gotten lost as the school fell into disorder. I remember veteran teachers at the school reminiscing about a time when parents were involved at Greenleaf, probably ten or fifteen years earlier. Parents had even cosponsored student groups such as the cheerleaders and choir. Such parental involvement was perhaps most notable in its effect on discipline in the school. One teacher, describing how she dealt with discipline problems in the past, appreciated parental involvement:

> There were kids that were disrespectful and stuff, but basically, you know, you dealt with their parents, and you sent them [the children] to the office. . . . I don't think it was real bad back then.

Such reliance on parents' support (and administrators' support, for that matter) had all but disappeared by the time I arrived at the school. The veteran teachers attributed the loss to a decline both in student achievement and in the level of trust between parents and other community members and the school's faculty and administration. The assumption was that parents felt that the drop in achievement meant teachers no longer respected or cared about their children. The shattered relationship did not, however, keep teachers from believing that a positive relationship with parents was important. Teachers continued to believe that parental involvement would help to solve the discipline and achievement problems of students. There were frequent discussions of what teachers could possibly do to bring parents back into Greenleaf, and teachers often attributed the lack of parental involvement to parents' thinking that middle school children did not need as much attention from their parents as elementary-school students did.

Data from Greenleaf indicate that teachers perceived that relations with parents and the community had improved after CMCD implementation. Before the school's decline, it had been a norm for teachers to participate in activities such as the PTO or open house; these activities helped them to have positive relations with parents. CMCD helped to revive such activities and created new ones such as positive notes sent home to parents, parent education nights, and CMCD workshops for parents taught by school-based faculty. Teachers quickly implemented these components, possibly because they supported their own values, and also because they believed these activities could restore the previous culture that had thrived on positive relationships between parents and the school. Their efforts were rewarded. One teacher said of the change in communication with parents after CMCD, "There is the discipline, cooperation and organization within the community. It is much better having the parents coming into the school to work with us."

Lorentz's (1998) survey data also attest to improved relations with parents and the community after CMCD. Teachers indicate in their survey responses that parent-teacher relations improved with the implementation of CMCD. Teachers more frequently notified parents about students' problems and needs, and they felt supported by parents and considered them as partners in educating their children. Furthermore, teachers believed that they were doing a better job of keeping parents informed and that the parents felt more comfortable coming to meet with them than they had before CMCD. The evidence suggests that the theme of community was easily understood and readily accepted at Greenleaf because it supported the kinds of relationships with parents and the community that were important in the history and culture of the school.

Norms of Collegiality

Thus far in the discussion of the connections between the CMCD themes and the culture of Greenleaf Middle School there has been no mention of the CMCD theme of care. Of interest, it is not a theme that was much talked about by the teachers at the school, although there is evidence of teachers' concern about their students throughout the data. Those data, however, more directly relate to other CMCD themes. I also know from my years at Greenleaf that the majority of the teachers there, past and present, truly care about the students. In support of that judgment, I offer the following information. Greenleaf teachers who did not appear to consider the disadvantaged backgrounds of their students were frowned upon by other teachers. Greenleaf teachers were always happy to see something good and positive happen for their students, perhaps because of the benefits that it would have on the students' character and self-concept and because students would be inspired to behave better and appreciate school. Greenleaf teachers often went out of their way to buy rewards and prizes for students and to sponsor extracurricular activities that met students' interests and needs. Teachers came early or stay late at school to provide tutorials and held weekend tutorial "sleepovers." Teachers and administrators sacrificed holiday and weekend time to take small groups of students fishing or camping. In addition, although I do not remember its happening before CMCD, teachers gave reward parties for students. In general, when teachers were inconvenienced for the good of their students, they did not complain the way they did when inconvenienced for some other purpose.

Perhaps one reason that care about students was not strongly articulated in the school was that there was so little care shown among the faculty for each other. In fact, when I arrived at

Greenleaf as a new teacher, the school was a hostile place for faculty. When I began teaching at Greenleaf, the Dean of Instruction advised me that teachers could be some of the most "vindictive and selfish" people I would ever encounter. This warning was quickly realized when, as a new reading teacher, I sought help from veteran teachers in the Language Arts Department. These teachers were not willing to share ideas, materials, or information about routine school operations. I was left on my own as a new, struggling teacher to figure things out. Not only did teachers not share instructional ideas; they did not agree to be consistent in the areas of discipline and classroom management. In 1994, the school had adopted block scheduling that allowed cluster teachers to be off during the same period daily. I remember hearing stories about how cluster members were not always in accord and of cluster meetings sometimes ending in heated, emotional, and unresolved arguments. In addition, faculty meetings at the time were often divided along racial lines that caused dissension among the entire faculty.

It became a norm at Greenleaf for teachers to feel alone and isolated from the rest of the faculty. Teachers took care only of their own classrooms. This "hands off" policy indicated a lack of concern about what happened in other classrooms, yet at the same time, teachers often discussed and gossiped about other teachers whom they considered to be poor instructors or disciplinarians. Teachers in the same departments never collaborated about instructional plans or methods. Students picked up on this culture of divisiveness and often "played" teachers against one another. This student strategy was possible because discipline management varied so much from one room to another and because teachers themselves were known to bad mouth their colleagues to the students.

Before CMCD the culture of Greenleaf was characterized by strong norms of individualism and personal survival, norms that are in sharp contrast to the CMCD theme of care. Probably the greatest accomplishment at Greenleaf since the implementation of CMCD is the development of a new cultural norm of collegiality among the faculty and administration that is arguably the strongest expression of care in a school culture.

Linking School Reform to School Culture

The question one asks is "How was collegiality able to so readily take root in the school culture at Greenleaf?" One possible explanation lies in the already described discussion of the CMCD theme of cooperation: the teachers' strong desire, even before CMCD, for students to get along and work well together. As teachers saw CMCD's positive effects on students who now were working in cooperative learning teams within the classroom and were scheduled within a cluster of students taught and disciplined by the same five teachers, the teachers themselves began to work more cooperatively with their colleagues, particularly those within their own cluster. The cluster structure arrangement both supports the value of teamwork, which Greenleaf teachers had come to value for students in their classrooms, and encourages the development of that same value of teamwork among the faculty as they work to plan instruction and manage the students within their clusters.

Further support for the developing norm of collegiality at Greenleaf comes from the theme of organization and the value that teachers place on consistency, which is a big part of that theme. As teachers begin to realize the benefits of consistency and agreed-upon structures, policies, and procedures within the school, they also come to accept the responsibility of working together to develop and oversee these elements of organization within their clusters and across the school as a whole. There is a synergy to the way implementation of CMCD strategies supported values of teamwork within the classroom and consistency within the clusters and across the school, and the way these values carried over to bolster teachers working relationships with each other.

I witnessed this change of norms at Greenleaf. Block scheduling allowed ample time for clusters and departments to meet for collaboration and the sharing of ideas. At the current time, it is frowned upon for teachers not to participate in these meetings and not to collaborate with colleagues. The norm is now so strong that teachers are reprimanded for not being cooperative members of the faculty, just as students are given consequences for not being good citizens. Lounge and lunchtime conversation has changed from "let's name all the negative things about

Greenleaf" to "let's discuss how we can work together to improve Greenleaf."

The comments from the teachers during their interviews corroborate my own remembrances and observations. One teacher, for instance, speaks of how her cluster had "really gotten this (cluster expectation) down to a science." She describes how the cluster had a basic set of rules agreed upon by the faculty that allowed parents to know what was expected of their children from one teacher to another. Another teacher, who was in her first year of teaching, describes the personal benefits of the emerging norm of collegiality at Greenleaf:

> I get to see what other teachers are doing and how they feel about the program. It also gives me an opportunity to see if I can improve something and get an idea if something is not working for me, how I can improve it.

This benefit of collegiality for new teachers at the school is recognized as well by veteran teachers, one of whom describes a situation that was a far cry from my early days at Greenleaf: "New teachers that came in felt comfortable because other teachers were there to support them."

Yet another experienced teacher explains that the benefits of improved collegiality also included working relations with administrators at Greenleaf. These interactions are now a meaningful part of the organizational structure of the school:

> Mostly I sit in meetings during the eighth grade floor meetings with our assistant principal. We've looked at the different behaviors and a lot of people were saying it wasn't consistent at times, and we got it straight. The majority of the people agreed on a set way to discipline kids, because some were being disciplined in a certain way and others were not. But we have come to a consistent way to discipline students.

It is important to note that the interview data do not contain evidence of a norm of collegiality at Greenleaf prior to the adoption of CMCD. It appears that a new norm of collegiality emerged as the CMCD model interacted with the Greenleaf school culture in such a way that teachers began to practice and value a norm of collegiality. The interaction consisted mainly of teachers extending the practice of teamwork beyond their classrooms and working to achieve and maintain consistency throughout the school. Communication and collaboration have become new values that are part of a new norm of collegiality for Greenleaf teachers. One can infer that teachers developed these values through their experience with the CMCD model.

One way that CMCD supports the development of collegiality is by providing fall workshops that encourage teachers to share implementation failures and successes with one another. Teachers are given the opportunity to help each other become higher implementers of CMCD strategies by discussing what worked and did not work, and by giving one another constructive feedback. A norm of continuous improvement developed out of these fall workshops that gave teachers the stamina to continue implementation even when the program's novelty had worn off or when problems were encountered.

There is, however, a caution contained in the data about the development of a new norm of collegiality at Greenleaf. That caution is found in Lorenz's (1998) findings about school climate at Greenleaf. Although the data indicate positive changes in teachers' perceptions about teacher-colleague relations over the four years of the survey, those changes are not statistically significant. Despite the comments of teachers in their interviews and contrary to my own experience at Greenleaf, teachers' survey responses indicate only limited improvement in their feelings of support, encouragement, and acceptance from their colleagues over the time that CMCD was implemented at Greenleaf Middle School.

It is difficult to explain this discrepancy in the data. Perhaps it is because the survey items have not captured the emerging norm of collegiality because the items do not inquire about such things as the level of communication and collaboration, the amount of time teachers spend sharing ideas, or the amount of time that teachers spend planning together as clusters and teams. Or, perhaps, the discrepancy may be attributed to a tendency in qualitative research to capture the interior mental perceptions of participants even before these perceptions have solidified as explicit norms or action. Whatever the reason for the discrepancy, it is necessary to recognize that the new value given to the norm of collegiality at Greenleaf Middle School lacks the strength and robustness of those values that are more deeply and historically entrenched in the school's culture. What this situation suggests is that, while new values and norms can develop as a result of a school's reform efforts, such values are fragile and require continuous attention and nourishment if they are to persist and become rooted in conscious perception of the school's culture.

Implications for School Reform Programs

Data from the case study of Greenleaf Middle School suggest that the CMCD model interacted with the school's culture in such a way that values and beliefs that existed at the school before its breakdown were revived or renewed by CMCD themes. By reflecting values and norms that were already part of the school's culture, these themes revived those values that had been lost sight of during the period when the student population at Greenleaf Middle School changed. The CMCD model for school reform also offered strategies that supported each of the themes, and these strategies helped teachers to reconnect with lost values and school norms. As a result, the school culture at Greenleaf is now stronger because its norms more closely reflect its long-held values, which also are enhanced by the emergence of a new norm of collegiality.

An obvious implication of Greenleaf Middle School's successful experience with the CMCD model of school reform is that whatever school reform effort a school may undertake, it should be consistent with existing and historical values of a school. In the case of Greenleaf, the CMCD model's synergistic interaction with the school's culture resulted in changes that were deeper than surface-level behaviors and reactions. Although such changes are more difficult to measure, they are more likely to be maintained and continually improved.

A perhaps less obvious implication of Greenleaf's experience is that the CMCD model is flexible enough not only to encourage teachers to make connections between the themes and strategies of CMCD and the school's cultural values, but also to allow teachers to contextualize those themes and strategies in ways that they themselves thought would improve or revive school culture. In a school where the values and beliefs may be different from those of the Greenleaf teachers, the CMCD themes would be implemented and emphasized differently. So, in a school using another model of school reform, that model should be flexible enough to be tailored to the culture of the school.

Another implication to be drawn from Greenleaf's school reform experience is that it is wise to examine a school's culture before introducing new programs or innovations. Although an awareness of the fit between the themes of CMCD and values that were already part of the culture of Greenleaf Middle School emerged in the course of this case study, prior to the introduction of the model and strategies to Greenleaf's teachers, a school climate survey had been conducted, and the staff was surveyed during one of the first workshops about what was important to them as teachers at the school. Thus, although the concept of relating school reform to school culture was not yet conscious and explicit, it was tacitly recognized. How much more effective might school reform efforts be if the fit and interaction between a reform program and a school's culture are from the very beginning matters of careful study in the program's planning and implementation?

Yet another implication of the experience of school reform at Greenleaf is that such reform takes time, both to implement in the first place and then to sustain. Although the values of the school's culture are much more evident at Greenleaf today and are more consistent with norms of behavior than they were when I arrived as a teacher a decade ago, continuous attention must be paid to whether those values and norms are ones that best serve the learning needs of students, and to the ways in which the CMCD model can support the continuance and expansion of the values and norms of the school's culture. By the time the open-ended interviews were conducted for this case study five years after CMCD was introduced at Greenleaf, teachers did not seem to remember the meaningful connection that had been made during the initial implementation of CMCD between the CMCD themes and values that already existed at Greenleaf, nor did they recognize how those themes and values continue to influence their practice and the culture at Greenleaf. Time spent to deepen in teachers' and administrators' conscious memory the connections between reform efforts and the school's culture empowers educators to bring forth innovations that continue to enrich the reform effort and to shape and reflect the culture of the school.

The final implication to be drawn from this case study of the interaction between the school culture at Greenleaf Middle School and the implementation of the CMCD school reform model is that a narrow focus on student achievement test scores as the only important measure of school reform would have missed an important outcome of school reform. The bottom line of any reform effort is its benefits to students, and those benefits include the opportunity to learn in a school whose culture reflects values such as those embodied in the CMCD themes of prevention, care, cooperation, organization and community—values that are beyond measure, but are immeasurably important.

References

Deal, T. E. (1993). The Culture of Schools. In M. Sashkin & H. Walberg (Eds.). *Educational Leadership and School Culture* (pp. 3–18). Berkeley, CA: McCutchan Publishing.

Deal, T. E., & Peterson, K. D. (1998). How Leaders Influence the Culture of Schools. Educational Leadership, 56, 28–30.

Deal, T. E., & Peterson, K. D. (1999). *Shaping School Culture: The Heart of Leadership*. San Francisco: Jossey-Bass.

Freiberg, H. J. (1999). Consistency Management and Cooperative Discipline: From Tourist to Citizens in the Classrooms. In H. J. Freiberg (Ed.). *Beyond Behaviorism* (pp. 75–96). Boston: Allyn and Bacon.

Freiberg, H. J. (1999a). Introduction in H. J. Freiberg (Ed.). *School Climate: Measuring, Improving, and Sustaining Healthy Learning Environments* (pp. 1–10). Philadelphia: Falmer Press.

Freiberg, H. J., Huang, S., & Stein, T. A. (1995). Effects of a Classroom Management Intervention on Student Achievement in Inner-City Elementary Schools. *Educational Research and Evaluation*, 1, 36–66.

Freiberg, H. J., Opuni, K. A., Prokosch, N., Stein, T., & Treister, E. (1989). Turning Around At-Risk Schools Through Consistency Management. *Journal of Negro Education*, 58, 372–382.

Freiberg, H. J., Prokosch, N., Stein, T. A., & Treister, E. S. (1990). Turning Around Five At-Risk Elementary Schools. *School Effectiveness and School Improvement*, 1, 5–25.

Hoy, W. K., & Miskel, C. G., (1991). *Educational Administration*. New York: McGraw-Hill.

Lorentz, J. (1998). Project Evaluation: Teacher Climate Survey. Houston, TX: CMCD, University of Houston, Unpublished manuscript.

Opuni, K. A. (1996). Project GRAD Evaluation. Houston, TX: Unpublished manuscript.

Stoll, L. (1992). Teacher Growth in the Effective School. In M. Fullan & A. Hargreaves (Eds.). *Teacher Development and Educational Change* (pp. 104-120). Philadelphia: Falmer Press.

Stolp, S. (1994). *Leadership for School Culture*. Eugene, OR: ERIC Clearinghouse of Educational Management. (ERIC Document Reproduction Service No. ED 370 198.)

6

Eliminating the "Christmas Tree School" Effect

Deborah Masterson

The biggest problem facing schools is fragmentation and overload. . . . Schools are suffering the . . . burden of having a torrent of unwanted, uncoordinated policies and innovations raining down on them from external hierarchical bureaucracies. . . . Collaborative schools are in a better position to work on connectedness under these conditions.
(FULLAN, *1999, p. 39*)

Angel Creek Elementary School (ACES),[1] was experiencing what Bryk and his colleagues labeled the "Christmas tree schools effect" (Bryk, Sebring, Kerbow, Rollow, & Easton, 1998, p. 123); i.e., it was offering a proliferation of special programs with scant attention to program coordination. The poor coordination created

---

[1]Angel Creek Elementary School (a pseudonym) is situated in a middle- to upper-middle-class suburban neighborhood that is on the outskirts of a large city located in a southwestern state. The student enrollment hovers around one-thousand students. Eighty-five percent of the students are white. Approximately ten percent of the students qualify for free and reduced lunch programs.

chaotic scheduling conditions for ACES faculty and students, and teachers complained that the scheduling problems were negatively affecting instruction. They explained that instruction was constantly interrupted in both the regular education classrooms and the special programs. Students were coming and going from classrooms every few minutes to attend an array of special programs. One teacher described the chaotic conditions this way:

> I had children pulled out of my classroom continuously in the morning, because I had ESL students. I had a special ed student. I had students going to speech. I had students going to PRIDE.... I did not have my ... homeroom ... more than about thirty minutes in the morning.

When students were pulled from regular education classrooms to attend special programs, they missed chunks of the curriculum, and there was no time to catch them up. Another teacher believed the problem was exacerbating scheduling problems: "If they were going to math, it wasn't necessarily at their math time."

Teachers questioned the need for so many special programs and felt that offering such an extensive list had become counterproductive. One teacher used the following analogy to explain her point of view:

> I think you can get too many ... It's kind of like when an old person goes to the doctor and is getting medicine from this doctor and this doctor and this doctor, and they end up very ill, because they've been over medicated.

Despite the number of conflicts related to program coordination and scheduling, no effort had been made to correct the problem. The depth of the problem did not appear to be general knowledge. The faculty and the administrators just accepted the conditions as inevitable and never discussed as a group how the conditions might be affecting instruction. Perhaps one reason for this laissez-faire attitude was the approach that had been taken to evaluate instructional needs.

Instructional needs had been evaluated based on an analysis of the scores from the state-mandated annual assessment of academic achievement. Because the overall scores remained high, the quantitative data gathered via these assessments did not reveal the growing level of programming chaos. Nevertheless, the chaos worsened each year as new programs were added and governmental mandates were changed. Eventually, the problems became so severe that two of the special reading programs had not yet started even though it was two months into the first semester. The teacher, who taught both programs, had not been able to find a conflict-free time for her students. This incident finally produced the impetus for change. It was in essence the straw that broke the camel's back. At this point, the principal gave me permission to establish a scheduling committee to redesign the master schedule of the school and to conduct a research project to study the change process that was about to take place.

Although it is safe to assume that the growing level of chaos would have affected the quantitative scores eventually, the reasons for that chaos could not have been revealed by applying only a quantitative approach. Furthermore, it would not have been possible to elucidate the factors that supported or impeded the restructuring project, and these are the factors that should be of greatest importance to administrators because they have a universal application regardless of the instructional problems to be solved. For these reasons, I chose to use a qualitative approach to study the process of change involved in redesigning a school's master schedule.

This project presented me with a unique opportunity to conduct a qualitative study of the change process as it occurred over a two-year period at one public elementary school. The project was divided into two phases: the development phase (year one) and the implementation phase (year two). During that time I collected data via observations and interviews. Data were also available from a qualitative survey instrument that I had administered the year prior to the actual study in order to identify the advantages and disadvantages of special programs.

Important Issues for Educational Leaders

From the data collected, I came to recognize and understand that three issues were at play that are important to educational leaders. One issue was the contrast between the intent of the special program laws and the practice of these laws at ACES. In other words, I wondered whether, with the number of programming conflicts that existed, this school could really be in compliance with the requirements of all of the legal mandates.

A second issue emerged about the relationship between leadership behaviors and the outcomes of this project. The data reveals that two distinct types of leadership existed: traditional-authoritarian and collaborative. As I explain in detail later in the chapter, the traditional-authoritarian style produced almost exclusively negative effects. Conversely, collaborative leadership produced positive effects.

Finally, I recognized a third issue concerning the impact that organizational structures have on the change process. The primary structures included the traditional bureaucratic structure of the educational system and the collaborative structure of the scheduling committee itself. The data clarified three distinct layers or levels within the educational system. These included the legislative level, the district level, and the campus level. As I describe later in the chapter, traditional structures were predominant at all three levels.

The framework for my explanation of the findings from this study was provided by a comparison of the underlying concepts from the traditional management theories (Fayol, 1949; Taylor, 1911; Weber, 1947) with underlying concepts from the complexity theory of organization model (Fullan, 1999; Stanford, 1998; Wheatley, 1999). The latter model explains why it has become necessary for complex organizations (systems) to develop adaptive process skills in order to continue to thrive in our rapidly changing world. As complexity theorists suggest, failure to learn how to adapt to the rate of change can lead to the decline or even the demise of an organization (Wheatley, 1999). Public school systems are one example of the kinds of complex organizations subject to this theory.

Legal Mandates: Intent vs. Practice

The first important issue for administrators is the question of whether or not the instructional practices at ACES were in compliance with the expectations set forth by the legal mandates. The answer to the question lies in the clarification of the specific intent of each of the special program laws. A closer analysis of these laws reveals that there is one overarching intent for all programs, including regular education programs, and that is the provision of a quality education for all students. Special program laws augment this intent by requiring additional instruction and/or services that ensure equal educational opportunities for students with special needs. Each of the special program laws is tailored to meet the specific needs of a certain category of students. In all, counting regular education, there were six different categories put into practice at ACES. Categorical programs included regular education, special education, English as a second language (ESL), dyslexia, compensatory education, and gifted and talented (GT). Under most of these categories various programs were offered. The following chart (Table 1) outlines the categorical programs that were offered at ACES in the 1999–2000 school year. The array of programs at ACES is similar to that offered in most large elementary schools across the country.

Table 1. Categorical Programs Offered at Angel Creek Elementary School, 1999–2000

Categories/Programs	Program Description and Students Served
Compensatory Education Programs	
PRIDE	Reading intervention for first and second graders
Learning Lab	Lab for assisting at-risk students in completing assignments and taking tests
PRIME	Math intervention program for at-risk third graders
KEYS	Mentor program for at-risk students
TRACK	Reading intervention for second to fifth grade students.
Special Education Programs	
Resource Language Arts	Intervention services and instruction for students who have been identified as having learning disabilities
Resource Mathematics	

(cont'd.)

Table 1. Categorical Programs Offered at Angel Creek Elementary School, 1999–2000 *(Continued)*

Categories/Programs	Program Description and Students Served
Special Education Programs *(cont'd.)*	
Life Skills	Primarily delivered in a pull-out setting
Adaptive Behavior	Intervention delivered in a pull-out setting
Speech and Language	Generally pull-out instruction
Helping Teacher	Support delivered within regular classroom
Other Services	Other services include but are not limited to occupational therapy, physical therapy, mobility training, adapted physical education, and vision or hearing impaired services.
Gifted and Talented	
Challenge	Pull-out instruction for identified students in grades K–5
English as a Second Language	
English as a Second Language	Intervention for students with limited English proficiency, less proficient students serviced in pull-out setting
Dyslexia	
Dyslexia Intervention Program	Dyslexia intervention delivered in a pull-out setting to identified students in grades K-12
Regular Education	
Core Subjects— English Mathematics Science Social Studies	Instruction provided daily to all students unless exempted by ARD decision
Health Drug Awareness Library Science Technology	Weekly instruction for drug awareness, library science, and technology
Physical Education (PE) Fine Arts (Art & Music)	Fine arts and PE offered on a rotating basis
Enrichment Math	Enrichment math for fifth graders was offered daily to students who qualified based on their math achievement in fourth grade.

Eliminating the "Christmas Tree School" Effect

When I compared the intent of these categorical mandates with the practice at ACES, it became obvious that a significant discrepancy existed. For example, an ESL specialist was discouraged with her students' progress. As she explained, she had to decide between teaching the content that they were missing when she pulled them from regular education classrooms or teaching her ESL curriculum. There simply was not enough time to do both. She generally chose to cover the content that was being missed, but this choice left her feeling that she was not able to "focus on ESL strategies, language, and the things that they are lacking." However, as the following excerpt shows, the intent of the ESL mandate is to develop the English language skills of students with limited English proficiency:

> English as a second language programs shall be intensive programs of instruction designed to develop proficiency in the comprehension, speaking, reading, and composition in the English language. (Texas Education Agency, 1996, p. 2)

A discrepancy also existed between the practice and the intent of compensatory education programs. As is evident in the following excerpt, the intent is that these programs should supplement and support the regular education program:

- use instructional strategies that
  - give primary consideration to providing extended learning time such as an extended school year, before- and after-school, and summer programs and opportunities . . .
  - minimize removing children from the regular classroom during regular school hours for instruction
- coordinate with and support the regular education program
  (Texas Education Agency, 1996, p. 1).

In contrast, the data reveal that virtually all of the compensatory education programs pulled students out of their regular education classrooms during essential instruction. This problem was exacerbated by the fact that a student could be pulled from one subject to receive instruction in another subject, and, as the teachers reported, there was no guarantee that the missed instruction would ever be delivered. Consequently, students who already had gaps in their learning were put at risk for slipping further behind. In addition, specialists from all programs complained that the hectic schedule left little time for collaboration with the regular classroom teachers to support or coordinate instruction.

The same condition existed for the students who attended other special education programs. They too were missing chunks of the curriculum because of being pulled from their regular education classes. In addition, the special education teachers were concerned about the quality of helping-teacher services. Evidence indicated that helping-teachers' daily schedules left too little time for them to provide in-class support. One specialist metaphorically spoke of helping-teacher services as a life and death situation, saying, "... helping-teacher, it was a big joke. Going around from room to room for five minutes to try and bandage a child who was bleeding to death did nothing."

Special education teachers also complained that they were frequently pulled from resource instruction to attend to other duties such as student testing or Admission, Review, and Dismissal (ARD) meetings. One specialist expressed her frustration by calculating that she was pulled from her resource class "in excess of 30 days of instruction." In addition, special education teachers asserted that there was no time to collaborate with the regular education teachers. Consequently, they were uncertain about what the general education curriculum and the related expectations were for each grade level.

The conditions reported at ACES contrasted with the intent of the Individuals with Disabilities Education Act (IDEA), which when authorized in 1997 placed more emphasis on allowing students with disabilities to participate in the instruction that is delivered within the regular education classroom (Wang, Walberg, & Reynolds, 1992). According to IDEA,

> The focus is intended to produce attention to the accommodations and adjustments necessary for disabled students to have access to the general education curriculum and the special services which may be necessary for appropriate participation. (PL 105-17, cited by LRP Publications, 1999, p. 12545)

Contrasts between intent and practice existed for virtually every special program. The contrasts improved but were not eliminated once the new schedule was implemented. As I explain, most of the remaining problems could have been resolved were it not for the barriers presented by the traditional norms of leadership and the bureaucratic organizational structure of the educational system.

Effects of Leadership

The second important issue for administrators to consider in a change process is the effect that leadership has on the process. Leadership at ACES had a profound impact on the scheduling project, and the effects of leadership came from three different levels in the educational system: the legislative level, the district level, and the campus level. The data indicate that at each of these levels the predominant style of leadership was traditional. The primary clue about the pervasiveness of a traditional management style was the use of authoritarian power by administrators and legislators. In other words, those in superordinate positions used their authoritarian power to give orders and to exact obedience.

As further explanation, legislators enacted special program laws that were prescriptive in nature specifying the population that was to be served, the instructional arrangements to be used (i.e., time, location, curriculum), how funds were to be dispersed, and how eligibility was to be determined. In contradiction to the intent of the laws, the tight regulations imposed by state legislators caused conflicts with other programs and with existing conditions at the campus level. Ultimately, there was a negative effect on instruction. However, noncompliance with these regulations could have meant a loss to the district of federal and/or state funds.

At the district's central office, administrators of the various special programs departments established written and unwritten policies about how they wanted their programs operated within the schools. While some of these policies were dictated by legal mandates, others were administrative decisions. One example of an administrative decision was the policy of the GT department that required GT students to be pulled from regular education classes for one full day per week to attend GT instruction. On this day, the regular education teachers were not to introduce new concepts or administer tests. Teachers complained that this infringed on the rights of the regular education students: "After all, GT kids are learning new concepts." Their concerns fell on deaf ears. Even when different members of the scheduling committee tried to set up a time to meet with the central office administrator about modifying policies to reduce program conflicts and improve instruction, the administrator avoided the issue by not returning phone calls or answering e-mail messages. In another department, an administrator simply refused to allow any changes or listen to the reasons for the request.

At the campus level, there was an interesting twist. The principal's leadership of the scheduling change process began in a laissez-faire mode with her choosing not to participate as a member of the scheduling committee and communicating only occasionally with the committee via the assistant principal or myself. Conversely, however, once the design of the master schedule was completed, she switched her leadership to an authoritarian style. The change in style actually produced some of the most interesting data for this study, as I explain later.

Leadership was also provided at the campus level by me as the chairperson for the committee and by the committee members themselves. Our style of leadership was collaborative. We used a democratic structure with the committee members acting as representatives for the various grade levels and special programs (teams). All decisions were made with input from the entire faculty. Tentative schedules and concepts were reviewed with each of the teams until conflicts were resolved and everyone was satisfied that we had designed a master schedule that would work and that would improve instruction for all students.

Teachers reported a high level of satisfaction with the collaborative committee process. One teacher said, "It is good to have somebody represent your team with your thoughts and concerns." Another teacher essentially summed up the perspective of all of teachers who were interviewed when she said,

> I don't think the process of doing the schedule in the past was ever opened for discussion . . . It was more of an administrative decision. The new schedule that we have was solely designed as a collaborative effort. . . . Administrators basically took a back seat and let us [teachers] develop a schedule that we knew would work for the students and the teachers. . . . It's an advantage, because we're the ones in the schedule.

While the committee worked collaboratively, there was a high level of energy and a commitment to the goals established by them for the project. Teachers felt empowered and motivated to improve instruction for all students. There was a positive atmosphere in the school. One teacher demonstrated the positive feelings and the commitment at the final meeting of the scheduling committee when she jumped to her feet, waved her fist in the air as if to signal power, and enthusiastically pronounced, "Now, we can accelerate everyone!"

The committee originally intended to reconvene in the fall semester of year two to support implementation of the new plan. Committee members wanted to assist the faculty in developing two new concepts that had been incorporated into the new master schedule. One concept was referred to as *extended learning time* (ELT), and the other was *co-teach*. Both were intended to reduce pull-out during core curriculum instruction and to provide more support to accelerate the learning of struggling students. ELT had been built into the master schedule to provide one hour each day that could be dedicated to delivering individualized small-group instruction to all students. During ELT, virtually all supplemental resources (specialists and aides) were to be focused on one grade level for one hour each day (obviously a different hour at each grade level) allowing teachers to redistribute students to smaller groups for remediation or enrichment instruction (Canady, 1990; Canady & Rettig, 1995).

Effective implementation of the new concepts would require some adjustments and training for teachers. To support the teachers during this time of adjustment, the scheduling committee intended to meet during the first year of implementation to provide a communication network that would give teachers the opportunity to discuss problems and share expertise. However, once the fall semester began, the principal changed her style of leadership from laissez faire to authoritarian. Two events signaled her decision to change her leadership style. First, she withheld permission for the scheduling committee to reconvene in the fall semester because she felt that the committee was infringing on administrative decisions by discussing what instruction should look like during extended learning time. Second, she directed the faculty not to discuss the scheduling project with anyone other than herself. She explained her decision to me saying that she believed teachers were asking several different administrators and me the same question and getting different answers.

Inevitably, problems arose related to the new ELT and co-teach programs, and without support some teachers were having difficulty resolving issues. Since they were not allowed to communicate with each other, those who had resolved problems were not able to share their solutions with those who had not. Teachers who were having difficulty deciding how to structure ELT and how to implement co-teach complained that they needed more support from the administration. They wanted an explanation from the principal about her expectations. She, on the other hand, did not want to "tell them what to do" fearing she would "stunt their creativity." However, as one teacher stated, "I understand her [the principal's] point of view, but . . . I want a framework. . . . It is easier to stray from a framework than to create your own."

Committee members became frustrated with not being able to meet to support the implementation of the new plan they had worked so hard to design. One member expressed the feelings of many when she said,

> We [the committee] should have met in the beginning of the year, and we didn't. I think that really stunted the whole process, and I think that's frustrating. . . . Last year [when we were able to meet] a lot of problems came out, and we talked about them and worked through them all. . . . Being able to meet like we did last year, this year would have been totally different.

In contrast to her perspective that she should not tell teachers what to do, the principal used her authoritarian power to restrict communication among teachers. In combination, these decisions eliminated virtually all support for implementation of the new concepts, and the momentum of the project slowed down. Her decisions led to teacher frustration and an unhealthy school climate. Consequently, open communication shut down, and a grapevine grew. Communication changed from being focused on a constructive pursuit (improving instruction) to being negative and counterproductive. Instead of talking about instruction, teachers were talking about their disappointment and their frustrations. For example, one teacher, trying to explain the faculty's difficulty with adjusting to ELT stated, "When I asked about Extended Learning Time itself, sometimes, I've felt a frustration there ... not knowing what to address with their kids." Another expressed her frustration with what she viewed as inadequate implementation of ELT:

> It is my personal feeling, it [ELT] was never followed through with. We spent a whole half of a staff development day making charts on what we wanted Extended Learning Time to be, but then I don't feel that was ever followed through upon. There was no structure.

The principal demonstrated inconsistency about the role that an instructional leader should play during a restructuring project. The indications were that she had some knowledge about the need to empower teachers; but, at the same time, she demonstrated a strong belief that, as the principal of the school, she should control the behavior of her subordinates. She explained the difficulty that she had with delegating power and responsibility by saying, "The buck stops here." In other words, she felt that she alone was held responsible by her supervisors for student achievement. Her perception may have been a reality in this bureaucratic organization. Overall, the evidence indicated that the principal operated primarily from a traditional management mind-set.

The contrast in leadership styles that developed between the principal and the committee indicated that the authoritarian approach presented barriers to achieving the goals of the scheduling project. Even though the committee, through collaborative leadership, was able to design a new master schedule that improved program coordination and instruction, the degree to which improvements could be made was limited by the parameters set forth by the legal mandates and by the directive decisions of administrators. Authoritarian behaviors negatively affected the climate of the school and slowed the development of ELT and co-teach; furthermore, because there was no support for implementation, some of the problems with program coordination continued to exist. For example, the reading specialist who taught two programs was unable to resolve her scheduling conflicts. She still did not have enough time to deliver two programs and had not been given any leeway to make changes in policies. In fact, although she believed she had worked out a solution with the principal in the spring, when she returned to school in the fall, the principal withdrew permission to make the necessary changes. In frustration, the teacher transferred to another school.

In summary, the evidence from this school shows that progress was made when the teachers were empowered, when collaborative planning was utilized, and when communication was open. Conversely, under the authoritarian style of management, progress slowed, communication was negative, and the atmosphere of the school declined.

The Relationship of Structure to the Change Process

The third issue affecting the change process is the relationship between organizational structure and the change process itself. Two types of structure affected the change process at ACES. Each type established norms for communication and for distribution of responsibility and authority. One type was inflexible in nature and was based on traditional theories of organization and management. Examples include the organizational structures of the local school district, the campus, and the state educational system. On the other hand, the scheduling committee was a flexible and temporary structure, having been created to address a specific need.

The data reveal that the inflexibility of traditional structures presented barriers to the restructuring project. Traditional organizations create an organizational pyramid that stratifies authority into layers, establishes a chain of command and a line of communication, and divides responsibilities into various departments. Individuals at the higher levels of stratification have the authority to give directives to those at lower levels in the organization and to exact obedience (Fayol, 1949; Taylor, 1911; Weber, 1947). At ACES, these characteristics of traditional bureaucratic structures were prevalent at all levels in the educational system.

In this case, the legislature had more power than the local school district because the legislature could enact laws requiring special programs and could require school districts to implement them. Evidence such as the number and the descriptions of educational mandates indicates that the legislature enacted special program laws in isolation from one another. These programs were then managed by separate departments within the state's educational agency. Because programs tended to conflict at the campus level, it appears that there was a lack of collaborative planning at the state level.

In addition, the structure of the local school district was also traditional in nature with the superintendent at the top and the teachers at the bottom of the organizational pyramid. Responsibility for operating the various special programs was delegated to separate departments under the supervision of different directors. Departments included Special Education, Gifted and Talented, Compensatory Education (which included dyslexia), and English as a Second Language. Administrators for each of these special programs had the responsibility of establishing policies for their own programs. The problem with this structure is that the separation of responsibility into different departments created what Wheatley (1999) has referred to as "well-bounded boxes" (p. 71) and what I have labeled as "departmental egocentrism," a territorialism that narrows perspectives and interferes with establishing collaborative norms. Capper, Frattura, and Keyes (2000) also explain the phenomenon of isolation metaphorically:

> [When] administrators, department heads, and coordinators are assigned the oversight of specific programs . . . most often such program monitoring is completed in isolation from others . . . Each program evolves as an individual island. (p. 5)

In the case of ACES, the narrow focus encouraged by the "well bounded boxes" created a sense of narrowly defined responsibility. Administrators did not demonstrate that they felt a sense of responsibility for the success or the wellness of the whole system. The evidence indicates that district-level administrators tended to focus only on the needs of their own departments and programs. They did not appear to understand that the poor coordination negatively affects programs as well, and they were not open to discussions about creating a better fit for all programs. Inquiries from faculty at ACES did not instigate an investigation into the conditions that created scheduling conflicts by those at the district level, and central office administrators provided no assistance in solving the problems.

The norms of the traditional structure were also in evidence at the campus level. Here too, responsibility was divided by departments and hierarchical levels. For example, teachers divided the responsibility for students by labels. Evidence shows that giving a student a special program label (i.e., special education, ESL) produces a "yours" and "mine" mind-set. According to special program teachers at ACES, responsibility for the academic, social, and emotional growth of students was not necessarily shared. One specialist perceived that

> special ed [had become] sort of a dumping ground for students that regular education teachers did not want in their class. It was very convenient to have them go to resource for large portions of the day so that they wouldn't have to mess with them.

At the campus level, there was also a lack of unity among departments. Evidence includes statements made by teachers about why they volunteered to serve on the scheduling committee. One teacher said, "I was there to give the views of the special education teacher." A physical education teacher stated, "I was there to protect our programs." In addition, specialists expressed their feeling of isolation from the regular education staff. They perceived a lack of respect, and they believed they were not viewed by their regular education peers as "real teachers." Fortunately, this mind-set began to change once the restructuring project was underway. This point is well illustrated by the teacher who enthusiastically exclaimed, "Now, we can accelerate everyone!" This particular teacher had never wanted special needs students in her regular education classroom.

The negative perceptions about students with special needs and special program teachers began to dissipate with the implementation of the new master schedule and co-teach. Teachers began to think more inclusively and to seek more equitable conditions for all students. As one specialist states,

> There used to be an atmosphere . . . that you were special ed or . . . regular ed . . . [There] wasn't a lot of collaboration . . . . I think they [regular education teachers] appreciate us more than they did in the past. . . . They . . . realize now that we're truly teaching and that it is difficult.

The principal's behavior also reflected the norms of the traditional structure. She too departmentalized and stratified responsibility. For example, she felt that her role as the instructional leader delegated to her rather than to the teachers the responsibility of making instructional decisions for ELT. She believed that teachers were overstepping their bounds when they began to have a conversation about how ELT should be implemented. In addition, she demonstrated her belief that she should uphold the actions of an assistant principal who had overruled a decision made by teachers about clustering students with special needs for the co-teach classrooms. The principal decided in favor of the assistant principal even though the teachers had been trained in this process and the assistant principal had not. It appears that the principal either associated knowledge with the level a person held in an organization or believed that supporting authority was more important than supporting expert knowledge.

In either case, such views were not hers alone. They reflect the thinking of early organizational theorists who believed that the higher one moves up in an organizational structure the more one knows (Fayol, 1949; Taylor, 1911; Weber, 1947). These theorists also advocated instituting control through establishing authority. Such opinions are evident in the following quotes from Weber (1947): "Bureaucratic administration means fundamentally the exercise of control on the basis of knowledge" (p. 339), and one should establish "a stringent hierarchy of higher and lower levels of authority ... [with] each lower level ... subject to control and supervision by one immediately above it" (p. 58).

Traditional theorists also advocated maintaining control by establishing a clear and direct line of communication. Fayol (1949) labeled this structure for communication as the Scalar Chain and suggested that to maintain authority and discipline in the organization, it was important to communicate one step at a time up or down the chain of command. Such a rigid line of communication was evident in this case study and proved to be detrimental to the change process. The problem was that communicating upward proved to be difficult. For example, requests from the faculty to consider making changes in policy fell on deaf ears at administrative levels in the organizational structure. Intermediate-level administrators did not pass the concerns on to their supervisors. As a result, the inquiries were stopped at the lower levels in the central office and never reached a level in the organization where someone had the power to institute and enforce collaborative planning.

In the case of ACES, traditional organizational structures placed constraints on the faculty's effort to improve instruction. The traditional structures that were prevalent at all levels in the educational system had an almost exclusively negative impact on the scheduling project. The one exception was that the impetus for improvement was an indirect effect of the legal mandates that required educators to continue to strive to improve instruction for all students, even those students considered to be at risk of falling behind their peers because of special circumstances. However, the overall effect of the traditional structures proved to be negative; they were not only inflexible, but also impenetrable.

Conversely, the collaborative structure of the scheduling committee proved to have generally positive effects. The structure provided a communication network or feedback loop that allowed information to flow freely back and forth between the committee and the faculty. With this communication network in place, the entire faculty was able to participate in the process of redesigning the school's master schedule. The network provided an avenue for sharing information about the need for change, developing a common set of goals for the project, and identifying conflicts via multiple perspectives (from different special programs and grade levels). The network empowered the faculty by allowing every member to participate in the decision-making process.

Key Underlying Concepts

Key underlying concepts of traditional organizational theories and of the complexity theory of organizations (complex adaptive systems) offer a conceptual framework that helps to clarify the phenomena that occurred during the course of the restructuring project at ACES. A notable point of such a framework is that the key concepts from the complexity theory model directly contradict concepts advocated by traditional organizational theories (Table 2). A discussion of these contrasting concepts, as well as their relationship to the findings of this study, is presented below.

From the perspective of complexity theorists, change is an evolutionary process called self-organization. Viable systems when "faced with increasing levels of disturbance . . . possess the innate ability to reorganize . . . to deal with the new information" (Wheatley, 1999, p. 80). Complex adaptive systems are "adaptive and resilient" (Wheatley, p. 80). Their resiliency comes from their "capacity to adapt as needed" (Wheatley, p. 27). Resilient organizations create *temporary flexible structures* to facilitate reorganizing into new forms as necessary to sustain themselves. In the case of ACES, the scheduling committee was the temporary structure formed to deal with the disturbances caused by the growing level of concern about the negative effects of scheduling conflicts.

However, the effectiveness of the scheduling committee was limited because it conflicted with the *rigid structures* and the

Table 2. Characteristics of Complex Adaptive Systems vs. Traditional-Mechanical Organizations

Complex Adaptive Systems	Traditional-Mechanical Organizations
1. Everyone a Decision-Maker Making (Stanford)	1. Hierarchical Power & Decision- (Taylor, Fayol, Weber)
2. Multiple Perspectives (Stanford, Wheatley)	2. Single Perspective (Fayol)
3. Self-Reference (Wheatley)	3. Control Functions (Taylor, Fayol)
4. Positive or Amplifying Feedback (Wheatley)	4. Regulatory or Negative Feedback (Taylor, Fayol)
5. Open Communication of Information (Fullan, Wheatley)	5. Restricted Flow of Information and Ideas (Fayol)
6. Non-Linear Thinking (Fullan, Wheatley)	6. Linear Thinking (Taylor, Fayol)
7. Flexible Temporary Structures (Wheatley)	7. Rigid Structures (Fayol, Weber)
8. Adaptive Processes (Stanford, Wheatley)	8. Plan of Action (Fayol)
9. Conflict Valued (Fullan, Stanford, Wheatley)	9. Conflict Feared (Fayol)
10. Coherence and Interdependence (Fullan, Stanford)	10. Division of Work (Fayol)

norms of the traditional style of management that were deeply ingrained in the educational system of which ACES was a part. Examples of this clash between the goals for improvement and the inflexible traditional norms of power and control are apparent in the behaviors of leaders at all three levels in the educational system (legislative, district, and campus). These leaders used their authoritarian powers as a *control function* to maintain the status quo. The use of the control function was especially evident when special program administrators would not allow modifications that would have altered their previously outlined plans and when campus administrators shunned teacher input about how instruction should be organized during ELT or how students should be clustered within co-teach classrooms.

The control function of traditional management was also used to restrict communication. Such restriction happened at both the campus level and the district level. At the campus level, the principal attempted to *restrict the flow of information* and ideas by shutting down the scheduling committee and by directing teachers not to discuss ELT or co-teach with anyone other than herself. At the district level, administrators, and in one case, a director's secretary, restricted the flow of information upward in the organization by acting as gatekeepers (not allowing the inquiries about policy changes to go past their own level in the organization). In bureaucratic organizations, information has traditionally been controlled by those at various levels, and only information that fits with the adopted plan of operation is passed through the chain of command. New information that is in *conflict* with previously held convictions is *feared*, and efforts are often made to suppress it (Wheatley, 1999).

Furthermore, information in complex systems flows through the organization via *feedback loops*. Traditional theorists and complexity theorists have opposing opinions about the function of feedback loops. From the traditional perspective, feedback loops serve a regulatory or a control function; i.e., information received is evaluated to verify "whether everything occurs in conformity with the plan adopted, the instructions issued and principles established" (Fayol, 1949, p. 107). Conflicts with the adopted plan are perceived as problems, and actions are taken to squash them. This approach was evident in this study when central office administrators refused to discuss or allow modification to their written and unwritten policies. Wheatley (1999) describes this type of behavior as producing regulatory or negative feedback loops.

The second type of feedback loop, the one advocated by complexity theorists, serves not as a control function, but as a device to amplify disharmony or conflicts. Wheatley (1999) labels this type of loop as positive or amplifying feedback. Instead of being viewed as something to be squashed, conflicts are perceived as a source of information about the possibility that there is a need to adapt the organizational plan. From this perspective, conflicts are *valued*, not feared. They are a signal that there is a misfit between the goals of the organization and the environment.

In the case of ACES, the conflicts signaled that the goals of the educational system were at risk because of the lack of program coordination, and this information should have signaled a need for change at all levels in the educational system. It did not. Only at the campus level, where the problem was most acute, was action taken to improve the negative conditions, yet the ability of the faculty to institute the needed changes was constrained by the traditional characteristics of the educational system. There were a number of constraints. First, the laws were too prescriptive, and they segregated students by labels rather than by instructional needs. Second, district-level administrators viewed conflicts from a regulatory perspective. Third, administrators at both the district and campus levels used their power to control the flow of information.

Attempts to control the flow of information had negative effects for the project and also for the relationships among faculty and administrators on the campus. For instance, information was too restricted to resolve a number of the instructional problems that existed. The climate of the school turned negative because of the teachers' frustrations about the unresolved issues (unresolved scheduling conflicts for some programs and the lack of support for developing ELT and co-teach). In addition, the teachers resented the restricted flow of communication.

According to Wheatley (1999), controlling information has become a counterproductive, if not an impossible, task in the technological age with new information being generated at an ever increasing rate. She cautions that having just a few people interpret data uncovers only a small portion of the potentialities, and she questions what happens with "all the data that goes unnoticed because we rely on these solitary observations?" (p. 66). Her concern is about the quality of the decisions that are made when information is limited. She advises that intellectual capacity can be increased by including many more individuals in the decision-making process. Adding to Wheatley's argument, other complexity theorists agree that educational systems today are so complex that no one person or limited group of people can see the whole picture. Stanford (1998) elaborates on this point by saying that schools are "systems within systems within systems [and] . . . making a change in one . . . system may have unexpected results in other systems" (p. 28).

On the other hand, Fayol (1949), a traditional theorist, recommends a linear approach and a singular perspective in organizational planning, asserting that planning is a function of management. He believes that it is the manager's responsibility to identify organizational objectives, outline a *plan of action*, delegate responsibility, and monitor progress. This argument is what complexity theorists refer to as *linear thinking*. In other words, it is the belief that there is a direct connection between cause and effect. Complexity theorists point out that in complex systems, there is no direct line between an action and an effect. Change in complex systems is nonlinear. Therefore, initiating changes in one part of the system without evaluating the consequences to the other parts can result in chaos. To avoid making this mistake, it is necessary to broaden our scope of information by employing *multiple perspectives* (Fullan, 1999; Stanford, 1998; Wheatley, 1999). In this way, we can see the whole and not just the parts.

At ACES, the process of designing the new master schedule was supported by accessing the *multiple perspectives* from the many smaller systems that compose the overall system of the school. These systems included the various grade levels and programs such as fine arts, physical education, special education, English as a second language (ESL), gifted and talented (GT), and compensatory education programs. Committee members found that the perspectives from each program and grade level were unique because of the differing needs of each program and of the students each program served. They considered each perspective when making changes to avoid the creation of new problems for some groups and when attempting to resolve problems for others. The process involved *everyone as a decision maker* and, in so doing, assured not only that the information gathered was that which was needed to make sound decisions, but also that everyone involved could claim ownership in the design of the new master schedule.

One of the major tenets of complexity theory is that complex systems have the ability to maintain a balance between order and chaos. That point of balance is referred to as "the edge of chaos" (Fullan, 1999, p. 24; Stanford, 1998, p. 12). It is at this point that open and flexible organizations have enough stability to sustain themselves and enough chaos to be creative. Complexity scientists have found that disorder can be a source of growth and that "disruptions, confusion, [and] chaos . . . are necessary to awaken creativity" (Wheatley, p. 20). On the other hand, systems that are not open and flexible have difficulty making the changes necessary for the maintenance of a healthy organization.

Complexity theorists explain, however, that being open and flexible "does not mean accepting anarchy" (Fullan, 1999, p. 24). To sustain themselves organizations need "both structure and openendness" (p. 24). The difference between the traditional approach and the complexity theory model is in the concept of structure. According to the complexity theorists, structure emerges via a *self-referencing process* and not from the control function of the traditional approach. Such self-referencing is the element in the *adaptive process* that facilitates orderly change. It exists when an organization has a "clear sense of identity" (Wheatley, 1999, p. 86), directly expresses organizational principles and goals, and demonstrates a strong commitment to them. A clear identity facilitates the process of filtering through the new information to decide upon appropriate actions to maintain a healthy system. Organizational identity establishes *coherence*, creating patterns in the choices that individual components of the organization make. It is this process that "creates order without control" (Wheatley, 1999, p. 168).

Coherence was created at ACES by the democratic structure and the communication network established by the scheduling committee. These structures provided the faculty with an opportunity to revisit and refocus on the goals of the organization (self-referencing) and to break down the barriers between the different programs on the campus. For teachers, the division of work and the division of responsibility for students by programs to a large extent vanished. Teachers began to work collaboratively across programs, and specialists felt more respected and accepted as teachers by the regular education staff.

Unfortunately, the same coherence did not develop between administrators and teachers. The traditional mind-set was steadfastly held within the administrative ranks. Consequently, qualitative information about instructional issues did not flow upward along the chain of command. Teachers did not have enough power to penetrate the rigid structures for communication, nor did they have the power that was needed to make changes without support from those in the higher administrative ranks. The inflexible structure of hierarchical power and decision-making ended up limiting the improvements that could be made.

Summary

In this case study of one school's efforts to redesign the master schedule, professional collaboration among the faculty provided the support that was necessary to make improvements in the instructional conditions at ACES. As a result of this collaborative effort, a new master schedule was designed that improved program coordination and allowed a better quality of instruction for most of the students. Students were no longer coming and going from regular education classrooms in the middle of instruction to attend special programs. According to the special program teachers, students with special needs were "getting more instruction . . . [and] not missing anything." In addition, the new schedule provided more time for special education teachers to assist students within the regular education classroom. The specialists believed that the extra time that they now had to spend in the regular classroom was "a big advantage" not just for the special education students, but also for struggling learners "who fall through the cracks" because they have "not qualified for special services." Likewise, the ESL teachers reported being better able to focus on their ESL curriculum and being able to introduce "language [vocabulary for upcoming units] before the language [was] presented in the [regular education] classroom," making the language more comprehensible and the students more successful. Teachers witnessed students with special needs demonstrating strong growth not just academically, but also socially. As one special education teacher said,

> Special education students never felt a part of the regular ed class . . . because they were in and out of the class. They never had a chance to bond with the regular ed kids. . . . I saw them learn to interact. . . . I saw them develop socially.

Although some of the problems with program coordination were resolved through collaborative planning, other problems continued even after the new master schedule was implemented. The persistent problems were the direct result of the traditional style of leadership and the traditional organizational structure that prevailed through all three levels of the educational system. For example, at the campus level, the principal's decision to use her power to disband the scheduling committee and to ban teachers from discussing the new schedule, co-teach or ELT essentially shut down the communication that was necessary to support the change process. As a consequence, the implementation process and the development of the new concepts were stunted; teachers became frustrated; and the climate of the school was negatively affected.

At the district level, administrators demonstrated a traditional style of leadership when they either refused to discuss the programming problems with faculty members or refused to allow changes in policies. Central office administrators, who focused on maintaining control of their respective programs, were not open to communication about the need to adapt. Their traditional mind-set created barriers to the accomplishment of all of the goals of the scheduling project. Without cooperation from these administrators, little could be done to create a better fit for some programs.

At the government level, an authoritarian or traditional mind-set was also demonstrated by the prescriptive nature of the special program laws and by the threat that funding could be lost to the district if educational mandates were not followed to the letter. The tightly prescribed laws presented constraints to how students could be served, splitting funding and instruction by labels rather than by need. These constraints contributed to the original scheduling conflicts and also presented barriers to improvement.

Structure, like leadership, was either traditional or collaborative in nature. While the organizational structures at the campus level, the district level, and the legislative level were traditional (bureaucratic), the structure of the scheduling committee was collaborative. Simply put, the traditional style presented barriers while the collaborative style provided support for the schedule change process. Traditional characteristics of the organizational system that presented barriers included (1) the hierarchical nature of authority, which gave overriding power to those in superordinate positions rather than serving to equalize power with subordinates who had expert knowledge; (2) the scalar chain (Fayol, 1949), which presented an inflexible path for communication that restricted the flow of communication from the faculty at ACES to the higher levels in the organization; and (3) the departmentalization of special programs, which divided responsibility for programs and inadvertently encouraged departmental egocentrism (narrowly focused perspectives).

On the other hand, characteristics of the collaborative structure directly, which contrasted with the characteristics of traditional structure, provided support for the change process. They included (1) a democratic approach to decision-making, which was provided by the schoolwide communication network, that allowed every faculty member to participate in the development of goals for the project and the design of the new master schedule; (2) the utilization of multiple perspectives so that the decisions made by the committee solved existing problems without creating new problems; and (c) the understanding that conflicts which were identified via the feedback loop were sources of information about a misfit between the goals of the committee, the needs of a particular subsystem (grade level or special program), and the tentative plan under consideration. Conflicts were the signal that the plan needed to be adapted to produce a better fit.

Comparisons of the characteristics of the traditional approach with those of the collaborative approach to leadership and organizational structure indicate that the traditional approach to management favors a control function to operate organizations, while the collaborative approach advocates shared responsibility and open communication of information. The collaborative approach proved to be more useful in this case study. Progress was made toward the goals of the scheduling project when the faculty was empowered to make decisions and given a forum for communication. In concurrence with the findings in this case, Bryk et al. (1998) suggest, based on their research on the Chicago public schools, that

> a control-oriented system will not produce the levels of individual commitment needed . . . to attain better schools. . . . Organizational control must rely more heavily on . . . a conception of "teachers as professional" rather than of "workers loyal to their superiors." . . . The transition from traditional domination to effective democratic localism places demands on leadership at the school building level . . . [to work] toward a shared professional commitment for student development. (pp. 100–101).

Conclusions

Because the overarching goal of the educational system is to provide a quality education for all students, it is necessary to create equitable educational opportunities for students who are at risk of failure and/or dropping out of school. Although this case study demonstrated that this goal is the intent of educational mandates, it is not necessarily what is happening at the campus level. The ACES study identified a gap between intent and practice that infringed upon the rights of students and frustrated teachers. The teachers sincerely wanted to improve conditions at their school. Unfortunately, however, even their collaborative effort failed to arm the teachers with the power necessary to improve instructional conditions within an entrenched bureaucratic structure to the extent that they desired. The implications from this case study raise questions for educational leaders at the legislative level, the district level, and the campus level.

One implication for legislative leaders is the need to reconsider their approach to developing categorical program laws. The current approach takes a prescriptive tack, tightly regulating eligibility requirements, program structure, and, in some cases, instructional content and methods. The complexity of these laws contributes to an atmosphere of chaos at the campus level. The unintentional consequences of the laws' prescriptive nature are instructional fragmentation and decreased educational opportunities for students. Instead of improving the educational opportunities for at-risk students, the the laws interfere with the delivery of quality instruction.

This study demonstrates the need to review categorical program laws to consider how these mandates can integrate rather than segregate programs and services. Perhaps legislatures need to move toward consolidating special program laws, focus on distributing funds based on the number of students who qualify for any special need, and leave the responsibility for improving instruction to professional educators. Legislators can then hold these educators accountable for demonstrating improved outcomes for all students.

A second implication for legislators is a paradox to the first. Chaos does ultimately provide the impetus for change. The educators at ACES were forced to evaluate their instructional practices and make improvements. The fact that the mandates created chaos was not the problem. Rather, the disjointed approach to enacting and managing mandates was. The message is that legislators should plan cautiously and collaboratively so that their mandates do not interfere with the goals of the educational system, but at the same time should continue to maintain the pressure that forces local districts and individual campuses to evaluate the effectiveness of their instruction and instructional arrangements (i.e., the models that they use for delivering special instruction and for collaboration among and between educators).

There are also implications for the district level. One implication is that the traditional structure of dividing responsibility for the operations of the various programs among different departments requires rethinking. This approach was shown in this study to have negative consequences for program coordination and improvement. Steps should be taken to break down the barriers that encourage isolated planning and departmental egocentrism. A second implication is that because the traditional structure for communication restricted the flow of information and devalued input from teachers, it should be replaced with open lines of communication. Although the traditional line of communication was meant to maintain control of the organization, in reality, it prevented those in command from receiving vital information about the needs of the organization and limited the improvements that could be made by the faculty. The traditional structure restricted the flow of information in both directions.

These two implications lead to a final implication for central office administrators and campus level administrators. As Fullan (1999) points out, "middle managers like principals [play a] crucial [role] in attacking incoherence resulting from overload and fragmented situations" (p. 16). Their role should be to facilitate knowledge creation. When administrators view their role as that of controllers of the status quo, their mind-set contradicts the attitudes and beliefs necessary for the facilitation of change. To be a facilitator of change, one needs to maintain an openness to information from the organizational members as well as from the community that may signal a need to adapt previously developed plans. To be a facilitator, one must view conflict as a source of knowledge about a possible misfit between the goals of the organization and the needs of the environment. Concisely stated, the traditional mind-set and the facilitator mind-set are incompatible.

Finally, there are implications for campus-level administrators. One implication is that principals play a significant role in creating the climate of the school and the conditions for school improvement. So it is important to keep in mind, as the evidence from this case study disclosed, that the use of authoritarian powers by the campus administrator has a negative effect on the school climate and is counterproductive to the goals of a school change project. Campus administrators need to adopt the mind-set of a facilitator rather than an authoritarian leader.

Second, for the creation of a professional climate to support school improvement, it is important to empower teachers to participate in the decision-making process to identify needs, develop goals, and create solutions. Third, an open-communication structure is necessary throughout the implementation phase of a change process to provide a framework that supports the adaptation or adjustment process. Through this structure, teachers can share their problems with implementation and can brainstorm solutions.

Evidence from this case study also demonstrates a need for educational leaders at all three levels to develop a less traditional mind-set and move toward creating flexible collaborative structures that facilitate the change process. Incorporated within this concept is the recommendation that the status of teachers should be raised to a professional level. Teachers should be made an integral and respected part of the team that makes decisions about instruction and improvements. The information to which they have primary access is invaluable to a system that must adapt to the needs of a rapidly changing world while attempting to provide a quality education for all students.

As explained by the complexity theory model, traditional structures tend to be rigid and are therefore less amenable to new information; consequently, they are slower to change. Rigid structures tend to be problematic in a rapidly changing world in which adaptation has emerged as a survival skill. Schools today must be able to adapt at a rate comparable to the rate of change in their environment. This study raises questions about what educational leaders—teachers as well as administrators—need to become facilitators of the change process.

References

Bryk, A. S., Sebring, P. B., Kerbow, D., Rollow, S., & Easton, J. Q. (1998). *Charting Chicago School Reform: Democratic Localism As a Level for Change*. Boulder: Westview Press.

Canady, R. I. (1990). Parallel Block Scheduling: A Better Way to Organize Schools. *Principalship*, 69(3), 34–36.

Canady, R. I., & Rettig, M. D. (1995). The Power of Innovative Scheduling. *Educational Leadership*, 53(3), 4–10.

Capper, C. A., Frattura, E., & Keyes, M. W. (2000). *Meeting the Needs of All Students with Disabilities: How To Go Beyond Inclusion.* Thousand Oaks, CA: Corwin Press.

Fayol, H. (1949). *General and Industrial Management.* (C. Storrs, Trans.). London: Sir Isaac Pitman & Sons LTD. (Originally published in France 1916).

Fullan, M. (1999). *Changes Forces: The Sequel.* Philadelphia: Falmer Press.

Making Sense of the New IDEA Regulations. (Vol. 2). (1999). Alexandria, VA: LRP Publications.

Stanford, B. (1998). *Charting School Change: Improving the Odds for Successful School Reform.* Thousand Oaks, CA: Corwin Press.

Taylor, R. W. (1911). *The Principles of Scientific Management.* New York,: W. W. Norton.

Texas Education Agency. (1996). *Texas Administrative Code.* Title 19, Part 2, Chapter 89, Subchapter D, Rule 89.63. Austin, TX. Available at http://www.tea.state.tx.us

Wang, M. C., Walberg, H. J., & Reynolds, M. C. (1992). A Scenario for Better-Not-Separate-Special Education. *Educational Leadership,* 50(2), 35-38.

Weber, M. (1947). *The Theory of Social and Economic Organization.* (T. Parsons, Trans.). New York: Oxford University Press.

Wheatley, M. J. (1999). *Leadership and the New Science: Discovering Order in a Chaotic World.* San Francisco: Berrett-Koehler.

7

Engaging Families: A Study of Parent Mentoring

Trish Gaffney

The study which led to this chapter began in 1987 when I first expressed curiosity about parents helping parents to Dave Stokan, the assistant principal at the middle school where I taught. We were overseeing the annual fund raiser. The school, then twelve years old, had just begun to develop a cadre of parent volunteers. Some of these parents were helping Dave with the mundane details of distributing fund raising items to students for delivery to their customers and collecting money from the students. It struck me that although generating funds for educational enrichment was worthy work, it was a severe underuse of these parents' capacity. They could much better serve the school community if their talents were put to use in relationship activities. At the same moment, I remembered a few other parents with whom I frequently communicated. They were overwhelmed by their children's adolescence and lacked survival tools. Their outlook contrasted with the perspective of these volunteer parents who seemed to have coping skills in abundance. I wondered what these two groups of parents could share with each other, given the opportunity. My thoughts turned to mentoring.

The literature on adolescence supports the idea that mentoring can make a difference. The Carnegie Council on Adolescent Development (1995) advocates reengaging families, strengthening parents' roles, sustaining parent involvement in schools, and developing parent peer support groups. Parent-to-parent mentoring has great potential for effectively nurturing these strategies.

My epiphany about parents' roles still haunted me over a decade later when I was a middle school administrator and doctoral student doing research. I began the groundwork for understanding how a project on parents mentoring other parents might look. My original plan, examining relationships in which parents mentor peers with early adolescent children, stalled. A conversation with Dr. Joyce Epstein helped me to consider the difficult ethical issue of drawing in parents to be mentored without labeling them as deficient. I continued to read, to study existing programs, and to talk with everyone who might have an interest in the topic. Many of these resources encouraged me to find a program to study rather than to invent one myself. Jan Farrand, a social worker, introduced me to Parent Share, a mentoring process well suited for my project, and connected me with the program's originator, Dr. Charles Smith of the Kansas State University Cooperative Extension Service. Dr. Smith shared materials that could be used to initiate parent-to-parent mentoring and offered access to administrators implementing the program at pilot sites, as well as the data resources of his graduate student, Kelly Kuhn.

Parent Share is designed as a community-based program that connects experienced parents with parents who are struggling. Training provided to the volunteer mentors emphasizes listening and providing encouragement to parents who seek support. The program responds to the isolation parents may feel as they raise children. Mediating parent isolation from family, friends, and community can contribute to the prevention of child abuse. A relationship with a caring mentor has the potential to positively influence the development of the struggling parent's children.

Dr. Smith gave me permission to contact the Parent Share pilot sites to learn about their progress in initiating the program and, if permitted by the sites' administrators, to interview the mentored parents about their experiences. Because of the geographical diversity of the sites, data collection was conducted through telephone interviews over the course of a year.

The Process of the Mentoring Cycle

Of the 26 pilot sites, those that moved forward with plans to implement the Parent Share curriculum depended on broad-based, inclusive planning, beginning with the end in mind. The words of the program directors reveal three themes or beliefs that inspire and inform the development of such programs. The first theme is that the mentoring approach can be an effective means of building community capacity to serve youth at risk. At many of the sites, schools partnered with the community organization providing Parent Share from the initial planning stages. The children were always a key force as programs evolved.

A second theme is illustrated by a program leader whose goal was to redesign the "only bad parents need parent education" approach by providing a program responsive to parents. His invitation question is calculated to engage parents: "How can we help you relieve stress?" Although every parent's stressful circumstances are unique, stress is endemic to parenting. Mentoring can help parents respond appropriately to stress and prevent it from becoming toxic.

A third theme suggests the power of relationships: "One-on-one is going to make the difference." This is an important theme to revisit when the difficulties of program development tempt one to try short cuts. Mentoring requires deep investments of time, but the results are incomparable to any other kind of support.

Launching the Mentoring Programs

Examples from six different sites provide a good cross-section of different conceptualizations and executions of parent mentoring efforts. The settings and situations are diverse. Each site faced unique challenges in implementing the Parent Share program. The common thread is the time and effort invested in collaboration with all stakeholders at the front end of the project, which is illustrated by these start-up stories. The first four programs have actually been implemented; the last two are programs still under development.

The first site, based at a Cooperative Extension Service office (Site 1), was developed in a joint effort with other community groups in the more rural sections of the midwestern city-based geographical area served. The site used the recommended Parent Share curriculum to initiate three unique mentoring efforts with three different groups. The projects occurred in sequence over the course of two years. The completion and evaluation of each project informed the implementation of the next one. The same basic program was used similarly with each group.

Social service agencies cooperated with the Extension Service to provide sessions for training the mentors, including mentors from True Colors (Miscisin, 2001). Topics included the definition of a mentor, problem solving, behavior change, self-esteem, information on elder and child abuse, and signs of mental illness. These topics are enhancements to the Parent Share preparation for mentors.

There was little money available to the program at this site. Funds to train the three groups of mentors came from three separate small grants. The Extension Service acted as a training consultant for each location, then turned over the established programs to the communities to be sustained. One of the three communities had an elementary school at its center. Another drew mentors from a faith-based community to serve a growing population of migrant families seeking farm work. As an extension of the Parent Share curriculum, but separate from the three projects, the Extension Service also sponsored training that targeted 19 city agencies which came together to learn about developing mentoring programs.

The results at Site 1 illustrate the various applications imaginable from a single concept, parent mentoring, and a single guide, Parent Share. Mentors learned to plan thoroughly, involve all stakeholders, and let go of programs once they are sustainable.

The second site was in a town 45 minutes from a large, southern city. The Parent Share program was paired by another Extension Service office (Site 2) with two other curricula, using some creative modifications. One supplement to the Parent Share program was a leadership curriculum, offered to an audience of parent partners from public housing. This curriculum resembled programs for developing community leaders in cities across the United States. The parent-mentors were volunteers from every corner of the town, who were coaxed into service by a visionary program director, Amanda. Mentors represented the public and private sectors. They were typically influential and outgoing. Later it became apparent that the first cohort of parents who were mentored shared these characteristics. A "friendship curriculum" provided a resource to help the mentors in relationship-building; the parent partners learned the curriculum experientially. Friendships even grew among the parent partners. These parents had enormous praise and respect for Amanda, who tapped every resource to serve the audience, including an unexpected contingent, the parents' children. They came because of the evening meeting time. Ernestine, a parent partner, reported:

> They didn't expect the kids to show up with the parents, so what they did, they really got involved in it, and Ms. Amanda was really happy that the kids was involved with it. They had more fun than we did. They loved the debates.

The evolution of parent-mentoring at Site 2 also involved three cohorts of parents, just as at Site 1. Whereas the three projects at Site 1 were in three geographic locations, the three cohorts at Site 2 evolved over time from the same community setting. The program director, Amanda, said, "It takes three years for people to catch on, unless they're much better than I am in getting the work done. Before three years you can't see much results, and some programs take so long." By the second year, some of the original parent partners were serving in helping roles. The third cohort of parent partners was assembled based on the recommendations of the original parent partners, now parent-mentor volunteers themselves. Including everyone improved and honed the mentoring process.

The results at Site 2 illustrate the evolution of a parent mentoring program within a single community and the potential offered by this arrangement to produce home-grown mentors for future cohorts of parents with mentoring needs. The lesson learned is that relationships are the key ingredient in developing programs which work and can be sustained.

The Parent Share curriculum provided the component which met the requirements of a Strong Families, Safe Children grant sought by an international, nonprofit organization (Site 3) in a town 45 minutes from a large city in the Midwest. The third site involved interagency cooperation through a Human Services Coordinating Body. This cooperation led to a coalition which supplemented a program designed to support youth achievement and youth mentoring. Other components of this site's program were Second Time Around, a curriculum for grandparents as caregivers, and The Achievers Program, an Afrocentric curriculum for youth at-risk. The three elements combined produced a strong family mentoring program. Twenty-five hours of training were provided to the first cohort of mentors by a state university Extension Service representative, Patsy.

The mentoring agency that received the grant provided ongoing relationship support to the mentors through monthly meetings. The mentored parents also met as a group every three months. The parents interviewed were unaware of the extent of behind-the-scenes collaborations necessary to produce the quality program that they valued.

The results at Site 3 show the strength of aligning several programs through a body seeking maximum impact on program participants and reduced duplication of effort by multiple social service organizations. The lesson learned is that one must seek collaboration! Time and effort are worthwhile investments that improve the results exponentially.

Site 4, in a medium-sized, southern university city, blended three women into a team to train parent-mentors and seek parent partners: Barbara, an Extension Service trainer who taught the mentors; Cara, an employee from the school district's Family Resource Center, who recruited the mentors and parents;

and an unnamed local college employee, who helped with group bonding exercises.

The neighborhood elementary school where the parent-mentors met and received training was a 100-year-old center of the community that had dwindled to 160 students. The parent partners came from the public housing adjacent to the school. The housing project was soon to be demolished, its residents dispersed. The rumored closing of the school also increased the mobility rate and expedited the move out of the neighborhood of some who planned to move anyway.

Of the four communities served by Cara in her school district capacity, this community was the closest knit, as well as the neediest, and the one on which a Parent Share program would have the most impact. The parent partners were receiving social support from the mentor-parents in making the welfare-to-work transition required by new state reform laws.

The mentors, mostly grandmothers, aged 40–60 years, would remain long-term residents of the community. Those whose parent partners moved needed support if they were to continue as mentors and take on new parent partners. Unused to the mobility to which schools are accustomed, and to the strategy of impacting children and families whenever and however that can be accomplished, the mentors met with the organizers to assess their feelings about the departures of their parent partners and to renew their energy for new matches. These mentors created a stronghold in a fragile community.

The results at Site 4 illustrate the various obstacles ready to thwart the launching of parent mentoring programs, even in communities with expertise, caring, and need. The lesson learned is that one must be persistent! Even if the timing is not right, one should not give up on establishing a parent-mentor program, especially in the face of demonstrated need. Bide the time; be patient. Continue to support potential mentors until conditions improve.

Not every collaboration resulted in a viable parent mentoring program. Pauline, an Extension Service program director in a small city in a southwestern metropolitan area (Site 5), invited three separate community partners to collaborate on a Parent

Share program. The parent facilitator of the school district and the manager of an apartment complex declined to participate, but a church already involved in a grant-funded youth intervention program considered the invitation. Because of its substantial previous commitment to its youth program, the church decided not to cosponsor a parent mentoring program at this time. Pauline hoped to leave the door open for a future collaboration.

The mentoring efforts at Site 5 and at Site 6, below, began with many obstacles, similar to the case at Site 4. Besides being persistent and patient, administrators must know when to take the project off the table and back to the shop for retooling. One lesson learned from Sites 5 and 6 is not to bury a stalled or dormant project. It may renew itself, phoenix-like, when the time is right. A prerequisite for this eventuality is continuing to maintain relationships with potential stakeholders. Sponsoring a mentoring program is a huge commitment. It can work only if all the resources are in place at the right moment.

Susan, an Extension Service program director in a smaller southwestern community (Site 6), headed a diverse board to implement a collaborative mentoring effort with a local agency. The original plan was to mentor one family. Agencies considered for partnership were the local adult and youth probation offices and a prison ministry. Another avenue explored was how parent mentoring could affect potential juvenile probation candidates under age ten. Parent mentoring efforts have remained in the planning stages because of the absence of full commitment by an influential community member.

Mentoring one family at a time, the plan at Site 6, is a different approach than the one outlined in the Parent Share curriculum, which recommends starting with a committee, obtaining and training six parent-mentors, and matching them with six parent partners. However, a review of the successful Parent Share programs shows them to be responsive to local needs. Sites that elected to delay implementation of a parent mentoring program should not be considered unsuccessful. Using the committee approach, some groups decided that the need was not sufficiently great or the resources sufficiently abundant to initiate a program during the time frame of the study.

The program development experiences at the six sites described in this section may help readers consider options for initiating their own parent mentoring programs.

Recruiting and Training the Mentors

Once the plans for a parent mentoring program are in place, the critical next step is recruiting and training the mentors. Examples from the three different sites represent different approaches to attracting and preparing experienced parents to mentor parents who may be struggling. Site 7 is in a large urban center. The other two sites are in rural areas. Two themes permeate the search for mentors: openness and timing. Although the Parent Share program recommends using experienced parents as mentors, other adults may also fit this role. If mentors are not forthcoming as a program implementation is planned, there may be a later, better time for a mentoring program to be started. Programs are underway at Sites 7 and 9. Site 8 has paused and waits for better timing.

Programs typically asked potential mentors to commit to a time frame ranging from six months to one year and to submit to a rigorous screening. Site 7, in a western Canadian city, was more successful than other sites in recruiting and training mentors. Michelle, the director of recruiting at an international, nonprofit organization, compared the relative difficulty of obtaining parent-mentors with attracting youth mentors, whom the organization also recruits:

> It's quite different being a mentor to a child than being a mentor to the parents. . . . It's really easy to recruit somebody to help a kid . . . but people often think that by the time somebody's 18, they're an adult and they should have their act together. But also even being matched to a child is different than being matched to the parent because somehow you see the child as blameless in a situation, and yet as a mentor you see the parent creating an unhealthy situation and not being prepared to do, or willing to do, anything about it. It's just a different dynamic entirely.

Despite the probability of lower yields of parent mentors compared with youth mentors, community organizations that recruit parent mentors have proven methods for recruiting and screening mentors developed by successful providers of youth mentoring. These methods include attention to agency reputation, media coverage, word-of-mouth efforts, staff composition and performance, and recruitment materials. Targeted recruitment strategies attract parent mentors who match the expressed preferences of the parent partners. For example, among parents seeking youth mentors for their children, a considerable portion prefer that their children be matched to mentors of similar racial or ethnic background (Roaf, Tierney, & Hunte, 1994). Targeted recruitment seeks to meet parent preferences, but the openness of recruiters to multiple mentor characteristics also yielded opportunities. This strategy brought in excellent mentors who might not meet the profile of the mentor proposed in the Parent Share guidelines. Michelle elaborated:

> We started off there, I think, saying that we hoped that they would be experienced parents themselves, and then we sort of changed our view of what *experienced parent* meant and realized that you could have experience with parenting issues without being a parent yourself by being an aunt or whatever, a good neighbor.

The results at Site 7 include a high rate of mentor recruitment and retention. Parents who were interviewed expressed satisfaction with their matches. One mentor interviewed following the original study was an elderly white man who mentored a middle-aged widowed father. The aboriginal widower grew up on a reservation, as did the mentor, the son of a minister. Although they had many differences, their common cultural experience anchored their match. The lesson learned here is that one must have recruitment strategies but be willing to be flexible.

Even though Site 8 was unsuccessful in recruiting mentors during the time frame of the study, there was support for the process of the Parent Share program. In a midwestern town surrounded by agricultural industry, community organizations supported starting a Parent Share program. Many were interested in filling the parent partner role. The only barrier to initiating the program was that potential volunteers in this small community were already committed to volunteering elsewhere. In the view of the Extension Service director, Karen, it was "just the wrong time." Without doing anything differently, she would try again to start a program, beginning with a small group and building, as the program originator recommended. There were already interested parents to be served through mentoring.

The results at Site 8 illustrate the optimism that an experienced administrator can safely express in the face of postponement of a program implementation. The lessons learned are a respect for timing and a commitment to the value of effective strategies like parent mentoring.

The Parent Share program at Site 9 developed over an extended period of time. Located in an agricultural town 75 miles from a medium-sized city in the Midwest, this site used a March-of-Dimes-supported grant to pay the salary of a part-time program organizer who would serve two locations and train ten parent mentors. Collaborative support was also sought through the local social services network. Following a state mandate to have different community organizations work together, collaborators developed a welfare-to-work vehicle designed to nurture families. Mothers, and then fathers, of families with young children were served through Parent Share and a fathering curriculum, It's My Child, Too.

According to Joan, the Extension Service program director, it was worthwhile to persevere through the long development process, building the groundwork and securing the administrative unit to run the program. The mentors were already recruited through several groups that Joan worked with regularly by the time the funding finally became assured. The lesson learned at Site 9 is to move forward with the planning stages even if lack of funds is a barrier to program implementation. The human element, mentor recruitment, can be more labor intensive than grant-seeking. A parent mentoring program can run on a shoestring, but it cannot run without mentors.

The three sites whose recruitment and training of mentors are described above represent three approaches typical across all the sites. One strategy is to look beyond the written guidelines of the Parent Share program to use people resources in a locally appropriate way. The result may be some unconventional choices as mentors. A second tactic is to postpone program implementation when enough mentors have not been recruited. This buys time while relationships with mentor candidates are established. A third approach is to seek mentors and train them even when other pieces of the program, like funding, lag behind.

The recruitment and training experiences of the three sites described in this section may help readers consider options for reaching their own potential audience of mentors.

Seeking the parent partners

Following the recruitment of mentors, program planners must seek parents to be mentored. Examples from three different sites illustrate that many contexts might yield parents who may be struggling and feel open to being mentored. Site 10 is in a large midwestern city, and Site 11 is in a large city in the Northwest. Site 12 is in a midwestern lake community with a mixture of affluence and poverty. Three themes thread through the search for parents to mentor at these and the other sites. One theme is need. Parents whose needs are compelling may be more open to the help that mentoring provides. The second theme is the formative assistance parents can acquire through mentoring. Mentoring is an additive rather than a deficit model of helping. Finally, progress with a steady supply of parents choosing mentoring contributes to program sustainability. Strong programs are underway at these three sites.

At Site 10, Carol, the Extension Service program director, inherited a well-formulated Parent Share program called Mentor Moms. In its second year, the program attracted 14 adolescents as its parent partners. The original pilot was done through a high school in a state with an initiative to support teen mothers through mentoring. Two teachers saw the need for mentors for pregnant teens. The Parents as Teachers program and the counselor at the school recruited the young women. They met weekly through a school seminar in which they were grouped. They chose to have an adult mentor if they found the friendship helpful.

The young women were eligible to remain in the program until they graduated. The goal was to keep them in school and prevent repeat pregnancies. Several mentors mentored a second parent partner.

The program was well accepted by the young women, and news of it traveled by word of mouth. In the following school year, the program expanded to two additional high schools. A high school in a nearby rural town with a high pregnancy rate asked to join in the program for the next year. A prerequisite to success was the school's ability to provide the seminar time. If the seminar is scheduled like a homeroom, students avoid missing regular classes.

The results at Site 10 show the sustainability of effective parent mentor programs. Although Carol was not the program initiator, several factors helped her to continue it. The school-community partnership had many stakeholders, both supporters and customers. Adolescent mothers continued to need mentors. Finally, the state initiative offered support from beyond the community level.

Based at a church-related service agency office, Samantha, program director at Site 11, used the Parent Share curriculum to develop a program for the women served by her organization. All of them are recovering addicts in treatment for substance abuse. "Confidentiality is extremely important in this program," she wrote. Her clients were "not very trusting." Several mentor pairs were described as having stormy, yet productive relationships that became more balanced over the course of the year. The substance-abuse issues that the parents faced may have contributed to the intensity of the pair relationships.

The incidence of substance-abuse issues may have contributed to the strong establishment and growth of the mentoring program at Site 11 and thus its sustainability. It now includes two additional service locations. The site regularly seeks opportunities for collaboration with other community organizations. The only missing pieces at this site are time and funding for program evaluation.

Where can planners reach and encourage the targeted mentees? A community organization left printed brochures in pediatricians' offices in an attempt to attract parents with children of all ages. Monica, a parent at Site 12, reported seeking a means of reducing the stress of parenting four children:

> I had first heard of the Parent Share from an article in the newspaper, but I didn't think I'd be eligible for it since I have older children, too. One day I took my son to a well child checkup, and they had a little brochure about it, and . . . the people there had told me that I was eligible for it. So I called and I met with Alicia [Extension Service program director], and she lined me up with my mentor now. And I meet with her once a week for a couple of hours, and I think it's great. I get a break from the kids, and the girl I'm hooked up with, she's raised four kids like I have, and so she sympathizes with a lot of problems I have now.

According to Alicia, Monica used the partnership to interact effectively with the local child welfare and mental health agencies:

> She'll be able to keep her kids because . . . we are involved with her. . . . As long as Parent Share and this other agency are involved, they won't make any home visits, and they won't feel any need to check on her and make sure that she is continuing to work on the things that they asked her to work on. That's a very, very big effect for her. . . . She can keep her kids, and she doesn't have to worry about somebody constantly coming in and assessing her parenting skills and what's happening with her family.

The results at Site 12, indicate, as the words of one parent attest, the success of mentor intervention in representing parent needs. Reaching parents with older children can be particularly powerful, especially if the family has many children and all receive some benefits through the mentoring process. For Martha, the formative assistance of the mentor is preferable to the deficit assessment of the welfare agency.

The three sites whose mentored parents are described above responded to needs identified by the community. Parenting adolescents, recovering alcoholics, and parents under legal scrutiny had needs that received attention. The three sources of parents to mentor described in this section may offer readers ideas for seeking parents open to mentoring in their own communities.

Supporting the Mentors

Once successful sites schedule inclusive planning, select and train mentors, and identify and match mentors with parent partners, one might imagine that parent mentoring programs would become self-sustaining. Although the strongest programs certainly have shown sustainability, even they require extensive effort to maintain. Resources supporting the mentors are carefully monitored and wisely expended. The following examples from two sites, Sites 12 and 7, show mentors' and program directors' perspectives on the kinds of support that are necessary and helpful in sustaining the programs.

Three themes guide mentor support. One is the objective perspective of the program director. A second theme is time as a resource. Finally, just as the mentor pairs give time to each other, the program director must schedule time for mentor renewal, a third theme. Even under ideal circumstances, the time frame for one mentoring cycle between partners can easily last more than a year, and the most giving mentors can be drained dry without scheduled respites. Mature mentors may be busy, travel, or have health problems. Yet the natural course of the mentoring relationship is at least six months, with an opportunity for formal closure. In addition, the timing for reassigning mentors to new parent candidates must be individualized.

Committed mentors are the fulcrums of sustainable programs. Frieda, the mentor of Monica, a parent at Site 12, is dubbed "the cheerleader" by the Extension Service office. But even she experienced some burnout during her relationship with a high-maintenance parent partner. Frieda's two-month trip to Florida was needed as a recess, according to Alicia, the program director. For relief within the program, the next step in the mentor-parent relationship is to concentrate on "how to have fun with your partner," instead of just doing serious work, because "real friends do go out and have fun." Alicia's strategy is to structure a socialization time for the mentor pair that is free of problem solving.

How Frieda, the mentor, perceives and uses the support provided by Alicia will certainly influence whether the closing months of the mentoring process are satisfying to her and whether she mentors another parent in the future. The program director provides the objective eye, builds in the time for reflection, and promotes renewal.

Mentors want support from program directors. They may need someone else to ask the hard questions they dodge with their parent partners. As the matches progress, their expectations may change. They may accept that they are unable to effect all of the changes they might like to see. Although some people's lives may look hopeless to their mentors, the program director's objective eye can help mentors to understand the determination that lies dormant in the parent partners. These thoughts from Kelly, the program director at Site 7, reveal her support for a frustrated mentor:

> I have one young mom . . . whose mentor's been really frustrated with her, but she has a very, very busy lifestyle and has a young son who has got a lot of health issues, and so it's been difficult for them to connect. I've had to talk to her [the mentor] a little bit about maybe being more structured with their time. I do go over with the parents what their commitment is to the relationship as well. They need to be available and they need to honor and respect the time the mentor's putting aside for them.

The program director provided a suggestion, reflected with the mentor (and the parent), and encouraged the relationship. How the mentor better structures the time in the relationship with the parent will influence her satisfaction with her role and her renewal as a mentor of other parents.

The mentors at the two sites described in this section experienced understandable frustration that was expertly mitigated by the program directors. The interventions illustrate that the directors' provision of objectivity, time, and renewal for the mentors is the required maintenance needed to sustain parent mentoring programs. Like vehicle maintenance, neglect of mentor support is costly and can disable otherwise well-running programs. The lesson learned from these examples is the importance of building in mentor support as a non-negotiable from the planning stages of the program.

Contexts of the Mentoring Cycle

Inside various contexts constructed through mentoring, relationship possibilities abound. It would be impossible for schools to know or even imagine the many contexts of mentoring parents. Having this knowledge is not necessary for schools to contribute to or benefit from mentoring partnerships. But glimpses of mentoring pairs' activities attest to the imagination and creativity of the community organizations most often responsible for designing the programs. Themes both public and private are found in each of the examples from the three sites which follow.

The interaction spaces of Monica, a parent at Site 12, and her mentor, Frieda, varied between public and private. Their weekly meetings were usually at a public place, and they talked on the phone as needed:

> We make arrangements to meet in town, and sometimes I have the kids along, so we'll go to McDonald's and they play on the playground, or I'll meet her in town in the evening for just the two of us.

As a mother of four, home schooling the two oldest children, Monica expressed appreciation for the mentor's role as another adult in her life: "Just the break alone, or at least getting out the house and seeing another adult is great." The presence of this mentor provides public perspective to Monica, generally immersed in the private life of the family. A concern of the public welfare agency was Monica's housekeeping and its effect on her children's development. As stated earlier, the program director can serve as a buffer between the parent and the public welfare agency. The support that Frieda provided helped Monica to cope better with the demands and responsibilities of her parent role—including her housekeeping.

Another pair indulged their shared interest in coffee and thrift-store shopping at various locations around the city while they built their relationship. The interaction spaces of Catlin, a parent at Site 7, and her mentor, also varied between public and private. Catlin described an outing:

> Both of us like to look around thrift shops, so we meet in the morning, and we go for coffee first; and then we pick a different thrift shop to look at, and we poke around in there. Then it's time for her to pick up her younger daughter from play school, so she has to go get her. That's what we usually do, and sometimes, if I need an errand or two, she'll take me for grocery shopping; or I wanted to go and get some potting soil, and the best place to go was across town, and I don't have a vehicle, so she took me to do that. Most of the time it's for pleasure, but sometimes I need grocery shopping done, and she'll take me.

When she is on her own, Catlin relies on public transportation in a city where owning a vehicle is the norm. Time with the mentor includes private transportation and an opportunity for customized shopping. This pair also followed the pattern of public interactions and weekly calls to arrange their meetings. Catlin assumed flexibility in the private dimension of their relationship: "I'm sure that if I phoned her up and needed to talk that she would take time to listen."

Some pairs meet in the home of the parent, which can lessen child-care needs and give the mentor a window on the mentee's parenting style. Jenny, a parent at Site 2, described how she met her mentor:

> Laura from this organization came with Sidney—that's my mentor—to the home to do a preliminary kind of an interview. I presume before that they had done research into both of our lives and our needs and goals . . . before matching us up. . . . We met for the first time for about a half-hour interview with each other and then we're happy, so the week after, we got together. And she comes weekly . . . for an hour or so and just chats basically. And if there are any issues outstanding for that week that I thought I might like to talk over with her, we do.

The interaction space may appear private, but introducing an outside element into a private space renders it public until the change becomes comfortable and routine.

Meeting in the public room of a low-income apartment complex as a home base, the community organization at Site 2 used a group-mentoring format together with a leadership-training curriculum. Meetings were also scheduled at the different venues of the leadership training throughout the city. For example, mentees attended a city council meeting under the tutelage of savvy group-leading mentors. Within these highly public contexts, many long-lasting private relationships formed, not only between mentors and parents, but also among the parents themselves.

Ernestine, a parent at Site 2, reported learning "how to control our temper, how to speak to people, how to approach them in a business-like manner, and how to conduct ourself" through the mentoring activities. Her 14-year-old daughter, Joline, who attended the sessions with her mother, "learned how to present herself as a leader because she was having problems in school too, in teachers and students understanding her" Would your school be enriched by two such transformations? Here is how the principal responded to the program, according to Ernestine:

> [The newspaper] had a big write-up with the girls, well most of them was girls that went to the classes that went to the high school, and they put them in the paper, and the principal recognized them and gave them a little ceremony and told them that they were very proud of them, and that made them feel good. She cut her little article out and posted it on her wall.

Ernestine further reported that her daughter was now in ROTC, played basketball, and was nominated for freshman homecoming queen. Joline improved her grades and "did a total turnaround." Public and private spaces came together in that newspaper article hanging on the wall in that high school student's room.

The mentor pairs at the four sites described in this section developed their relationships in a variety of contexts, both public and private. Schools have little influence over the relationships, nor do they need this influence. The lesson learned from these examples is that schools can benefit from the mentoring programs by connecting families to them and supporting families who subscribe to them.

Connecting Schools with Community-Based Partnerships

Community-based partnerships that provide mentoring for parents can parallel the efforts of schools. Such mentoring can extend the reach of the school through resources that ultimately benefit the students. Three levels of school involvement are possible. First, the school may be the unknowing beneficiary of the mentoring, when it is unaware of the existence of this resource in the community. Second, the school can link families to mentoring opportunities or respond to parent participation in mentoring programs. Third, the school can partner with a community agency to co-create a program of mentoring that is the most responsive to the particular parents it serves.

In a program design not involving a school, the county agency at Site 1 recruited mentors through responses to a notice in a church bulletin in a small rural town and accepted the congregation's offer of space for training the mentors. The prospective mentors included a retired school counselor, a nurse, a mother and her teenaged daughter (who will mentor a child through a connection to 4H), a minister, and a single mother (once on welfare). It was this agency's third cohort of mentors and its first attempt to include teens in the six-week mentor training period recommended in the Parent Share curriculum.

The intended audience of parents was Latino migrant farm workers new to the community. Although there was no school connection to the mentoring, Parent Share could complement the district's Title I migrant program and fulfill some of its requirements. Previous cohorts of mentors at this site were linked more directly with schools in two other areas of the county, and the agency left the door open for another school connection to emerge. The lesson learned is that the process of training three cohorts of mentors is similar. In the first two cohorts, where the local school was directly involved, the communities were quicker to take ownership of the parent mentoring programs.

In another program not explicitly involving a school, Alice, a mother at Site 7 in a small city, was mentored through a leadership project. She spoke passionately, as did other parents, about the increased patience she developed. Alice was convinced that mentoring helped her deal effectively with her adolescent daughter's oppositional disorder, and it gave her tools for communicating clearly with the student's teacher. At this site, children were welcomed to participate with parents in the leadership meetings and activities. Ernestine, a parent in the same program, reported the following changes in her 14-year-old daughter Joline:

> Before she got into it she, Joline, was real difficult because she was outspoken. She never wanted to listen, and she believed that it had to be her way or no way. So when she got into the program, she learned how to really communicate with other people to listen. She learned how to listen and word her phrase.... She cares about other people's feelings more now than she did at first.

Ernestine also praised the program's effects on her 18-year-old son, Tony, also a high school student. The school was aware of the program and responsive to its effects, as revealed by the principal's response to the newspaper article covered earlier. The lesson learned is that a lack of initial awareness of a parent mentoring program by the school is not fatal and is mitigated by appropriate and timely responses to the program's benefits for families.

The program in an urban center at Site 2 was not designed for direct involvement with schools. But an older mentor made it his business to intervene with the school when he saw a need. As the son of missionaries, he grew up on a reservation. As a mentor, he assisted a middle-aged aboriginal man whose adolescent children experienced low expectations from the school. By serving as the father's coach and the students' advocate, the mentor helped to bridge the cultures of home and school. The students became more successful and the parent received more respect from the school. The lesson learned here is that parent engagement generated through mentoring programs may upset "business as usual" in schools. Teachers and principals may gain a window of understanding that can shape individual response and policy development.

Family-community partnerships such as the three programs described at Sites 1, 7, and 2 can become more powerful just from schools' awareness of them. Because schools frequently operate in isolation, effort is required if they are to become involved in established and functioning family-community partnerships. What are the benefits for schools and their students?

The lessons learned are that awareness and support of family-community partnerships may mitigate competing demands on the time of principals and teachers (Moles, 1993, p. 43), and that schools are unable to serve all parents who care about their children's progress in school and want to know how to assist their children (Epstein, 1987, p. 131).

Deeper and longer lasting benefits can be the result for schools and the families they serve when a school is willing to take the plunge and sign on as a partner with a community organization in support of a parent mentoring program. Counselors and social workers can help teachers and principals become aware of opportunities for connecting families to mentoring programs offered to parents by community organizations. Agencies like the ones described below offered mentoring to parents through a partnership with schools.

At Site 3 outside a large midwestern city, a school supported a partnership between the Extension Service and the YMCA to mentor parents and students. Program director, Ray, recounted the tedious start-up task of recruiting parent partners:

> We made an initial contact with the principal, and we followed that up with the school counselor, who in turn helped us to disseminate information to the teachers, who then passed that information on to the kids, who then took that information home, shared it with their parents; and those parents that were interested enough to inquire further filled out the application form, and actually we just went through that process in reverse. They returned it to their teacher; their teacher returned it to the counselor; and the counselor then forwarded that information to us. Originally we wanted to make a direct contact with the parents, but because of issues of confidentiality, we weren't able to do that. So it was necessary for us to go through the counselor and then the teacher and so on. . . . We had information going through a lot of different hands, and at any point along the way the process could break down.

The process was tolerated with impatience by the organizing stakeholders, but resulted in satisfying self-referrals by the families seeking mentoring.

By identifying families it believed could benefit from participating and providing invitations from the community organization, the school compressed the implementation timeline of the program and was poised to receive progress reports on the families from the mentors. To monitor and enhance the mentoring process, the school and the community organization developed a plan to share data on the families over time. Through data sharing, they learned a valuable lesson. The students at this site were in the upper grades of elementary school, and the organizations learned that vertical teaming with the next level of schooling influences whether deep and long-lasting benefits for the families served can be sustained.

At the Mentor Moms site (Site 10) in a small midwestern city, the partnership between high schools and a community agency underwent a program evaluation, which calculated the benefits of matches between parenting students and adult mentors. Using the criteria of no repeat pregnancies and continuing enrollment in school, the evaluation found only one case in which a young woman had a second child, but she graduated and married. There were no official dropouts from the program, but this year a few parent partners still enrolled in the program did not attend school.

One student who was mentored by a middle school counselor experienced child care problems and stopped attending school. The mentor planned to help her enter a GED program if she persisted in nonattendance. High school graduates were still listed as "with" their mentor, but the mentor was reassigned to yet another high school student. The relationship between a graduate and the mentor has the potential to grow into a post-program friendship. The Mentor Moms program became known among local school districts, which asked to be included in it through the community agency.

The lesson learned is that resources dedicated to program evaluation help to measure a pilot's sustainability and suggest refinements. Without direct school involvement in this program, the benchmark of continuing enrollment, which is so important to schools, might have been absent from the evaluation. Continuing enrollment is likely to provide deep and long-lasting benefits to parenting students.

School-family-community partnerships such as the two programs described at Sites 3 and 10 affirm that schools exercising full commitment to mentoring partnerships position themselves to gain the most for the families they serve. Given the opportunities presented by these community organizations, would your school have made the commitment?

The three sites described below illustrate how schools might have made the difference in attracting parents to be mentored. In each case, a well-organized community organization sought a partnership with a school to serve parents through mentoring. Mentors were selected, trained, and ready to interact with their parent partners. In each case, disappointment resulted because of the school community members' failure to connect effectively with targeted parents.

A community organizer in a rural area of a southeastern state (Site 13) classified her inability to implement a Parent Share program together with a school as the single biggest disappointment of her long career. Although her organization and a local elementary school in the town had worked closely together over time and the program had developed to the point of training mentors, no parents ever applied to be mentored. The director attributed this failure to transportation issues, as the community served by the school spanned an expansive rural area. What role could a stronger commitment by the school have played in attracting parents to be mentored?

Another passionate community organizer in a similarly rural town in the Midwest (Site 14) also developed a Parent Share program to the point of recruiting mentors. Located across the street from a high school, the community organization had mentoring parenting students as its program goal. Although the high school had some parenting students, none ever became connected to the mentoring organization. This disappointed project director felt that the resources he had assembled were wasted, but he did not blame the high school. Might a stronger commitment by the school have meant a successful program implementation and benefits to families?

At another midwestern site (Site 9), the program director followed all of the guidelines for implementing Parent Share. A faith-based contingent of mentors was recruited and trained by a community organization that had a standing relationship with a local K–6 school. Tracy, the program director, reported:

> We have not actually enrolled any parents in it.... We were working with an elementary school that was in a target area for limited resources. During the process, when we were just ready to bring on our mentor parents, they had a change in the principal of the school. So, since we were working with the school, we did not proceed... We only got to the point that we were working with a church in the neighborhood to gain some experienced parents to work with the other parents, and we were really targeting fathers of boys that were in fifth and sixth grade, [who] are about nine to eleven years old.

In a follow-up, Tracy reported that the school employee who worked with her to initiate the program, a community resident assistant, left the school and was not replaced. As with any project in which the initial contact person changes, it made things different, she said. The local school board was studying declining enrollment on the aging east side of town, with the possibility of school closures. This was not a good time to pursue the parent-to-parent exchange project, but she planned to keep the materials ready for an opportune moment because the program had potential.

Although there was no shortage of fathers of early adolescent boys to be mentored, the change in principal of the school, the loss of the contact employee, and the issue of declining enrollment caused the planned program of mentoring parents to be tabled. As with the other sites where no mentees emerged, the school, and perhaps the district as well, played a stronger role than it acknowledged or realized in making an opportunity available to families.

The three sites described above illustrate how the absence of schools' full commitment correlates with missed opportunity for parents who might have been mentored. The lesson learned involves timing. Unseized opportunities are windows that are likely to remain closed. Their closure may even disrupt other partnership opportunities with the community organizations. Schools can never predict with certainty the outcomes of a partnership. Given the opportunities presented by these community organizations, how would your school have responded?

At the sites with successful school-family-community partnerships, the community organization took the initiative and held the responsibility for developing the program, working in concert with the school. Answers to questions about the needs of school families, obtained through the school's community liaison or counselor, guided program development. By maintaining the information flow, the school continued to have input and the program results informed the practice of the school.

At the sites that lacked successful school-family-community partnerships, the flow of information broke down. Community organizations intent on partnerships with schools were less successful in securing the schools' commitment. Parents who might have been mentored were not served.

Schools may connect with parent mentoring programs initiated by a community organization at three levels of commitment: as a passive beneficiary of increased family engagement; as a link between families with needs and mentoring opportunities or in response to families' participation in a program; or as a full partner with a community agency to customize a mentoring program for the parents it serves. In any case, it benefits schools to make a connection.

Banking on Relationships: The Difference a Year Makes

Across sites, parents reported feeling supported, and they knew that their children had made gains associated with schooling. Caring is difficult to construct in isolation, and that difficulty is a reason to include schools, families, and communities in the process. The mentoring process offers parents opportunities for dialogue and interaction over the course of a year and beyond. Mentors screened and trained through community organizations can meet the distinct needs and preferences of the parent partners.

Although Danielle, a Francophone parent partner at Site 7, spoke English, she was very glad to have a parent mentor who spoke French. When asked if the match with her parent mentor, already lasting a year, would continue, she said,

> Oh, yeah, if she don't transfer. I hope not; she's French, too, and we've got very good communication. I hope she's not going away. She still wants to talk to me, and I still want to talk to her.

Monica, a parent partner at Site 12, reported that the parent mentor made a six-month commitment to the match; however, Monica believed a friendship was developing between them that would outlast the original timeline.

When asked if the payback was worth the intensity of the effort in establishing parent mentoring programs, Kelly, the director at Site 7, was emphatic:

> Definitely... I've seen some moms really grow, and I've seen some mentors really grow, too. They love this program. They get a lot out of it. They learn a lot from the moms that they're mentoring. I had one mentor who said, "I can't believe this mom lives on such a limited budget.... She's teaching me how to really appreciate the value of a dollar, and I just get so much inspiration from her strength." So I've seen real changes in families. I've seen the kids happier, moms more confident, so that really has a trickle-down effect with the kids, and I think this program is absolutely wonderful.

Kelly also expressed confidence that a program of parent mentoring based on Parent Share could be replicated elsewhere from the model that evolved at Site 7.

Of the twelve sites with active and developing programs, five were family-community partnerships, and seven were school-family-community partnerships. The results of this study suggest that embracing the opportunities provided by community organizations can lead schools to deeper family engagement in support of student achievement. Even though relationships with community-supported programs are time-consuming for schools to develop, the payoff can be substantial. When parents feel supported and satisfied with their children's gains in school, everyone associated with the school benefits.

Implications for Schools

My current work in a secondary school serving first-year immigrants exclusively pushes me to find new ways to apply the lessons learned through the study of mentoring parents. In our school, the need is great for parents and guardians to quickly understand and use the opportunities presented by a free public education. Many of the high school students arrive overaged and undereducated. For example, an eighteen-year-old student who completed only six years of schooling in his home country can "age-out" before graduating unless he takes advantage of intense acceleration. Guardians may be aunts, uncles, cousins, or siblings just slightly older than the students themselves. Families that have been open to informal mentoring often express willingness, as their year at the school ends, to provide mentoring to the next cohort of immigrant families.

The Investment Capital Fund Grant, a competitive grant awarded by the state of Texas, brought the school together with a community organization affiliated with the Texas Industrial Areas Foundation (Murnane & Levy, 1996; Rothstein, 2002). A benefit of this community connection has been the opportunity to meet periodically with other principals of high-need schools together with the community partner, Allied Communities of Tarrant (ACT). During the 15 months funded by the grant, a series of parent events has been planned in which ACT will lead information sessions. Supporting this effort is the formation of an advisory group consisting of parents and community members. ACT also uses community walks and rallies to build parent interest, energy, and commitment.

The framework of the grant application supported a plan for mentoring parents. The application process took place during a year and a half. The grant specifies that parents, teachers, and students receive training that leads to academic improvement for students and increased engagement for parents and teachers. The plan is to build a cohort of parents who are engaged and savvy, and who will help to guide the parents who follow them through mentoring.

A factor complicating the plan of a parent mentoring process in this school is that students are permitted to spend only one transitional year at the school. On the plus side, every year "graduates" a new cohort of parents who might serve as guides for the next annual contingent of newcomers. On the minus side, parents of second-year immigrants are still shy and unsure of their new roles, not unlike middle and high school parents everywhere. Nevertheless, we intend to maintain contact with families who have completed their year and encourage them to mentor new families.

Why do we think it is so important to engage families? Although our school statistics compare favorably with those from traditional middle schools and high schools in this urban district, among the largest in Texas, the effort to achieve well on standardized measures of school quality is high. Our work has shown us that working one-on-one with both students and their parents or guardians makes a difference. We maintain attendance through vigilance, cajoling, caring, calling, and making home visits. We connect families with needed services whenever possible. For example, we bring immunization shots to the campus at no cost to the students so that students avoid missing school to visit a clinic. We scour the planet for dropouts, following trails growing cold which might lead to California, Cuernavaca, or Cambodia. We grow lines of communication with parents to encourage them to contact the school before moving and to lobby for continued schooling for students at the new destination. Until now, all of this work has fallen on the staff alone. Developing an active cohort of parent mentors will offer one more resource to safeguard student attendance and intention to graduate.

Achievement at the school is high, as measured both by teacher-assigned grades and course completion, as well as by standardized testing. Achievement happens despite poverty (94%), mobility (50%), homelessness (3%), and long work weeks for many high school students. We need parent mentoring to mitigate the consequences of high employment rates among high school students who may have enrolled simply to learn English, not necessarily to achieve the state and district goal of graduation. Parents of middle schoolers may have immigrated primarily for students' educational opportunity. We want these parents to help their children plan for high school and beyond, to stay the course with their children, and to learn English themselves. Big goals? Certainly. Can mentoring parents help? That is a reasonable expectation. And although the professional school staff members are now the primary mentors, we will continue to find ways, through the support of receptive parents and guardians, and with the help of our community partner, to grow parent mentors for the next generations of immigrants who pass through the school annually. The evidence from the study encourages us to make the effort to engage parents through mentoring.

Where does one start? Other schools' needs may be less compelling, or even more so. One should reconsider the recommendations that stem from the evidence accumulated from the other parent mentor programs. One should start small and build the process one step at a time. One should engage a community partner; find or reallocate resources, especially a person to direct the process; and, most importantly, connect with parents, however hard they are to reach. Parents are critical advocates whom the school must develop. They can become the most important allies in support of student achievement.

Engaging parents in a mentoring process is something that does not gain attention often enough in schools. Why is this so? Deep engagement of parents in the life of the school is difficult to schedule, maintain, and monitor. Engagement of parents is a high-energy commitment of the school leader. Years may pass before the results of parent engagement are known, acknowledged, or felt. The effects of parent engagement are beyond measure; and, as the evidence presented in this chapter shows, the opportunity for the engagement of all parents is an important element of a good school.

References

Carnegie Council on Adolescent Development (1995). *Great Transitions: Preparing Adolescents for a New Century.* New York: Carnegie Corporation.

Epstein, J. L. (1987). What Principals Should Know about Parent Involvement. *Principal, 66,* 6–9.

Miscisin, M. (2001). *Showing Our True Colors.* Sacramento, CA: True Colors, Inc.

Moles, O. C. (1993). Collaboration Between Schools and Disadvantaged Parents: Obstacles and Openings. In N. F. Chavkin, (Ed.). *Families and Schools in a Pluralistic Society* (pp. 21–49). Albany, NY: State University of New York.

Murnane, E. J., & Levy, F. (1996). *Teaching the New Basic Skills: Principles for Educating Children to Thrive in a Changing Economy.* New York: The Free Press.

Roaf, P. A., Tierney, J. P., & Hunte, D. E. (1994). *Big Brothers/Big Sisters: A Study of Volunteer Recruitment and Screening.* Philadelphia: Public/Private Ventures.

Rothstein, R. (2002, August 7). Schools Can Use Help Teaching Parents to Get Involved. *The New York Times.*

Smith, C. A. (1998). *Parent Share: The Parent Mentor Program* (Rev. ed.). Manhattan, KS: Cooperative Extension Service.

8

Understanding the Language of Values in Educational Accountability

Patricia E. Holland

By now it is something of a cliché to point out that values are at the heart of evaluation. Yet, however trite this observation might seem, it is unarguably true that any evaluation reflects what is important, at least to those who establish the evaluation process. In the case of the 2001 legislation commonly known as the No Child Left Behind law, the values behind what is intended to be a landmark overhaul of public education throughout the United States are clear. In the first place, the very words—"No Child Left Behind"—convey the importance of learning for all students, including those minorities and non-English speakers who traditionally have not experienced the same levels of academic achievement as other students. Second, the emphasis on basic literacy and mathematics and on high-stakes testing in these areas reflects not only the value placed on learning these particular skills, but also the importance of measurable demonstration of them by students. Furthermore, the promise to award $5 billion over a six-year period to schools and districts that use "scientifically based" methods of teaching, particularly in the area of reading, reflects what *New York Times* journalist James Traub has described as "the moment when education came to be treated more like medicine—a science that advances according to the findings of impartial research—than moral philosophy or folk wisdom" (Traub, 2002).

A consequence of the No Child Left Behind law is that school administrators and teachers now pay considerable attention to those aspects of schooling that are consistent with these explicitly prescribed, funded, and tested values, but little time examining what the values themselves are, and even less time considering what other values are being ignored. It is easy to understand this response when test results determining whether or not standards have been achieved are linked to administrators' and teachers' annual job performance evaluations, to monetary rewards for those schools and individual educators who exceed performance standards, and to penalties such as increased inspection and oversight by governing agencies for those schools and individuals who do not perform to the standards. Furthermore, for both successful and unsuccessful schools there is additional pressure in the form of public identification of schools' performance that often appears in local newspapers as a ranking of schools based on their scores on a single, mandated, standardized achievement test.

None of this is new, of course. Improving schools through the use of standards, high-stakes testing, and public report has dominated accountability in public education for the now nearly two decades since the publication of *A Nation at Risk* (National Commission on Excellence in Education, 1983). However, while criticism of the dangers inherent in placing so much emphasis on accountability in the form of high-stakes achievement tests has been mounting over the past couple of decades, the critics' voices have been muffled by policymakers and educators who are busily shaping schools and educational programs in response to policies that make such tests a primary concern and a central focus.

What is missing from the discussions of current policies and practices of accountability is the recognition that any system of accountability is, as David Blacker (2003) points out, inherently normative. As he puts it, accountability standards serve "socially desired ends rather than natural ends written into the fabric of the cosmos." He goes on to say,

> Accountability thereby becomes a form of accounting, and this magic trick of quantification allows for "no nonsense" attention to be paid to polling data, *kids' test scores, school "report cards,"* Standard and Poor's ratings, or whatever else might allow marking off a numerical threshold [italics mine]. (Blacker, p. 1)

Recognizing and acknowledging these normative implications in current standards and test-based accountability practices make it possible to broaden the discussion about accountability to include a wider scope of the values to be considered in education and to be more aware of the values that are being promoted.

The problem, though, is how to achieve that wider scope and move out of the box that has been created by test-driven accountability. Surely it is not by dismissing the importance of tests and the academic standards they address. Who could argue against the values that no child be left behind, that students learn to read and develop mathematical skills, that they develop a knowledge of academic disciplines, and that the materials and strategies of the curriculum used in schools reflect the findings of research about what is effective? Unfortunately, what too often happens is that any effort to question how these values are addressed, or whether there might be other important values as well, is dismissed as criticism of the very notion that schools and educators should be accountable for what and how much students learn. As Blacker points out, the advocates of the current standards movement consider their prioritization of standards as "obvious and beyond discussion" (Blacker, p. 3). He sees this as a tactic that "attempts an end-run around questions concerning [the standards movement's] own normative implications" (Blacker, p. 3).

Perhaps Blacker is too hard on the proponents of standards and testing. Their failure to acknowledge normative implications that he ascribes to the standards movement can be seen as a flaw that extends more deeply into the fabric of American education and American society. From colonial beginnings on, the notion that the community holds teachers responsible for providing students with certain knowledge and skills deemed important by the community has been a fundamental assumption. Within the context of America's system of public schooling, in which schools are held accountable to representative boards of citizens, that assumption has been raised to the level of a principle of governance for a democratic society. The consequence of so framing accountability is that it has become a sacred touchstone by which to judge commitment to an educational system that is "public" both in the sense of being universally available and in the sense of being open to scrutiny and evaluation. Accountability and public education have become so intertwined that to question what is done in the name of accountability is to question the very nature of public education in our society. Thus, the form that accountability takes at any particular period of time attains in that time a kind of "sacred" status that is beyond question. This sacred status affords two types of credibility, both that of being answerable to a higher, formal authority, and that of providing a true and accurate account of the conditions and needs in American schools. Because the authority that adheres to accountability in general also covers the current forms in which accountability is cast, i.e., standards and high-stakes testing, it becomes difficult to mount any challenge to these forms.

The case can be made that this deep-rooted sacred status accounts for the perception that the only objections to current standards and test-based accountability that can be safely raised and entertained are those which remain within the confines of the existing approved standards and the measures by which they are tested. Although such objections may offer important critiques of the pedagogy framed by the standards and of the measurement flaws in methods of high-stakes testing that are being used, they provide only refinements of the existing machinery. What remain unexplored are the values underlying the current forms of accountability themselves, whether the forms are appropriate to the values, and whether both the values and the forms offer a complete enough range within which to determine accountability.

Furthermore, failure to consciously examine the relationship between the values and the forms of accountability has the unintended effect of conflating the values for which schools are to be held accountable with the forms of evaluation used to find out whether those values are being upheld. To recognize this confusion of substance and form is to begin to untangle it and open the possibility of a more dispassionate consideration of both the values being advocated and the ways they are being evaluated. One way to approach such a project is to look closely at the language—or, to be more formal, the "discourse"—that is being used to discuss accountability, standards, and testing.

The following sections of this chapter attempt to examine the current discourse of accountability. This examination begins by considering—some might say "deconstructing"—a few examples from the major document containing the language of accountability, the No Child Left Behind Act of 2001. These examples are by no means exhaustive and certainly are not intended to cover all possibilities for interpretation. Rather, they are just that—examples, and they are presented to sensitize the reader to the ways the discourse of accountability works to shape thinking and practice. Following the discussion of the No Child Left Behind Act, the ways in which various criticisms of standards and high-stakes testing help to shape a larger realm for the discourse of accountability is examined. Finally, a conceptual framework is offered that explains what appears to be a conflict in the discourse about accountability between the managerial values that characterize current policies and practices and the professional values that motivate the various criticisms of those policies and practices.

Discourse of Accountability—No Child Left Behind

One place to begin an exploration of the discourse of accountability in the No Child Left Behind Act is with the observation made by journalist James Traub (2002) that "the phrase 'scientifically based research' occurs more than 100 times in the Bush administration's No Child Left Behind Act of 2001." This emphasis on a particular way of thinking and of gathering information points clearly to values about what counts as knowledge and how that knowledge is legitimated. One way to characterize these values is to say that they reflect a functionalist view. The late Bill Foster (1986) has elegantly summarized the functionalist view and related it specifically to schools, saying that functionalism

> embraces the assumptions that the social world is objective, real, and concrete; that scientists standing, as it were, outside of this world can record and accumulate facts about it. . . . All things have a function, all serve some ultimate interest. Thus, schools are functional social systems insofar as they prepare youngsters for the outside world. (pp. 55–56)

Foster also notes functionalism's dominance in educational research. He describes the functionalist scientist as one who seeks and documents "underlying regularities that guide the social structure" without making any effort to critically examine them. As Foster puts it, the functionalist view is to "treat the organization as a given reality" (p. 56).

Functionalism as a view that underlies current views of accountability is also the basis of a recent criticism by Fred Erickson and Kris Gutierrez (2002) of another important policy document about educational accountability, namely the National Research Council report, *Scientific Research in Education* (2002). Erickson and Gutierrez criticize that report's emphasis on the value of a narrow view of science and research on what are essentially functionalist grounds. According to them, the report has "produced a statement that risks being read as endorsing both the possibility and the desirability of taking an evidence-based social engineering approach to educational improvement nationwide" (p. 21). In other words, these authors fear that under what he calls "a warrant for certainty in social policy" (p. 23), those "underlying regularities" that Foster described will be accepted uncritically and manipulated in the guise of improving schools and increasing student learning.

The functionalist view of scientifically-based research culminates in the unquestioned practice of the standardized testing of students and the implicit assumption that such testing is the ideal form of accountability by which schools can be judged. The assumption that such tests offer the best evidence of the success or failure of schools is certainly nothing new in the discourse of accountability. It has been evident in the now two decades long effort to reform America's public schools. Beginning with *A Nation at Risk* (1983), which sounded the alarm about "the rising tide of mediocrity" in America's schools, the standards for determining the quality of schools have been assessed by standardized testing of students. That landmark document's jeremiad about the state of America's schools was based on data about declining SAT scores and the Second International Assessment of Educational Progress' (IAEP-2) comparison of the performance of American students with those from other nations. Since the publication of *A Nation at Risk*, standardized testing has become an increasingly important source of evidence, to the point where the No Child Left Behind Act makes it a matter of law that every state must implement annual testing of all students in grades 3–8 to assess the states' accountability to standards for student achievement in reading and mathematics. Naturally, those standards for student achievement are defined in terms that lend themselves to being tested in uniform and manageable ways across the wide range of participating schools in any given state and in ways that allow for the comparison of districts and schools.

The use of standardized tests as a primary source of evidence for accountability is just one example of the functionalist view that pervades the discourse of the No Child Left Behind Act. Another is the unquestioned implication that the purpose of schools is to prepare students for the outside world, particularly the world of work. This functionalist value is reflected in the language of No Child Left Behind and is closely linked to what can be described as a marketplace mentality. The assumption contained in this view is that education serves the needs of business and industry. Accordingly, the role of education in American society is cast as part of a larger economic agenda that requires workers who have the knowledge and skill to function in the kind of "high performing work organization" that must become the norm in American business (NCEE, 1990).

This marketplace mentality is evident in the No Child Left Behind Act in the three concepts of "accountability," "choice," and "flexibility" that are described as the means for improving America's schools (Executive Summary, 2001). The interpretation of each of these concepts has the effect of supporting the view that schooling itself is a product-producing process. The products, of course, are students who are guaranteed to have certain, specified attributes, namely reading and mathematics skills. The first of these concepts, accountability, in its reliance on the standardized testing of students, presents such tests as a tool for quality control of the student product. Data from each state's annual tests are required to be "broken out by poverty, race, ethnicity, disability, and limited English proficiency to ensure that no group is left behind" (Executive Summary, 2001). The implication is that disaggregating student test data according to this list of variables will somehow yield information that can be useful in producing student products of uniformly acceptable quality. Thus, the careful monitoring of test data becomes an important part of the "annual report cards on school performance and on statewide progress" (Fact Sheet, 2001). Furthermore, these data are made available to the public as a kind of management report to shareholders.

Another part of the management of the accountability process reflecting a market mentality is the creation of an incentive plan for districts and schools that is modeled on those commonly found in business and industry. This plan imposes penalties on schools and districts that fail to meet defined accountability standards and rewards those that do. The use of such accountability procedures that have clear counterparts in the business world has the effect of subsuming education within a business model.

The influence of this business model and of the market mentality it reflects is also found in the view that public education should operate as a market economy. Parents and students come to be viewed as consumers within the marketplace of education, and, as such, deserving of choices about the schools their children attend. While the No Child Left Behind Act only "increases the choices available to the parents of students attending Title 1 schools that fail to meet State standards" (Executive Summary, 2001), the highly charged rhetoric about children being trapped in failing schools or in schools that are "persistently dangerous" (Executive Summary, 2001), as well as language about the benefits of such choice in terms of incentive for low-performing schools to improve rather than lose both students and annual funding based on enrollment, makes clear the value of school choice. Furthermore, there is the market economy notion that schools which fail to make "adequate yearly progress (AYP) toward statewide proficiency goals" (Executive Summary, 2001) are the educational counterparts of a failing business. Under No Child Left Behind, these failing schools "run the risk of reconstitution under a restructuring plan" (Executive Summary, 2001)—an educational version of a business Chapter 11 reorganization.

Finally, the No Child Left Behind Act grants schools the greater flexibility they need if they are to improve and achieve statewide proficiency goals. This flexibility is granted "in exchange for strong accountability for results" (Executive Summary, 2001). Most notably, No Child Left Behind offers schools flexibility in the form of discretion in their use of up to half of the federal funds received for several state grant programs. The effect of this trade-off is to shift the accountability system in schools from one that emphasizes the uniformity of schools' organizational, management, and budget structures to one that emphasizes the uniformity of the schools' performance in terms of student outcomes.

With this shift, the value placed on learning as a commodity within an educational market economy is solidified. As a commodity, the learning that students are to acquire can be standardized; it can be measured; its production can be managed; and it can be marketed by schools to student and parent consumers. This commodification of learning is apparent in the discourse of accountability. It has become suffused with language reflecting a functionalist view that public education is to be held accountable for providing students with knowledge as a commodity to be taken to, used in, and bartered within the economy of the marketplace.

Critiques of Accountability
Instrumentation Perspectives

Another way to explore the values within the discourse of accountability is to consider the criticism that has been leveled against the standards and, particularly, against high-stakes testing. Much of this criticism focuses on the form of the tests themselves, particularly the advisability of high-stakes testing in general, but also on particulars of the "standardized" instruments that are being used to assess students' performance.

An excellent example of the generalized criticism of high-stakes testing is found in the American Educational Research Association's Position Statement Concerning High-Stakes Testing in PreK–12 Education that was adopted in July 2000 (AERA, 2000). The position is clearly identified as grounded in research and in the 1999 Standards for Educational and Psychological Testing. The authority of these standards is described as representing "a consensus concerning sound and appropriate test use in education and psychology" (AERA, 2000). This statement can be read as an effort to trump the authority of the high-stakes testing advocates and policymakers who have implicitly made support of high-stakes testing a litmus test for support of school improvement. However, the AERA position statement does not challenge high-stakes testing per se, but only the *conditions* under which such tests are administered and the ways in which their results are interpreted.

AERA's position is politically savvy. By not challenging the worth and value of high-stakes testing itself, this organization of educational researchers and academics is ensured a voice in the ongoing discourse about such tests. Perhaps the greatest potential for AERA to affect the discourse about high-stakes testing lies in its support and dissemination of research to study the conditions and use of high-stakes tests. Although the political diplomacy represented by AERA's coolly reasoned position may be sufficient to temper the often fervent rhetoric of high-stakes testing, it is not enough to expand the discourse to a point where such tests become only one element in a broader examination of what values are and should be reflected in educational standards and the ways in which our schools can be held accountable for such standards.

Another approach to the critique of high-stakes testing involves close scrutiny of actual tests, both in what they measure and in how results are computed. An example of this is provided by what became a media argument during the 2000 presidential campaign about the so-called "Texas Miracle in Education." In the late 1990s data made public by the Texas Education Agency indicated that student achievement was going up and the school drop-out rate was going down. This information received broader media exposure and closer analysis than might have been expected as part of then Texas governor Bush's presidential campaign. Perhaps the best-known critique of the Texas Miracle is the research by Walt Haney of Boston College, which earned him mention in the *Washington Post* (Mintz, April 21, 2000) as well as visibility in other media.

The aspect of Haney's work that is of interest here is his critique of the Texas Assessment of Academic Skills (TAAS), a system of state-mandated high-stakes achievement tests in reading, writing, and mathematics that culminates with an "exit"-level test in grade 10. According to Haney (2000), "analyses comparing TAAS reading, writing, and math scores with one another and with relevant high school grades raise doubts about the reliability and validity of TAAS scores." Furthermore, Haney presents data indicating that the gains reported in TAAS data do not correlate with student scores on national tests such as the SAT or NAEP exams. Haney's critique of the TAAS exams is an internal one; it remains focused on whether the tests themselves are reliable and on the ways in which scores are manipulated by school policies that have been crafted to exclude low-achieving students (most of whom are minorities) from taking the exit-level TAAS.

The value of Haney's critique of the instrumentation and procedures of high-stakes testing is that, like the AERA position statement, it engages the discourse of high-stakes testing on its own familiar terms. Rather than charging that advocates of high-stakes tests are wrong, such a critique simply calls on them to look more closely at the testing instruments and procedures that they are supporting. Although this strategy is quite likely to be rhetorical, one that requires considerable time and patience, and is unlikely to extend the discourse on high-stakes testing beyond issues of measurement, it is nonetheless an important perspective that can lead, as it has in Texas, to improvements in current forms of accountability.

More pointed criticism of the nature of the high-stakes tests that are currently being used comes from James Popham, a noted scholar in educational evaluation. According to Popham, the standardized tests that states are using are not capable of measuring whether standards have been achieved (frontline, 2001). As Popham explains,

> If you look at the degree of match between any commercialized standardized achievement test and a state's content standard, it's not good enough to make a judgment about whether those standards have been achieved, and you certainly don't know which standards have been achieved. So this is simple a pretend assessment. It's not useful for helping teachers or parents judge whether their kids are really learning what they're supposed to learn. (frontline, 2001).

Furthermore, according to Popham, the tests that are being used are not capable of providing what they claim is a measure of the quality of schools. Rather, Popham explains, "they measure what children bring to school, not what they learn there. They measure the kind of native smarts that kids walk through the door with" (frontline, 2001).

Even though Popham's criticism of the current standardized tests is meant to raise awareness and concern about the form of the tests themselves and about their misuse, it has not, to date, expanded the discourse of accountability among educational policymakers, who continue uncritically to promote the use of these tests for accountability purposes.

Curriculum Perspectives

Another perspective from which criticism is leveled against standards and high-stakes testing that does attempt to extend the discourse on accountability concerns the effects of these standards and tests on curriculum. Among many critics of standards, Marzano (2000) questions whether there is time within a school year for teachers to address the ever-increasing numbers of curriculum standards for which they are responsible. Another critic of the standards is again Popham (2001). It is not the quantity of standards, but rather their quality that concerns him. He claims that the language in which many curriculum standards are cast is vague and lacks the descriptive rigor necessary to tie them to instruction and—even more importantly—to evaluation.

Much of the criticism of standards and high-stakes testing from a curriculum perspective expresses concerns that the scope of curriculum is being increasingly narrowed to focus only on the subjects that are tested and the kinds of test-taking skills the tests require. Alphie Kohn (2000) makes this point with an eloquence and passion that capture the frustration often expressed by teachers about the reductionist effect of testing on the curriculum:

> Schools across the country are cutting back or even eliminating programs in the arts, recess for young children, electives for high schoolers, class meetings (and other activities intended to promote social and moral learning), discussions about current events (since the material will not appear on the test), the use of literature in the early grades (if the tests are focused narrowly on decoding skills), and entire subject areas such as science (if the tests cover only language arts and math). Anyone who doubts the scope and significance of what is being sacrificed in the desperate quest to raise scores has not been inside a school lately. (p. 46)

Despite evidence that a curriculum engaging students in more sophisticated thinking and communication correlates with higher test scores (Darling-Hammond, 1997), enormous effort and time continue to be spent aligning formal curricula with test objectives. Especially hard hit are schools with high rates of student poverty. Curriculum in many of these schools has been reduced to instruction and drill on the limited skills and subject matter that appear on high-stakes tests. Content and objectives not covered by the tests are simply no longer part of the curriculum. This trend continues despite research which shows that high-performing, high-poverty schools teach "solid content" and have a "rich curriculum" (Toenjes, et al., 2000; Reyes, et al., 1999).

One of the strongest proponents of the importance of expanding the discourse of accountability to include these considerations of the effects that standards and testing have on curriculum, particularly the curriculum in high-poverty schools, is Linda McNeil. Her criticism of the Texas accountability system (McNeil, 2000a & b) claims that the emphasis placed on high scores on the Texas Assessment of Academic Skills (TAAS) test led many schools in Texas to "mandate a non-curriculum" that limited instruction to just the specific content of the TAAS test and replaced a genuine curriculum with "test-prep" (McNeil, 2000a). She describes the development of a growth industry of expensive curriculum materials geared to TAAS preparation and points out that many of these materials involve little more than mind-numbing drill. McNeil concludes that the narrowing of curriculum and instructional focus done in the name of accountability in Texas substituted a test-based program for a serious curriculum.

McNeil also recognizes the difficulty of inserting these concerns into the current discourse of accountability that she characterizes as "expert technical language." Such language, she maintains, sets up a scenario that drives out other, more "public languages":

> When educational practice and policy are subsumed under a narrow set of indicators, then the only vocabulary for discussing those practices and policies and their effects on various groups of students is the vocabulary of the indicators—in this case, scores on a single set of tests. (McNeil, 2000a)

Social Perspectives

A third perspective taken by critics of standards and high-stakes testing is based on their negative effects on schools and communities as social organizations. Often these social concerns elide into moral considerations about democratic schooling. These concerns are expressed as challenges to the dominant discourse of accountability's claims that standards and testing offer assurances of greater equity in education, particularly for minority students whose teachers and schools are now responsible for their students' achieving to the same standards as their more advantaged peers.

Expressions of social concern about standards and high-stakes tests are often embedded in criticisms of their impact on curriculum. The previously mentioned work of Alphie Kohn and Linda McNeil provide good examples. McNeil, in particular, decries what she describes as "a new kind of discrimination—one based not on a blatant stratification of access to knowledge through tracking, but one that uses the appearance of sameness to mask persistent inequities" (McNeil, 2000a, p. 731). Students are not the only victims of such discrimination, according to McNeil. Educators, parents, and other community members are also ill-served by "an accountability-based control system, because it is a closed system [that] structures out possibilities for external criticism" (McNeil, 2000a, p. 734). Lest the larger social implications of such a system be missed, McNeil points to the premise that "maintaining our democracy has been cited as the fundamental justification for public support of schools" (ibid.). She argues that the current accountability system that legislates and controls learning puts democracy at risk by reducing the possibility for public involvement through discourse and the democratic governance of schools. (McNeil, 2000a & b).

Deborah Meier's (2000) concerns about the consequences to democratic schooling of the current top-down accountability system of standards and testing also originate in a recognition of their effects on curriculum. Meier criticizes the efforts of states and the federal government to impose standards on the grounds that those standards are generally superficial and that they are being imposed on schools in an overbearing manner. Meier also contends that heightened emphasis on the testing of such standards deprives educators and communities from participating in decision making about the curricular programs and practices in their schools. Furthermore, she argues, the tests themselves not only fail to provide evidence of the achievement of a democratic society's ultimate educational goals, i.e., creating responsible citizens and life-long learners, but may actually jeopardize those important social goals.

Meier is but one member of a growing backlash of criticism and resistance from educators and parents that is taking shape to protest the social consequences of accountability systems that centralize control of educational programs and practices through uniform standards and testing. Scholarship such as that by Natriallo and Pallas (1998) has criticized the growing use of testing as a high school graduation requirement in the United States because of the inequitable performance patterns of students from different racial and ethnic groups. Sheldon and Biddle (1998) examined a twenty-five year body of research that warns of the danger of accountability systems based on "rigid standards, narrow accountability, and tangible sanctions." Such accountability systems, they contend, will destroy the social structure of schools, erode teacher morale and professionalism, and actually result in declines in student achievement. They dramatically conclude that such accountability systems result in

> chaos within schools, teacher alienation, student indifference. Lower levels of achievement and long-term declines in American invention, innovation, and industrial productivity are likely to follow if reforms focus on setting high standards, testing, and tangible sanctions for teachers and students. (p. 178).

Criticism in the form of protests and boycotts of high-stakes testing also has emerged from parents and other community members. They claim that current accountability systems jeopardize democratic schooling because they ignore community views about quality education and because they perpetuate inequities among schools. Massachusetts, New York, Ohio, Virginia, and Wisconsin have all seen controversy over state mandated testing (Schrag, 2000). Student boycotts of the tests have been organized; petitions to put a referendum on the ballot to change state testing laws have been circulated; editorials have been published; and an activist in Oakland, California, has sold t-shirts proclaiming, "High stakes are for tomatoes" (Schrag, 2000). Alliances of educators and other citizens such as Coalition for Authentic Reform in Education (CARE) and FairTest (a national anti-standardized testing organization) have also been organized and are pressuring legislatures and school boards to abandon high-stakes tests in favor of more "authentic" forms of student and school assessment (Fox, 2001).

It must be stated, however, that both the scholarly and the community-based social criticism and protest of standards and high-stakes testing remain, at best, marginal in the discourse of accountability. Diane Ravitch is reported to have dismissively referred to the critics of high-stakes testing as "crickets-few in number, but making a lot of noise" (Schrag, 2000). The support for an accountability system based on uniform standards and high-stakes achievement tests remains strong among those who have the power to control the discourse and to shape educational policy in this country.

The examples that have been presented of different perspectives from which accountability in the nation's schools can be criticized are intended to illustrate possibilities for expanding the current discourse of accountability. Limiting accountability only to externally imposed standards assessed by standardized test items is criticized for seriously constraining not only the way standards are set and measured, but also—and perhaps more importantly—the process of deliberation that is at the heart of curriculum as it is developed, implemented, and assessed by schools that are accountable to the communities they serve and to the goals of democratic education that underlie public education nationally.

The criticism of standards and testing by scholars and citizens alike implicitly questions whether the current discourse and practice of accountability are adequate and effective. From the instrumentation perspective, critics pose the question from within the discourse of accountability by exposing problems with the standards themselves and with the measures that are being used. From curricular and social perspectives, however, the critics stand outside of the discourse to challenge it for what is missing or ignored. These critics of accountability share a common concern that humanistic and social values suffer within standardized test-based systems of accountability.

Managerial Values and Accountability

Before the discourse of accountability can be expanded, it is important to recognize that the criticism of the current accountability system in American public education reveals an important question about values. That question is whether accountability should be shaped according to managerial or professional values. Before that question can be answered, however, it is helpful to consider both sets of values more carefully.

Oversight

It is readily apparent that managerial values are dominant in current accountability policy and practice. Take, for example, the value placed on oversight within a managerial system. The very practice of management is essentially defined in terms of its responsibility for overseeing the work done within the organization and for monitoring the quality of what that work produces. In the context of educational accountability, the value placed on managerial oversight is reflected in mandates for the annual testing of students in order to gather evidence of their learning and also of the quality of schools they attend. The mandate by the Federal government for this oversight and the requirement that it be administered within the governing bureaucracies of the respective states are also features consistent with the notion that managerial oversight is carried out by persons or agencies not directly involved in the process of production. Thus, the managerial value of oversight gives implicit support to a bureaucratic structure that not only separates the work of production from the work of decision making, but also subordinates production to decision making, which is considered the prerogative of management. The ultimate effect of this separation is to make authority external from the work of production.

Standards

Standards are another important managerial value. The establishment of standards to which workers and products must conform and by which their quality is judged is a key aspect of the decision-making function of management. Accordingly, the standards favored by management have particular characteristics that provide evidence for the decisions they are expected to make. One such characteristic of standards is that they are objective; they describe features or characteristics that are actual or real, as opposed to thoughts, feelings, or states of mind. Standards stated in these

The Language of Values in Educational Accountability

objective terms can be measured or quantified in some way, thus making it possible for management to specify the degree or level at which a standard is successfully met. Particularly in terms of production standards, performance below that specified level is viewed as evidence of unsuccessful performance. Performance at or above the level indicates relative degrees of success.

This ability to quantify and measure standards is closely related to another characteristic—uniformity. When standards are uniformly applied, they may be used comparatively to gauge the relative success—or lack thereof—across persons or units. Thus standards define expectations, although because those expectations are expressed in terms of what are actually minimum levels of expected performance or production, they may tacitly create a state of mind in which the minimum suffices as the maximum to which it is necessary to aspire and perform.

The value placed on standards in the current scheme of educational accountability needs little explanation to any educator. Standards have become a familiar form for identifying curriculum and instructional objectives and for determining acceptable levels of student achievement of those objectives. Because each state is required to apply standards uniformly to all of its public schools, and because these standards are stated in ways that make it possible to measure and quantify the attainment of objectives, it has become a common practice—although according to evaluation and measurement scholars, not a legitimate one—to make comparisons across the districts and schools within a state.

Applications

The emphasis on standards is tied to yet another managerial value, namely that of having explicitly identified applications for each standard. These applications take the form of specific requirements that define the procedures and materials to be used in order to achieve certain standards. Again, a high value is placed on these applications being used uniformly, not only because the applications themselves are believed to be the best practice, but also because administrators want to ensure the reliability and validity of the measurement of their results. The effect of the value placed on applications is to create job descriptions that are highly prescriptive and rigid and that confine the work to be done within finite limits.

The managerial value placed on applications shows up most clearly in educational settings in the use of so-called "teacher-proof" curricula. These highly detailed curricula are most often well-researched commercial products in the areas of reading and mathematics. Because the annual testing of students in these areas was put in place by the No Child Left Behind Act, increasing numbers of districts and schools have purchased these curricula to prepare students for the required high-stakes annual tests in these subjects. Teachers are expected to follow to the letter these curricula, which specify exactly what material is to be taught on a given day, how it is to be taught, and even the exact amount of time to be spent on each instructional activity. The uniformity of teaching required by this kind of curriculum controls what are often major variables in the learning equation, thus making it possible to compare student learning across campuses and classrooms.

From any analysis of these managerial values of oversight, standards, and applications, a couple of generalizations emerge. The first is that managerial values are results-oriented. They focus on ends that are specified in the form of standards to which staff are expected to produce. This focus on results in educational accountability results in standards and high-stakes testing becoming the major topic of attention in many schools. Second, managerial values rely on external authority, i.e., management, to determine the conditions of work and to establish the criteria by which to assess the quality of that work and its products. Management has both the responsibility and the power to make decisions that affect these things. When managerial values are applied to educational accountability, the power to manage teaching and learning rests with federal, state and district officials, not with teachers or even with principals.

Professional Values and Accountability

It is on this very issue of decision-making power that professional values rest. Professional values place that power within the work structure itself, with those who perform particular jobs. Thus, professional values rely on internal authority and decision making. In educational settings, this reliance means that teachers and principals have the authority to make curricular and instructional decisions that are, in their opinion, best suited to the students for whose learning they are responsible.

Trust

Confidence in such internal authority requires trust in the ability of people within the organization and confidence in the decisions that they make. Such trust is an essential professional value, and one that works both from inside and outside of the organization. In fact, the word *professional* comes from the Latin word for a public declaration with the force of a promise. Those who would present themselves as professionals are in effect making a promise about the quality of what they do, particularly about the quality of the complex decisions they are called upon to make in the course of their work. It is the promise to make such decisions and take responsibility for them that distinguishes professionals from technicians or unskilled laborers. As support for that promise, however, professionals must offer evidence that they have the knowledge and skill that are necessary to make important decisions about what they do and how they do it. One important way to provide this evidence is in the form of credentials attesting to the levels of education and experience they bring to their work. Of course, credentials alone do not inspire trust; professionals must also continually provide evidence that they are capable of making good decisions in the form of the results of their decisions. This process differs, however, from a managerial value system where standards are established and monitored externally, in that the professionals themselves have the authority to determine what the nature of those results is to be, and to define both the means that are used to achieve them and the criteria by which they will be judged.

Another way in which the process differs from a managerial one is that professionals provide services to clients, as opposed to products for consumers. Clients must trust professionals to exercise their authority responsibly and to make good decisions that lead to the kind and quality of service that the clients as well as the professionals desire. In the context of educational accountability, legislators, parents, the general public, and even students must trust educators to make decisions that are in the best interests of students' learning and therefore also in the best interests of all parties concerned about the quality of public education.

Judgment

A high value is also placed on judgment in professional organizations. The decisions that professionals make require a considerable element of judgment about the right course of action in circumstances that quite often involve either new elements or the combination of familiar elements in new ways. Professionals are required to develop their understanding of each unique set of circumstances, come to opinions about them, compare them with previously encountered situations, and decide upon a response. This complex of activities comprises the process that is often referred to as "professional judgment." It is a major part of the work of those who would call themselves professionals. In making such judgments, professionals certainly must rely on their education as well as their experience. They must also be able to rely on being able to carry out what they have determined to be an appropriate course of action without constraints that might jeopardize its success.

This is not to say, however, that professionals are not accountable. They are, both to their clients and to colleagues within their profession. To their clients, professionals owe what is legally described as a "fiduciary duty." In other words, they are strictly bound by professional and ethical norms that require them to serve the welfare of their clients, even at some sacrifice to themselves. These are standards to which professionals are held, both by their clients and by the public. Professionals are also held accountable for standards of practice by governance organizations for their particular profession. An important feature of such governing bodies is that they are comprised of members of that profession who are responsible for upholding standards of practice determined within the profession and for disciplining any violators of those standards.

Although education is described as a profession, its status as such is threatened by current accountability policy that erodes educators' authority to make judgments about their practice. While it is fair to say that the large number of teachers required to staff the classrooms of America's public schools makes it more difficult to maintain a professional community, that difficulty does not absolve educators from being accountable as professionals. It also must be pointed out that the No Child Left Behind Act includes efforts aimed at strengthening the quality of teacher preparation and training in the form of an Improving Teacher Quality State Grants program (Executive Summary, 2001). Whether such efforts will provide only technical training in "using practices grounded in scientifically based research" (Executive Summary, 2001), or whether they will prepare teachers to make complex professional judgments is yet to be seen.

Interpretation

A professional value system also requires professionals to be able to interpret situations and information in order to make sound judgments. This ability involves more than just the accumulation and presentation of data. It involves a process of sifting through the various kinds of information produced by the circumstances of their work, and then selecting the right information to use in analyzing situations and making decisions about what to do. This process requires professionals to construct their own understanding of the situations they encounter in their practice; they cannot simply rely on a set of standard explanations and procedures from which to choose a course of action.

The value placed on interpretation depicts professionals as needing to be open and flexible in their work. Calling upon professionals to continuously interpret the circumstances of their practice also involves them in an ongoing process of accountability that requires them not only to evaluate what has already occurred, but also to create new knowledge about their practice in the forms of better understanding about its complexity and better responses to its circumstances. These responses then become the context for further assessment. For educators, such a process would certainly expand what is considered relevant information beyond the current scope of students' test scores. It would also give educational practitioners a voice, along with policymakers and the public, in determining the nature of their work and criteria by which it will be evaluated.

Toward a Reconciliation of Managerial and Professional Values

It should be readily apparent from the preceding discussion of managerial and professional values that a conflict exists between them in current discussions of accountability in education. While this conflict is an unfortunate condition, particularly for teachers and principals whose professional status is jeopardized by the current dominance of managerial values, it is not an inevitable one. Managerial and professional values do not have to be incompatible. This is an often overlooked point made by Donald Schon (1987) almost two decades ago in his theory of reflective practice. Schon's description of technical rationality offered a view of the knowledge necessary for practice that is squarely based in managerial values. According to Schon, "technical rationality holds that practitioners are instrumental problem solvers who select technical means best suited to particular purposes" (p. 3). His argument is that all too often "the problems of real-world practice do not present themselves to practitioners as well-formed structures," but rather as "messy indeterminate situations." It is the job of the professional practitioner to make sense of these situations and to "construct" them as problems in a way that "sets a direction for action" (p. 4). This process is the basis for what Schon called reflective practice. It is a process that reflects the operation of professional values.

The point of Schon's distinction between technical rationality and reflective practice that is often overlooked is that reflective practice and the professional values associated with it does not supplant technical rationality and the managerial values it embodies. Rather, they work in tandem. Technical-rational knowledge, often the type of scientifically-based knowledge that is so valued in managerial systems, is assumed to be important for addressing some of the problems that practitioners confront. However, because such knowledge is insufficient to address problems that are unique or unfamiliar, in those instances reflective practice takes over. Tom Sergiovanni (2000) pointed to how such an interrelationship could work in education with his call to school superintendents to recognize that standards advocates care about schools and to work together

> to improve the validity of the standards movement rather than oppose it. Superintendents should join with the standards advocates to make this movement less a crusade that clouds rationality and more of a well-conceived and carefully thought-out strategy for school improvement (p. 6).

Sergiovanni's position is one within which managerial and professional values can coexist. In the case of educational accountability, to the extent that managerial values support teaching and learning to clearly identified standards that both educators and the public support, and to the extent that managerial values serve to provide evidence of the extent to which standards are achieved, they are necessary. However, to the extent that these managerial values fail to account for the complexity of teaching and learning in the public schools of this country, and to the extent that they fail to provide educational practitioners with sufficient latitude to address the complex problems and circumstances of their work, they are insufficient. It is at that point that professional values offer better ways to address situations of practice that lie beyond what can be accounted for by standards and tests—that lie beyond measure.

References

American Educational Research Association (2000). AERA Position Statement Concerning High-Stakes Testing in PreK-12 Education. Http://www:aera.net/about/policy/stakes.htm (May 3, 2001).

Blacker, D. (2003). More than Test Scores: A Liberal Contextualist Picture of Educational Accountability. *Educational Theory*, 53 (1), 1–18.

Darling-Hammond, L. (1997). *The Right to Learn: A Blueprint for Creating Schools that Work*. San Francisco: Jossey-Bass.

Erickson, F., & Gutierrez, K. (2002). Culture, Rigor, and Science in Educational Research. *Educational Researcher*, 31 (8), 21–24.

Foster, W. (1986). *Paradigms & Promises: New Approaches to Educational Administration.* Buffalo, NY: Prometheus Books.

Fox, D. (2001). Radical Dilemma in the Anti-High-Stakes-Testing Movement. *Radical Teacher* 61. Http://www.uis.edu/~fox/papers/mcas-dilemmas.html (October 21, 2001).

Haney, W. (2000). The Myth of the Texas Miracle in Education. *Education Policy Analysis Archives*, 8:41. Http://epaa.asu.edu/epaa/v8n41/ (October, 23, 2001).

Interview: James Popham. (2001) http://www.pbs.org/wgbh/pages/frontline/shows/schools/interviews/popham.html (November 14, 2002).

Kohn, A. (2000). Standardized Testing and Its Victims: Inconvenient Facts and Inequitable Consequences. *Education Week*, September 27.

Marzano, R. (2000). Implementing Standards in Schools. Updating the Standards Movement. *NASSP Bulletin* 84 (620), 2–4.

McNeil, L. (2000a). Creating New Inequalities: Contradictions of Reform. *Phi Delta Kappan*, 81 (10), 728–734.

McNeil, L. (2000b). *Contradictions of School Reform: Educational Costs of Standardized Testing.* New York: Routledge.

Meier, D. (2000). *Will Standards Save Public Education?* Boston: Beacon Press.

Mintz, J. An Education Miracle, or Mirage? *Washington Post*, April 21, 2000, A-1.

National Center on Education and the Economy. Commission on the Skills of the American Workforce (1990). *America's Choice: High Skills or Low Wages.* Rochester, NY: NCEE.

National Commission on Excellence in Education (1983). *A Nation at Risk: The Imperative of Educational Reform.* Washington, DC: Government Printing Office.

National Research Council (2002). Scientific Research in Education, R.J. Shavelson & L. Towne (Eds.), *Committee on Scientific Principles for Educational Research.* Washington, DC: National Academy Press.

Natriello, G. & Pallas, A. (1998). The Development and Impact of High Stakes Testing. Presented at the High-Stakes Testing Conference, New York, December, 1998.

No Child Left Behind Act of 2001, Pub. L. No. 107-110.

Popham, W. (2001). *The Truth about Testing: An Educator's Call to Action.* Alexandria, VA: Association for Supervision and Curriculum.

Reyes, P., Scribner, J., & Paredes-Scribner, A. (1999) (Eds.). *Lessons from High-Performing Hispanic Schools*. New York: Teachers College Press.

Sergiovanni, T. (2000). Standards and the Lifeworld of Leadership. *The School Administrator*, September 2000, 6–12.

Schon, D. (1987). *Educating the Reflective Practitioner:Toward a New Design for Teaching and Learning in the Professions*. San Francisco: Jossey-Bass.

Schrag, P. (2000). High Stakes are for Tomatoes. *Atlantic Monthly*, August, 19-21.

Sheldon, K., & Biddle, B. (1998). Standards, Accountability, and School Reform: Perils and Pitfalls. *Teachers College Record*, 100 (1), 164–180.

Toenjes, L, Dworkin, G., Lorence, J., & Hill, A. (2000). The Lone Star Gamble: High Stakes Testing, Accountability, and Student Achievement in Texas and Houston. Houston, TX: The Sociology of Education Research Group (SERG), Department of Sociology, The University of Houston.

Traub, J. (2002). Does It Work? *New York Times, Education Life*, November 16, 2002, 24–25.

U.S. Department of Education (2001). The No Child Left Behind Act of 2001: Executive Summary. http://www.ed.gov/offices/OESE/esea/exec-summ.html (June 13, 2003).

U.S. Department of Education (2001). Fact Sheet: The No Child Left Behind Act of 2001. http://www.ed.gov/offices/OESE/esea/factsheet.html (June 13, 2003).

For Product Safety Concerns and Information please contact our EU
representative GPSR@taylorandfrancis.com
Taylor & Francis Verlag GmbH, Kaufingerstraße 24, 80331 München, Germany

www.ingramcontent.com/pod-product-compliance
Lightning Source LLC
Chambersburg PA
CBHW062008220426
43662CB00010B/1270